Edge of Empire

Edge of
Empire

*Documents of Michilimackinac,
1671–1716*

Translated by Joseph L. Peyser

Edited by Joseph L. Peyser
and José António Brandão

Introduction by José António Brandão

MICHIGAN STATE UNIVERSITY PRESS

MACKINAC STATE HISTORIC PARKS

EAST LANSING/MACKINAC ISLAND

♾ The paper used in this publication meets the minimum requirements of
ANSI/NISO Z39.48-1992 (R 1997) (Permanence of Paper).

Michigan State University Press
East Lansing, Michigan 48823-5245

Printed and bound in the United States of America.

14 13 12 11 10 09 08   1 2 3 4 5 6 7 8 9 10

LIBRARY OF CONGRESS CATALOGING-IN-PUBLICATION DATA

Edge of empire : documents of Michilimackinac, 1671–1716 / translated by
Joseph L. Peyser ; edited by Joseph L. Peyser and José António Brandão ;
introduction by José António Brandão ; foreword by David Armour.
    p.   cm.
Includes bibliographical references and index.
ISBN 978-0-87013-820-1 (cloth : alk. paper)   1. Fort Michilimackinac
(Mackinaw City, Mich.)–History–Sources.   2. Mackinac, Straits of, Region (Mich.)–
History–Sources.   3. Fur trade–Michigan–Mackinac, Straits of, Region–History–
Sources.   4. Trading posts–Michigan–Mackinac, Straits of, Region–History–
Sources.   5. Michigan–Discovery and exploration–French–Sources.   6. Indians of
North America–Michigan–Mackinac, Straits of, Region–History–Sources.   I. Peyser,
Joseph L., 1925-   II. Brandão, José António, 1957-   III. Mackinac State Historic Parks.
    F572.M16E44 2008
    977.4′88–dc22
    2008020048

Cover design by Erin Kirk New
Book design by Claudia Carlson

g green
press
INITIATIVE   Michigan State University Press is a member of the Green Press Initiative
and is committed to developing and encouraging ecologically responsible publishing
practices. For more information about the Green Press Initiative and the use of recycled
paper in book publishing, please visit www.greenpressinitiative.org.

Visit Michigan State University Press on the World Wide Web at:
www.msupress.msu.edu

This work is dedicated to
Joseph L. Peyser
in Memoriam

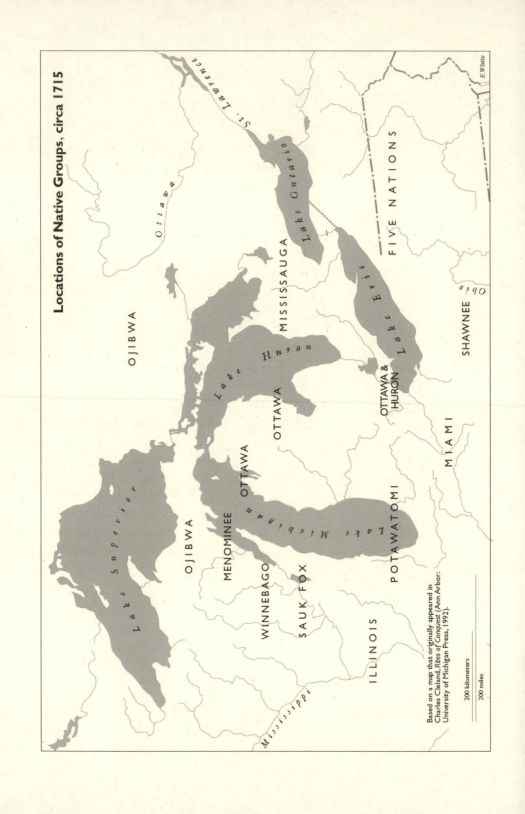

Locations of Native Groups, circa 1715

St. Lawrence

Ottawa

OJIBWA

Lake Superior

OJIBWA

MENOMINEE

WINNEBAGO

OTTAWA

Lake Michigan

SAUK FOX

OTTAWA

Lake Huron

MISSISSAUGA

Lake Ontario

FIVE NATIONS

OTTAWA

OTTAWA & HURON

Lake Erie

Ohio

ILLINOIS

POTAWATOMI

MIAMI

SHAWNEE

Mississippi

Based on a map that originally appeared in
Charles Cleland, *Rites of Conquest* (Ann Arbor:
University of Michigan Press, 1992).

200 kilometers

200 miles

E. White

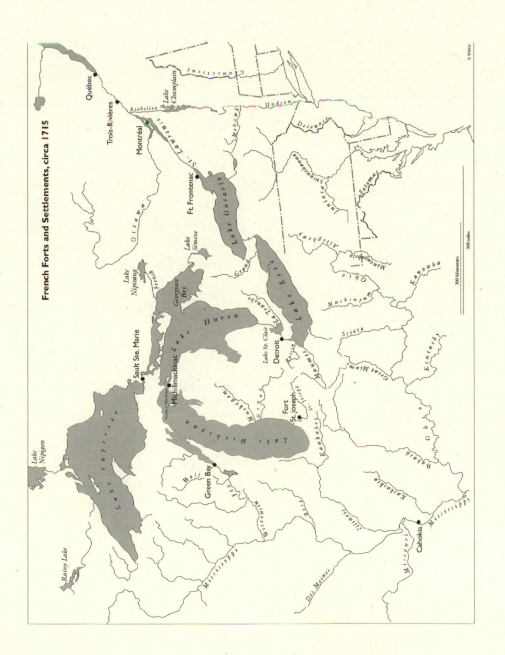

French Forts and Settlements, circa 1715

Québec
Trois-Rivières
Montréal
Ft. Frontenac
Sault Ste. Marie
Michilimackinac
Fort St. Joseph
Green Bay
Detroit
Cahokia

Lake Nipigon
Rainy Lake
Lake Superior
Lake Nipissing
Lake Simcoe
Georgian Bay
Lake Huron
Lake St. Clair
Lake Erie
Lake Ontario
Lake Michigan

Ottawa
French
Grand
La Tranche
St. Clair
Miami
St. Joseph
Kankakee
Maumee
Sandusky
Muskingum
Scioto
Great Miami
Ohio
Kentucky
Wabash
Kaskaskia
Mississippi
Missouri
Des Moines
Wisconsin
Fox
Rock
Illinois
Maumee
Straits of Mackinac

Richelieu
Lake Champlain
St. Lawrence
Mohawk
Hudson
Delaware
Connecticut
Susquehanna
Juniata
Potomac
Alleghany
Monongahela
Ohio
Kanawha

Wolf
Green

Strait of Mackinac

E. White

300 kilometers
300 miles

Contents

Foreword

Piecing together history is much like working on a gigantic jigsaw puzzle. The problem with the former is that many of the elements have been destroyed, and sometimes they are scattered all over the world. The challenge is to find the pieces, figure out how they could fit together, and then imagine what the complete picture of the past looked like.

Mackinac State Historic Parks (MSHP) is committed to discovering and preserving the remains of the past at the Straits of Mackinac, Michigan, and then presenting the results of the research to an interested public. This volume, which has been years in preparation, is the latest effort to share the results of careful and meticulous research.

Our understanding of the French experience at Mackinac and Michigan is very limited, and few researchers are actively trying to find the pieces of the French past. One of the great barriers to this understanding is language, because few researchers are fluent in seventeenth- and eighteenth-century French. Fortunately, Dr. Joseph L. Peyser built a strong foundation of copied and translated French documents. Working closely with Dr. Keith R. Widder, curator of history for Mackinac State Historic Parks, Dr. Peyser set out in 1991 to locate, copy, translate, and publish French language documents relating to Michilimackinac. Dr. Peyser's diligent research in archives in Canada and France, and his political acumen in obtaining permission to secure copies of the documents, enabled the project to amass one of the largest collections of copied French Colonial documents in the United States. Currently housed at Western Michigan University and ably managed by Dr. José António Brandão, the microfilm copies of the primary documents collected by Dr. Peyser are available to the scholarly community.

Dr. Peyser (deceased in 2004) was a meticulous researcher and his work has been assembled in three volumes in this series: *Jacques Legardeur de Saint-Pierre: Officer, Gentleman, Entrepreneur* (1996), *On the Eve of the Conquest: The Chevalier de Raymond's Critique of New France in 1754* (1997) and, with José António Brandão, in this volume, *Edge of Empire: Documents of Michilimackinac, 1671–1716*. What has been published in these three volumes is only a portion of the assembled documents. Much remains to be studied and presented. Careful translation is very time consuming. Thus it will be some years before future volumes appear. In the meantime, the Mackinac State Historic Parks' Petersen Center in Mackinaw City houses Dr. Peyser's unpublished translations, which are used by staff and are available to qualified researchers.

I have had the personal pleasure to follow the progress of the French Michilimackinac Research Project since its genesis, as well as to have managed it from Dr. Widder's retirement in 1997 until my own in 2003. By that time all of these documents had been translated and Dr. José António Brandão had become the principal researcher for the project. This assured a smooth transition in collecting and translating under the direction of Steven Brisson, chief curator of Mackinac State Historic Parks and with the enthusiastic support of Director Phil Porter and the entire Mackinac Island State Park Commission.

This book represents the work and resources of many people and institutions. Mackinac State Historic Parks has been active in historical and archaeological research since 1957 under the guidance of Dr. Eugene T. Petersen and subsequent directors David L. Pamperin and Carl R. Nold. Dedicated to protecting, preserving, and presenting the history of the Straits of Mackinac, MSHP has sponsored the publication of original documents, photographs and archaeological reports in a consistent and expanding way. Since 1962 more than 100 titles have appeared, and others are in process. We are grateful to Chairman Frank J. Kelley and the entire commission for fostering these publications that provide an additional venue to make available the history of Mackinac.

Partners such as the University of Indiana at South Bend and Western Michigan University have contributed their expertise. We are most appreciative of the ongoing partnership with our co-publisher, Michigan State University Press. Financial support has come directly from Mackinac State Historic Parks, Mackinac Associates, The University of Indiana, Western Michigan University, The National Endowment for the Humanities and especially the Florence Gould Foundation.

Within this book, based in large measure on unpublished court records, you will meet some of the ordinary people of French Canada. Marie Felix recently returned from trading at Michilimackinac testifies against the "Lame One" for stealing furs. René Fezeret accuses Jean Boudor of getting his son Guilhebaud drunk at Michilimackinac and cheating him out of ten packs of beaver and one hundred half-pints of brandy through gambling. Voyageurs Pierre LeBoeuf, Jean Verger, Pierre Mongeault, and Jean Gautier are imprisoned for deserting and not going to fight the Fox Indians in 1715.

These new pieces of the historical puzzle help reveal the complexity and richness of the French Colonial past at Michilimackinac which is still only imperfectly understood.

David A. Armour
Deputy Director–Retired
Mackinac State Historic Parks

Preface

The documents that make up this volume are, for the most part, previously unpublished and untranslated French-language records. They are drawn from among the thousands of documents (in paper, microfilm, and microfiche copy) collected from archives in France, Canada, and the United States, which make up Mackinac State Historic Parks' French Michilimackinac Research Project Collection. A few of the documents have been published before, some in translation, and are offered here in new translations. The contents of these few previously published records were considered too relevant to the themes of this collection to omit, and in a few cases the translations needed corrections. In all, the vast majority of the documents deal with the French fur trade and those people and places in New France involved in that business. In particular, the documents relate to the fur trade, traders, and others dealing with the "post at Michilimackinac" in the period from 1671 to 1716. During these years, the "post at Michilimackinac" was located at the Straits of Mackinac, first in what is now Saint Ignace, and then at Mackinaw City, Michigan.

Throughout this early period, Michilimackinac was an important trading post and key location for negotiations and other interactions with the Native groups upon which the French colony relied for its economic and political well-being. For reasons of space, we have chosen to concentrate on the fur trade at Michilimackinac. Future offerings in the series are planned for, and will deal with other aspects of Michilimackinac's history and culture.

The documents translated here were for the most part produced by, and in, the legal system of New France as people sought to protect their interests in the fur trade. Most of the documents are "legal" in nature. The documents are either contracts for carrying on trade, or records of legal proceedings related to the fur trade. In addition to shedding light on the people and place of Michilimackinac, the documents provide insight into at least three broad "topics." Regarding the fur trade in New France, and at Michilimackinac in particular, the documents identify many of the people involved in the trade, and tell us much about the personal and professional relations among people who traded. The documents also reveal clearly the process by which the trade was carried out, the roles of Natives in the trade, and the roles of women in the trade. At the same time, the documents also illuminate how the legal system in New France worked, and offer a window into French colonial society, the place of the fur trade in it, and the role of rank and order—social class—in New France. The documents suggest that French Canadian society, while similar to the patriarchal and hierarchical one of France, was also remarkably fluid. Nobles interacted with, and took on as partners in the trade, commoners. Women, who in principle had a very restricted legal status in French Canada, were actively engaged in the fur trade on behalf of their husbands, and in many cases appear to have been the ones running the businesses. Native women appear in the records as business partners and as agents for French firms trading out of Montreal and Quebec, and had legal standing in French Canadian courts.

The volume is divided into several parts. The introduction seeks to offer an overview of the French fur trade, and of the place of Michilimackinac in that network, and present some sense of what Michilimackinac was like in the years up to 1716. The legal system in New France is also briefly outlined. It is hoped that these overviews will allow readers to contextualize, and therefore better understand, the information in the documents. This is followed by the translated documents, and the third part offers a glossary of untranslated terms used in the documents, a glossary of French legal terms and their English equivalents (which serves to indicate the basis of the translation of the legal terms), and lists of the commanders and missionaries who served at Michilimackinac.

NOTE ON TRANSLATION AND EDITORIAL PRACTICES

Unless otherwise indicated, the documents were translated by Joseph L. Peyser.

The aim of the translation was to provide an accurate and readable English-language version of the French document while still retaining the flavor of the original. To that end, grammatical errors were corrected, capitalization and punctuation were standardized, and literal translations—which produced stilted English—were avoided. The written record of legal proceedings often produced documents, many pages in length, without punctuation and/or paragraphs. To translate these documents, it was necessary to create "mental" breaks and punctuation. It seemed disingenuous not to indicate that in the translation. Every effort, however, was made to keep such changes to the bare minimum to ensure that corrections of grammar, punctuation, and awkward syntax did not alter the original meaning.

Some things, however, were not changed. All spelling and capitalization of proper names of places, people, and groups are as found in the original document. Rules of spelling were not as firmly set in the seventeenth century as they are today, and people often spelled their own names differently. In the case of place names, and the names of Native peoples and/or groups, spelling could be quite erratic depending on the pronunciation of the speaker, the "ear" of the listener, and the particular regional accent of the person sounding out the word to write it down. (The variant spellings of Michilimackinac alone are a testament to creativity.) To standardize spelling in many such cases might alter meaning or hinder efforts of other researchers who might use this collection to identify places, people, or groups. Modern renderings of names, etc., are provided, whenever possible, in the notes. Where the original French was difficult to decipher, or the meaning of a term or word was unclear, the original word or passage is provided in a note.

Some words were not translated at all and are not set apart in italics in the translation to indicate that they are French words. It was simply not possible to translate some words into English without altering their meaning, and some words, especially those related to units of currency, have no English equivalent. Rather than produce awkward paraphrases of some words, or clutter the text and distract the eye with numerous italicized words, the French remains as is. Such words and their meaning are discussed in the glossary of untranslated words in appendix 1.

In addition to notes to explain matters related to translation, we offer notes to try to identify people and places mentioned, and subjects raised, in the documents. It is hoped that this editorial matter will assist readers in understanding the documents more fully. Often, however, it simply was not possible to locate a specific place or to identify a particular person. Place names changed over time; some place names were specific only to the people who traveled a route, and never made it onto early maps—let alone onto modern ones—while other names were used more than once, and at different times, to refer to varying locations. Similarly, it was not always possible to identify the people mentioned in the documents. The inconsistent spelling of family names and/or lack of recorded first names, and the common nature of many names, often made it impossible to identify a person or to be sure which of several people with similar names it might be. In other instances, a location or person does not warrant a note because the place or person is identified later in the document. Rather than add needlessly to the already long list of notes, it was thought best not to add a note to the effect that the identification would appear evident in the course of the document or that no more information could be found. In general, then, if a personal name or place name does not attract a note, it is either because no unambiguous information could be found, or because extant information added nothing to what is provided in the document translated here. Names in italics at the end of documents, or set apart within documents, represent signatures on the original documents.

When identifying persons or subjects, we have striven to keep the notes as short as possible and focused on the subject at hand. Many of the people mentioned in the documents lived full and interesting lives. We have touched only on those aspects of their lives that relate to understanding their role in the document's creation, or in the events mentioned in the document.

Acknowledgments

This work was written by Joseph L. Peyser and myself, José António Brandão. I came to be Joe's coauthor because he invited me to participate in the French Michilimackinac Research Project (FMRP), which is sponsored by Mackinac State Historic Parks and described in the foreword to this volume. Joe had prepared many volumes worth of translations for the FMRP, had already brought two to press, wanted to slowly withdraw from active research and publication, and was looking for someone to take over his role in the FMRP and help him bring a third volume of translations to press. David A. Armour, then deputy director of Mackinac State Parks and the person who oversaw the project for that wonderful institution, accepted Joe's decision to withdraw and leave me in charge. I am deeply grateful to David and Joe for asking me to participate in the FMRP. Working with the vast collection of documents that they have gathered for the FMRP is the opportunity of a lifetime. Both men, moreover, welcomed me as a full partner in the project and made me feel as if I had been part of the team from the start. As the FMRP moves ahead, it will rest squarely upon the very substantial foundations that they established.

I was saddened by David's retirement from the project, and devastated by Joe's death on December 27, 2004. I knew of Joseph L. Peyser long before I met him in 1999. I had come across his work on the Fox Indians and admired his command of the documentary record of French–Native relations. Although Joe thought my addition to the FMRP would allow him to ease out of the project, I exacted a price from him: he had to promise to stay on as a "consultant," and I contrived every excuse I could think of to visit him to discuss the FMRP in general and the current manuscript in particular. Although I viewed our roles as that of mentor and student (although Joe was too polite to ever treat me that way), we became friends as well as colleagues in a very short time. I miss his counsel and friendship. I am indebted to David for his continued support and advice as I worked to complete this manuscript.

By the date of his death, Joe had completed all the translations (which included some notes identifying individuals and places) that came to be used in this work. Because he had translated the documents included here over many years—not necessarily in chronological sequence, and at the time, not with an eye to publication—it was necessary to make changes.

My task was to edit all the material for consistency, to research and find answers for questions that had come up during the translation process, to add the needed editorial matter to identify people and places, and to provide the historical context for some of the events mentioned in the documents. I also agreed to write the introduction to the volume. I completed the bulk of the needed changes and additions in good order and to Joe's satisfaction. I had also prepared a rough outline of the introduction, which he commented upon. However, delays on my end, and his untimely passing, meant that he was not able to cast his keen and critical eye on the final version of the introduction and edited translations. Thus, I take sole responsibility for this work's completed form and all decisions related to bringing the book to press.

Joe and I often discussed our good fortune at having such a wonderful project to work on, and we both wanted to thank Keith Widder and David Armour, who got it all started, and Mackinac State Historic Parks, the Parks Board, and the Gould Foundation for their funding support. We were grateful to Steven Brisson, curator of collections at Mackinac State Historic Parks, for assuming David Armour's place in overseeing the FMRP, and to Phil Porter, director of Mackinac State Historic Parks, for his continued support of the project. Joe and I were also very grateful to Monsieur Raymond Dumais, the project's researcher in Quebec. He identified and transcribed for Joe many of the documents presented in this work and arranged for the images of documents reproduced here. Without his knowledge of New France and its documentary record, this book would not have been possible and the project as a whole would be much the poorer.

Western Michigan University and Mackinac State Historic Parks have provided me directly with assistance that must be acknowledged. The FMRP collection, on indefinite loan to Western Michigan University, is now housed in Western's Regional Archives. I am indebted to Dr. Sharon Carlson, head archivist, Dr. Joseph Riesh, dean of libraries, and Dr. Marion Gray, chair of the Department of History, for their support in helping to bring the collection to WMU. Keena Graham, a graduate student in public history at WMU, with funding support from the department, prepared an inventory of the FMRP collection. A one-year sabbatical leave from WMU, generously subsidized by Mackinac State Historic Parks, allowed time for my portions of the work on this book. Grants from Mackinac State Historic Parks have also underwritten the costs related to the daily administration of the FMRP. My thanks to David Armour, and now Steven Brisson, for their support, and to Kristine M. Blakeslee and Julie L. Loehr at Michigan State University Press, to copyeditor Barbara Fitch Cobb, and to the anonymous reviewers of the manuscript for their work and suggestions to improve it. Joe would have been very pleased with their detailed attention to the manuscript and I am most grateful for all the errors they have spotted and corrected. The errors that remain are, of course, my doing.

As usual, Mary and Robert provided unfailing support. Traveling "back" to the world of New France is made far more enjoyable by knowing the welcome that awaits me outside my office door in my more contemporary world.

Joe was a private man and I hesitate to speak for him in matters of personal gratitude. Still, I know that he cherished his family, children Jan and Randall, and grandchildren Ben, Lisa, and Jason. Joe's great love was his wife Julia. He would have dedicated his portion of the work to her. I leave the last word to Joe's son Randall who, in a very fitting tribute to his father's broad interest in the history and culture of New France and its Native and Euroamerican inhabitants, has created at Western Michigan University the Joseph L. Peyser Endowment for the Study of New France. "For several years, as my father contemplated retirement, he searched for a colleague to continue his work. In Joe Brandão my father found a kindred spirit. More important than the work, however, was the close friendship that the two of them shared. It is fitting that my father's final book was a collaboration between Joe "l'aîné" and Joe "le jeune" who became the younger brother my father never had."

Introduction

NEW FRANCE, THE FUR TRADE, AND MICHILIMACKINAC

The history of northeastern North America—from Hudson's Bay to Chesapeake Bay, from the Atlantic coast to the Mississippi—involves the history of five groups of peoples: the French, English, Dutch, Swedish, and Indians. The latter can be divided into many subgroups based on cultural and linguistic differences. What linked these people—in addition to geography—was the fur trade. The fur trade was an important economic activity in the North American colonies created by these European powers and in the Native communities that had contact with Europeans. The fur trade also served as a means to establish political and military links between Natives and Euro-Americans. These connections and alliances helped some European nations, such as the French, to extend their power in North America over Natives and over the colonies of their European rivals. The connections supported by the fur trade also helped some Native groups, such as the Iroquois of New York, to extend their power over other Native groups and over some European colonies. Michilimackinac in particular, and what is now Michigan, in general, occupied an important place in the French fur-trade empire.

✳

The fur trade in northeastern North America was, in reality, a consequence of Christopher Columbus's failed search for a water route west to Asia. The possibility of finding this route, or places with vast riches such as Columbus's Spanish successors had found, attracted the efforts of French, English, and Dutch rulers. Unable to explore the lands claimed by Spain, which also clearly blocked the way to the east, the other nations searched for a northern passage.[1] Italian John Cabot (Giovanni Caboto) sailed for England, and in 1497–98 explored along the Newfoundland coast. In 1534 French explorer Jacques Cartier traveled up the St. Lawrence River into the interior of the continent. In 1603 Samuel de Champlain, also sailing for France, returned to the area to continue Cartier's explorations, but he too could not find the passage. In 1608 Englishman Henry Hudson, sailing on behalf of the English Muscovy Company, tried an arctic route, but also failed to find the elusive Northeast passage.[2]

While a western passage to Asia proved elusive, explorers in northeastern North America found a land that they liked and that had resources they felt they and their sponsors could use. The ocean was filled with fish, furs traded by local inhabitants proved to be sought after in Europe, there was a vast amount of land, and the people they met could be converted to Christianity. There seemed to be some value, if not readily evident stores of gold and diamonds, in northern America, and European nations each strove to claim some part of it for themselves. The French, English, and Dutch promoted (with varying degrees of enthusiasm) the establishment of colonies in North America to stake claim to areas they had explored and the resources they had found (although the settlements did not always end up where the explorers had first gone). By 1608 Champlain had founded the village of Quebec by a cliff overlooking the St. Lawrence River. The Virginia Company of London had established a settlement at Jamestown, in Virginia, by 1607. In 1609 Henry Hudson, trying a more southern route and now sailing for the Dutch, traveled up the Hudson River, where in 1614 the Dutch built a fort that eventually became Albany, New York. And in 1620, a group of English Protestants founded a settlement in Plymouth.

Despite not finding the fabled route westward to Asia, the French never really stopped trying. Of the fifty-three major voyages of exploration launched by the French up to 1751, twenty-six were attempts to find a water "passage" westward, and by the mid-1700s, an overland route to the Pacific. Of those exploratory voyages, thirty-nine, or 73 percent, took place before 1701.[3] Just as importantly, the French realized that in addition to the fish they could catch on the East Coast, the interior of North America also had valuable resources. Of the latter, furs were the most important. Of those fifty-three voyages of exploration, thirty were also undertaken to find more fur-bearing lands and to develop trade relations with the Natives who trapped the furs.[4] This combined passion for exploration and for expanding the fur trade (for both the wealth and political power that could result from claiming the land and its resources) had led the French as far west as the Rocky Mountains by the 1750s.[5] Not surprisingly, it was a group of French traders—led by Alexander Mackenzie, another fur trader based out of Montreal—who were the first Europeans to travel overland to the Pacific in July 1793.

A number of factors made this exploration and expansion of trade possible. French explorers had support from the French Crown, relied upon knowledge of the interior gained from Natives, were remarkably tough explorers, and were motivated by the desire for wealth, as well as a desire, fueled by national pride, to discover new lands before other Europeans got there.[6] But most important of all, the French sat on the access route to the interior. Quebec, and later Montreal, were located on the St. Lawrence— the central river system that linked the Atlantic with the Great Lakes, from which the west, north, and south were accessible. The French recognized their good fortune and did everything they could to maintain that advantage. They worked hard to explore westward, and made alliances with Native groups in the hope of gaining exclusive trading rights with them. They worked to ensure peaceful relations between Native groups so that they would hunt for furs and not war against each other (warfare hindered trapping and trading activities). Sometimes, as against the Fox/Mesquakie in the early 1700s, they sought to destroy those who opposed their plans.[7] In support of this policy, they built a vast network of forts and trading posts.[8] In all, the French built 106 settlements, posts, and missions.[9]

By the late 1690s, however, the fur trade had become a problem for the French. The lure of adventure and wealth, aided by lack of government control, was leading men to trade rather than farm, and according to Crown officials, was undermining the colony's development.[10] No more than 800 men were ever engaged as legal or illegal traders, but that represented a large proportion of the male population.[11] Even worse, the demand for beaver pelts weakened, and the fur trade was no longer as profitable. In 1696 Louis XIV, king of France, ordered the posts in the interior closed, and traders were prohibited from going out to trade. Officials in Montreal suggested that for economic and military reasons, the forts at St. Joseph and Michilimackinac not be closed down, but by 1698 all the western posts were ordered closed and trading was proscribed.[12]

How, then, can one explain the continued exploration and expansion of the trade? The answer is that the fur trade, while less profitable, continued to provide wealth, and became even more vital for other reasons. While the fur trade had been very profitable, the French had competed with the English in seaboard colonies, and with the Dutch in New Netherland, for control of the land and for the allegiance of the Native peoples who traded them furs. As the vast extent of North America became known, mostly through French efforts, the French and English raced to claim lands for expansion and to prevent their European rivals from growing more powerful. By 1700 both countries had developed visions of strong settlements in North America that would produce goods not found in Europe and serve as markets for European goods. The French were less enthusiastic about this than were the English, but they were not prepared to let the English take over North America.[13] For the French, who by 1700 numbered only 10,000 people and by 1760 only 70,000, this meant reliance on Native peoples. The French needed the military support of Natives to fend off the English, and the Indians wanted goods and weapons for a variety of reasons. To stop trading was to lose the connection to the Indians and the support they provided.[14] In the end, the fur trade became more important to maintain, even as it began to cost money to operate.[15] Indeed, the French Crown subsidized the costs of some goods, and maintained posts in some areas for military rather than economic reasons.[16]

Few places were as important in the overall scheme of things as the *pays d'en haut*. This term means "upper country" and refers to the western Great Lakes (Huron, Michigan, and Superior) and the areas immediately north, south, and west of them. This region was important because of its large Native population, because it had an extensive riverine system needed for beaver populations, and westward expansion. It was vital, then, that the French control the region and be on good terms with its peoples. A quick glance at any map will reveal the centrality of what came to be Michigan in this system.

To maintain good relations through trade and diplomacy with the nations in the *pays d'en haut*, the French built a number of posts, including one at Michilimackinac, one on the St. Joseph River (Niles, Michigan), and one at Detroit. Some posts, often where the value of trade was surpassed by their strategic value, were run as Crown monopolies. Others, such as Michilimackinac, Detroit, and the post at the St. Joseph River, were garrisoned by French troops and run by French commanders, who contracted with merchants to actually manage the business end of matters.[17] Throughout the country, the trade was carried out by *congé*, a fur-trade license. A licensing system had been developed in 1681 to try to control the number of men who could go into the interior. Limiting the number of traders was meant to control the volume of trade and who would have contact with Natives. The latter was an important consideration, since bad traders could cause diplomatic problems. The *congé* specified where the holder could trade, the type of merchandise he could send, and the number of canoes and men he was permitted to send in any one trading season. The holder would then make contracts with the men who took the goods upriver.[18] The latter were called *engagés*. Wages, length of service, how much (if any) personal trade items the canoe men could take, and even what spot in the canoe the *engagé* was to occupy were all listed.[19] *Congé* holders either were merchants in Montreal or Quebec, or contracted with merchants to bring in trade items from France. *Congés* were also given to widows and orphans, who then sold or leased them to merchants.[20] The license holders then had to sell the furs either to a Crown monopoly, or to a group of private citizens who had been granted the monopoly, depending on the period, to buy and ship all the fur to France.[21]

At the height of the fur trade in 1755, Michilimackinac had eighteen licenses assigned to it. Detroit, established in 1701, had thirteen licenses in 1755, and the post on the Saint Joseph river, operational since 1691, had four licenses assigned to it. All in all, these three forts shipped 1,950 packs of furs and hides, or about 195,000 pounds of furs/hides (97 tons).[22] This volume of trade represents 29.3 percent of all furs and hides traded in Canada, Louisiana, and Hudson's Bay districts, and about 38 percent of all furs from Canada.[23] These forts, in the same order, ranked first, second, and fourth among all French forts in terms of volume of furs shipped through their gates. The volume of trade varied, of course, from year to year; but the general importance of these places in the French trade, and in the military and diplomatic scheme of things, did not.

✳

In the late 1600s and early 1700s, few places were as important to the French as Michilimackinac. The historical record is replete with references to the place and the important events, both diplomatic and economic, that took place there.[24] Despite this, historians struggle to develop a complete picture of the daily life and material culture of the place. We know much more about the later history of the fort because the site of the post-1716 fort has been located, excavated, and rebuilt.[25] But the first incarnation of the fort has never been found.[26] Still, the written record offers some tantalizing images, if not a complete picture, of Michilimackinac and its residents.

Michilimackinac was, properly, the name of an island (today known as Mackinac Island), located in what is now the Straits of Mackinac. The island sits a few miles east of modern day St. Ignace, Michigan. St. Ignace itself is situated on a large spit of land, in Mackinac County in the Upper Peninsula of Michigan, that juts out southward into the straits. Most authorities concur that Michilimackinac derives from the Ottawa Algonquian word for "turtle," which the island is said to resemble in shape.[27] Before 1716, French sources used the word to refer to the straits region as a whole, and to the area of modern-day St. Ignace, which was home to several Indian villages, a Jesuit mission, a French village, and a garrisoned French post. After that date, it came to refer to both the straits and the area on the south side of the straits (now Mackinaw City) where a new fort was built.

The Michilimackinac area was home to the Ottawas, the Huron-Petuns—known also as Wyandots (Ouendat, Wendat)—and other Indians. At the time of first contact with the French, the Ottawas had lived in the straits area and on Manitoulin Island, which was located in the northeastern portion of Lake Huron. The Hurons were a powerful confederacy of Iroquoian speakers who had lived around Lake Simcoe, Ontario. They had served as important allies of the French and as key partners in the French fur trade. By about 1670, as a result of warfare with the Iroquois Indians, the Ottawas, Hurons, Petuns and many other groups had moved, or were driven, further north and into the Michilimackinac area.[28] By 1671 the Society of Jesus, better known as the Jesuits, had established a mission there to minister to the Ottawas and others. The Jesuits were a Catholic missionary order, founded by Ignatius Loyola in 1534. (Loyola was later canonized, and the mission at Michilimackinac was named St. Ignace in his honor.) The order began its sustained work in New France in 1625 with just five missionaries. The Jesuits went on to become the most powerful and important of the Catholic orders working to convert Indians to Christianity in North America.[29]

The number of Ottawas and Wyandots who lived at the mission at Michilimackinac is hard to determine. The Indians left us no records, and the Jesuits were not very precise and did not undertake systematic censuses of their charges. Still, most of the reliable information about Indian population in the area comes from the Jesuits, and it is clear that, over time, the number of Ottawas outstripped that of Wyandots. In 1672 the Ottawas were said to number 60 and the Wyandots 380. By 1679 those numbers were 1,500 and 500 respectively. In 1698 the Ottawa number, again, was 1,500 and the Wyandot 300.[30] These figures, approximate as they are, stand in stark contrast to the population estimate provided by Antoine Laumet *dit* Lamothe Cadillac. In 1695, shortly after he arrived to take command at Michilimackinac, Cadillac estimated that there were "six or seven thousand souls" living within a "pistol shot" of the French fort.[31] It is possible that this number represented the Native population in the whole region, but the Indian population in the immediate vicinity of the fort was most likely closer to the estimates provided by the Jesuits.

The French population at Michilimackinac is not much easier to determine. In the 1680s and early 1690s, before Louis XIV closed down the fur trade and required traders to return to the villages and towns along the St. Lawrence, the entire French population of the *pays d'en haut* was likely little more than 700 male inhabitants.[32] In 1695, Cadillac estimated that in addition to an unspecified number of men in the garrison and of year-round inhabitants at Michilimackinac, there were over 200 more seasonal residents, living in sixty houses in two neat rows.[33] This number appears to be exaggerated. It is unlikely that only five years after the post was first opened, so many homes would have existed. Later, when the fort was established on the south side of the straits, and after some fifty years of occupation, and with a vastly expanded fur trade, there were only forty houses in the fort.[34] In 1716, when the fort had been reestablished on the south side of the straits, it was said to contain a "commander, some settlers, and even some French women."[35] There are no references to French women living at Michilimackinac before 1716. The post commanders, who served as military leaders and diplomats at forts, and who might be expected to have taken their wives along to help create a suitable home environment for them, apparently did not do so.[36]

The two populations at Michilimackinac lived in close proximity to, but separated from, one another. The Ottawas and Wyandots each lived in their own village, the Ottawas to the north of the Wyandots. And according to Louis-Armand, Baron de Lahontan, who wintered in Michilimackinac from 1688 to 1689, the Jesuits had a "House, or Colledge adjoyning to a sort of a Church, and enclos'd with Pales [poles] that separate it from the Village of the Hurons." French *coureurs de bois* had houses nearby in a "very small settlement" south of the mission.[37] There is no mention of a French fort in 1688, but when the French later built a fort, which came to be called Fort de Buade, it was constructed south of the mission.[38] Surrounding the settlements, to the west, were fields where the Indians planted their crops.

There is some ambiguity in the historical record, and thus in the secondary literature, about the exact date of the fort's construction. As early as 1683, Olivier Morel de La Durantaye had been sent to Michilimackinac to exert royal authority over the French in the region and keep New France's Native allies in good humor. Some writers have concluded that La Durantaye built the fort, which they call Fort de Buade, that year.[39] It is likely that some sort of structure was built around 1683, but it was probably little more than a fortified house, which is what most of the early posts, in fact, were.

According to Antoine de Bougainville, "the house where the commanding officer resides, being surrounded by stakes, is honoured by the name of fort."[40] The Jesuit missionary Pierre Charlevoix, visiting Fort St. Joseph in lower Michigan in 1721, noted that the "commandant's house, which is but a sorry one, is called the fort, from its being surrounded with an indifferent pallisado."[41] But whatever may have been built at Michilimackinac in the mid-1680s, it was not called Fort de Buade. Lahontan makes no mention of any fort at Michilimackinac, nor does his detailed map show one. Nor would it make sense for La Durantaye, sent north by Governor-General Joseph-Antoine Le Febvre de La Barre, to name the post after the disgraced and recalled Louis de Buade, comte de Frontenac (who had, in any case, a fort already named after him), instead of naming it after La Barre or some other official whose favor he might want to curry.[42]

The structure that came to be called Fort de Buade was not built until after 1687. In that year, Governor-General Jacques-René Brisay de Denonville was given permission by Louis XIV to build posts in the *pays d'en haut*, as he had requested, and ordered La Durantaye to "borrow" goods from those who traded to Michilimackinac to sell in order to raise money to build a post at the straits.[43] Such an order clearly indicates that no fort existed at Michilimackinac, or that whatever structure, or structures, that may have existed either were no longer standing or did not meet the colony's needs. It is unlikely that La Durantaye built the fort in 1687, as he was actively campaigning against the Iroquois that year. And again, one must conclude that Lahontan's failure to show a fort on his 1703 map, based upon his stay at Michilimackinac in the winter of 1688–89, indicates that if La Durantaye started construction of the fort, it was not completed by the spring of 1689 when Lahontan left the area.

That La Durantaye did, at least, begin to construct the fort is evinced by a 1692 letter from Governor-General Frontenac (who had returned to the colony) and Intendant Jean Bochart de Champigny in which they state that La Durantaye used the funds he gathered in 1687 to "build the said" fort.[44] Yet in an earlier letter, signed only by Frontenac, he claims that it was Louis la Porte, sieur de Louvigny who built the fort.[45] It is possible to resolve the contradictory claims about who constructed the fort, and who named it, if one accepts that La Durantaye began the construction and that Louvigny completed it, or put the finishing touches on it. La Durantaye was not incompetent, but he was removed from his post by Frontenac in 1690. It is unlikely that he would have chosen to name the structure he began/built

Fort Buade to commemorate his dismissal. Louvigny, Frontenac's acolyte, was given the post to facilitate the growth of his and Frontenac's wealth, and whether or nor he had any hand in building the fort, it was likely he who named the post after his benefactor.[46] Frontenac's letter crediting Louvigny with a hand in the construction of the fort was most likely meant to cast Louvigny in a good light to justify Frontenac's removal of La Durantaye and appointment of Louvigny. In the end, the fort built at Michilimackinac can only be referred to (and rarely ever was in the documents of the period) as Fort de Buade starting in 1690, the year that it was completed.[47]

There is very little that can be said with certainty about Fort de Buade. Denonville's instructions from Louis XIV were to build light fortifications, each with a "wall [rampart?]," a "reasonable [sized] ditch," and a "palisade" beyond that.[48] In suggesting a solid wall and trench, Louis XIV was already calling for far more than most forts would ever see. Still, one can assume that La Durantaye was given some version of these instructions, and he did raise over 29,000 livres for constructing forts at the St. Clair River and at Michilimackinac.[49] The St. Clair River post, named St. Joseph, was garrisoned by eight men in 1688 and likely did not take up much of the funds La Durantaye raised.[50] And if Cadillac's estimate of sixty houses within the fort at Michilimackinac is to be trusted, it was a substantial fort. Even forty houses would have made for a large structure.

Fort de Buade most certainly had some sort of wall, likely of poles or logs stuck in the ground.[51] There was, of course, a garrison house for the soldiers. In 1693 the structure was damaged by fire and had to be rebuilt at a cost of 300 livres.[52] It is likely that there was a separate dwelling for the commander and a powder magazine, but none are mentioned in the documents of this period. A lengthy report attributed to Cadillac provides a few more details about the fort and surrounding area.[53] The fort was built so as to command a clear view of the straits in order to keep an eye on it for passing canoes.[54] The French homes in the fort were made of "wood, one piece upon another" and covered with cedar bark; "only those of the Jesuits are covered with planks."[55] The soldiers apparently had more than one "dwelling" in the fort, or also had their own homes in which, according to the missionary Étienne Carheil, they met with local Native women.[56]

Father Carheil, as might be expected of a priest, found much wanting in the conduct of the French at Fort de Buade. He accused the traders and soldiers of drinking to excess, gambling, and using Native women as prostitutes. Nor were the post commanders much better, since they permitted this sort of conduct and used allocations from the Crown, intended for gifts for Indian allies, for their own purposes. Indeed, the commanders were not spared from the charges of gambling and extramarital sexual relations. According to Father Carheil, while La Durantaye was a "chaste" commander, one of those who followed him (either Cadillac or Louvigny) "has more than one child in the [Native] village."[57] If the picture that emerges from the quill of a devout man is that of an amoral society, one can nonetheless argue that it might not be far off the mark. If the documents that follow, especially the case of Fezeret versus Boudor, reveal anything, it is that drinking, gambling, and theft were a very real part of the fur trade out of Michilimackinac.[58]

Still, if those at the fort needed distractions to pass the time, they also came to Michilimackinac to work, and needed to live. Those who traveled to Michilimackinac either left Montreal in the spring and then continued on their voyages north, or arrived in the late fall to winter at Michilimackinac in order to get an early start on their trading voyages the following spring.[59] The French relied on the nearby Indians for corn, which after being dried and pounded was turned into "sagamité"—a boiled mush.[60] The corn was also used to make a corn bread, baked in the embers and ashes of a fire.[61] French and Native alike relied heavily on fish, mainly whitefish, caught nearby, and upon "grease or marrow" brought to Michilimackinac from the Illinois region.[62] The French at Michilimackinac in this, as in the later, period were not much given to farming. There is not even mention in the documents of garden plots at Fort de Buade.[63]

The ban on trading ended the official French stay at the fort in 1698, and the opening of a new fort at Detroit in 1701 drew away a number of Natives from the area.[64] In 1705 the Jesuits, frustrated by the lawlessness in the region and by the lack of Crown support for their goals, burned their mission and left the area.[65] Still, the region was not without a missionary for very long. Louis XIV was surprised to learn of the Jesuits' departure and instructed the governor and intendant to send Father Marest back to Michilimackinac, which they did in 1706.[66] Nor did traders ever fully leave the area. In 1708 a visitor to the region reported a fire in the Ottawa village at Michilimackinac, and efforts by traders and missionaries to prevent its spread.[67] Whatever may have been its state, some sort of French settlement, in or outside of a fort, still existed on the north of the straits in that year. A 1713 report put the number of Frenchmen living at Michilimackinac at around forty, but by then it is not clear if the French in question were in the Fort de Buade area.[68] As in the case of Fort de Buade, there is some (although less) uncertainty about when the new fort—named, but rarely called, St. Philippe—was built.[69] The anonymous "Plan de Missilimakinak" makes it very clear that a fort was built on the south side of the straits, because it was a "more convenient" location, by 1716. And the events that led to the new fort are well established in the historical record. As early as 1710, Governor Vaudreuil and Intendant Raudot had called for the restaffing of Michilimackinac. Furs were making their way to Albany, the Fox Indians were causing problems with French allies, and it was feared that the English wanted to move into the western Great Lakes. Reestablishing Michilimackinac was the first step to restoring order in the area and to begin to address the larger problems related to the imperial contest with England.[70] Constant Le Marchand de Lignery was sent to Michilimackinac in 1712 to begin the reestablishment of the place, and he commanded there until Louvigny arrived. Still, he was instructed not to incur any major expense while there, and it is unlikely that he built the new post in the years before Louvigny arrived.[71]

Louvigny, assigned to command the area in 1712, did not get to Michilimackinac until 1716. As late as 1715, still in the main colony, he reported that he had been laid up by illness for four months.[72] In 1716 he finally traveled to take up his command at Michilimackinac and led the war against the Fox Indians. It makes sense to suggest that the fort was built sometime between 1715, when a large group of men were waiting in the Michilimackinac area to go to war, and the end of 1716, when Louvigny finally engaged, and defeated, the Fox Indians. Louvigny would have the authority to build a fort in order to have a fortified position from which to wage war, and the decision to go to war was only finalized in 1715.[73]

It is less certain when the north-side location was abandoned.[74] If the Ottawas had moved to the south side of the straits shortly after the fire in their village in 1708, it is likely that the French sent up in 1712 to reassert control in the region would have gone there as well.[75] After all, it would be wise to be near those one was to influence, and Fort de Buade would have been in shambles and of little use. The illegal traders, also to be brought under the rule of law, would also likely be found with the Ottawas, with whom many had married.

Yet the date of the Ottawa move is not clear. In 1708 they were said to be on the north side of the straits, occupying an area with poor soil.[76] In 1711 a visiting missionary made the same point about their land.[77] This would suggest that they had yet to move by 1711, since after all it would hardly make sense to move from one place with poor soil to another. On the other hand, Lignery was under orders to keep the cost of reestablishing the French presence at Michilimackinac to a minimum, and using the old fort, dilapidated as it may have been, might have saved time and trouble. Yet again, if Lignery had built up the Fort de Buade position, the move to the south shore would only have increased the cost of reopening Michilimackinac. Moreover, if the new fort built by 1716 on the south side was put there because the site was more convenient, would that same situation not have obtained in 1712? The latter reasoning would lead one to conclude that after 1712, references to Michilimackinac are to the south side of the straits, but the evidence is too scant to arrive at an incontrovertible conclusion about when the Fort de Buade area was abandoned, other than by 1716. The story of the new fort lies beyond the scope of the present work.

*

The fur trade, then, was vital to New France's growth. It provided economic incentive for settlement, and furs were an important export commodity. In the 1600s the fur trade accounted for almost all exports from New France. In the 1700s, well into the period of British takeover of New France, it accounted for 60 percent of exports. Throughout the 1700s, trade averaged 176,000 livres weight per year—about 88 tons.[78] It provided incentive for exploration, which in turn helped the French explore and claim most of North America. The fur trade was a major link to Native nations, and without those links, the French could not have gained economic mastery of the trade. Without the economic links, there would have been fewer military alliances, and without those, the French would never have been able to withstand the pressures of the far more populous British colonies as long as they did. Michigan was a key to the French plan: it was located astride all the major water routes into the vast interior, was in the middle of a territory that was home to large numbers of Native peoples, and had three forts vital in the economic and military schema of the French. In the years before 1716, none of those posts was as important as Michilimackinac.

THE LEGAL SYSTEM OF NEW FRANCE

In the period covered by the documents in this collection, New France was a Crown colony ruled by officials appointed to govern the colony on behalf of the Crown's interests. While the principles of governance and law were imported directly from France, in many instances New France gave Louis XIV an opportunity to modify those practices he felt detrimental to the national (read his) interests. The result was a more orderly rule of law.[79]

✳

The colony along the St. Lawrence was divided into three administrative jurisdictions: Quebec—the seat of colonial government and where the governor and the intendant resided—and Montreal and Trois-Rivières. Each of the latter two had its local governor and district of control. The *pays d'en haut*, where Michilimackinac was located, was under the direct control of the authorities at Quebec.[80] But, as the following documents make clear, those with dealings in the pays d'en haut undertook legal proceedings related to matters at Michilimackinac in the jurisdictions in which they lived. The intendant was responsible for justice, as well as finance and civil administration, and he presided over the Sovereign Council, which served as a court of both first instance and last appeal in civil and criminal matters.[81] Each jurisdiction had a royal court to judge both civil and criminal cases. A judge, deputy judge (sometimes called the king's attorney), clerk, and a bailiff made up the staff at each court.[82] In the absence of royal courts, and sometimes in the same jurisdiction, seigneurial courts fulfilled the same roles.[83] Private civil law in New France was based on the Custom of Paris, which in turn reflected Roman Catholic values and notions of justice and punishment.[84] Civil law was further defined by the Civil Ordinance of 1667, and commercial law, master-servant relations, and partnership rules were covered in the Merchant Code of 1673. Both the Ordinance and the Code were modified, at times, by local regulations drafted by the Sovereign Council and the intendant.[85] The Custom of Paris assumed a society that was "aristocratic, patriarchal, [and] agricultural." Women had limited legal rights and could not, in principle, make contracts or alienate property without the consent of a husband (if married) or a father (if still single).[86] The Custom of Paris also assumed the existence of "universally valid human principles for human behaviour and social relationships. . . . Magistrates guided by the king's attorney . . . identified the general principle pertinent to a case and then applied it."[87]

As a means of keeping the costs of justice low (and thus for those seeking it), lawyers were not allowed to practice in New France. For this reason also, positions in the judicial system were awarded, not bought, and legal and notarial fees were set by the Crown.[88] Still, "people versed in law and legal procedures" were allowed to speak for those involved in court cases.

It was up to judges to determine what offence, if any, had been committed. In order to make such a determination, judges needed two witnesses, preferably of good reputation, who made identical statements.[89] In criminal cases, there were "twenty different types of punishment," including "capital punishment, torture, perpetual service in the king's galleys, permanent banishment . . . publicly asking forgiveness . . . and fines."[90] In civil cases, the decisions reached related to restitution by the guilty to the aggrieved.

Notaries were an integral part of the legal system in New France. Not only did they draw up legal agreements in their role as public notary, but they also could act as defense attorneys for the accused and sat in judgment in civil suits.[91] A notary's signature on a document "gave it an authenticity that could not be challenged in court."[92]

People interested in bringing civil suit against others, usually to collect debt, had to follow one of two procedures.[93] In a simple case, the person was required to contact a bailiff to have him prepare a summons. The latter would indicate "when the case would be heard" and "the motive of the case." On the designated court date, the plaintiff pleaded his case, the defendant raised what objections he could, and a verdict was rendered then and there by the judge. In more complicated cases, the plaintiff had to present to a judge a detailed written version of his claim, provide copies of pertinent documents, and stipulate what he considered the appropriate remedy/sentence in the case. If the case was found to be meritorious, those involved in the case were summoned before the judge and both parties were questioned by him. A final resolution to the case could await the opinions of outside experts or witnesses whom the judge could call. The judge then awarded damages or set fines as the case warranted.

✳

This, then, is the broad outline of the legal system in which most of these documents were created. The system appears to have been remarkably accessible for people at every level of society, and those who administered it seem to have taken their roles as guardians of order seriously. That was fortunate, because the fur trade to Michilimackinac, and those who traveled to, and traded at, the edge of the French empire in Canada seem clearly to have needed help in maintaining order.

NOTES

1. The French, however, did not entirely concede the southern regions of North America to the Spanish, and continued to explore and colonize in the Gulf of Mexico and the Caribbean. See James Pritchard, *In Search of Empire: The French in the Americas, 1670–1730* (Cambridge: Cambridge University Press, 2004).

2. W. J. Eccles, *The Canadian Frontier, 1534–1760* (1969; Albuquerque: University of New Mexico Press, 1978), 12–34; Jerry H. Bentley and Herbert F. Ziegler, *Traditions and Encounters: A Global Perspective on the Past*, 2nd ed. (Boston: McGraw Hill, 2003), 607–35.

3. Richard I. Ruggles and Conrad E. Heidenreich, "French Exploration," in *The Historical Atlas of Canada: From the Beginning to 1800*, vol. 1, ed. Richard C. Harris (Toronto: University of Toronto Press, 1987), plate 36.

4. Ibid.

5. W. J. Eccles, "French Exploration in North America, 1700–1800," in *North American Exploration*, vol. 2, *A Continent Defined*, ed. John Logan Allen (Lincoln: University of Nebraska Press, 1997), 149–202.

6. Conrad E. Heidenreich, "Early French Exploration in the North American Interior," in *North American Exploration*, vol. 2, *A Continent Defined*, 68–71.

7. The story of French exploration is carefully laid out in the works of Eccles and Heidenreich cited above. On French-Native policy and relations in the Great Lakes region, see Richard White, *The Middle Ground: Indians, Empires, and Republics in the Great Lakes Region, 1650–1850* (Cambridge: Cambridge University Press, 1991); R. David Edmunds and Joseph L. Peyser, *The Fox Wars: The Mesquakie Challenge to New France* (Norman: University of Oklahoma Press, 1993); Gilles Havard, *Empire et métissages: Indiens et Français dans le Pays d'en Haut, 1660–1715* (Sillery/Paris: Septentrion/Presses de l'Université de Paris Sorbonne, 2003).

8. Gilles Havard, "Postes français et villages indiens: Un aspect de l'organisation de l'espace colonial français dans le Pays d'En Haut (1600–1715), *Recherches amérindiennes au Québec* 30, no. 2 (2000): 11–22; Joseph Zitomersky, "The Form and Function of French-Native Settlement Relations in Eighteenth-Century Louisiana," in his *French Americans-Native Americans in Eighteenth-Century French Colonial Louisiana: The Population Geography of the Illinois Indians, 1670s–1760s* (Lund, Sweden: Lund University Press, 1994): 359–87.

9. Conrad E. Heidenreich, "Settlements to 1760," in *Historical Atlas of Canada*, ed. Harris, plate 37.

10. Eccles, *The Canadian Frontier*, 110–11.

11. Louise Dechêne puts the number of the voyageurs at the turn of the seventeenth century at around 668 men, or 12 percent of the male population of New France at that period. *Habitants et marchands de Montréal au xviie siècle* (Montréal: Librairie Plon, 1974), 220–21. Some communities, such as Montreal and Three Rivers, provided a disproportionately larger number of men for the trade. The proportion of voyageurs also varied across time. From 1690 to 1709, about 17.5 percent of the male population undertook at least one trade voyage. See Hubert Charbonneau et al., "Le comportement démographique des voyageurs sous le régime français," *Histoire sociale/Social History* 11, no. 21 (mai/May 1978): 120–33, esp. 125.

12. Eccles, *The Canadian Frontier*, 125–28; Yves F. Zoltvany, *Philippe de Rigaud de Vaudreuil, Governor of New France, 1703–1725* (Toronto: McClelland and Stewart, 1974), 37–38. See Joseph L. Peyser, *Letters from New France: The Upper Country, 1686–1783* (Urbana and Chicago: University of Illinois Press, 1992), 61–62, for a translated version of Louis XIV's edict. However, as the documents that follow reveal, it was one thing to declare an end to trade, and quite another matter to make it a reality. See, for example, documents 41–43. Despite the ban on fur trading in the west, at least 617 contracts were made between 1701 and 1715. In 1705 alone, 111 were made. Gratien Allaire, "Les engagements pour la traite des fourrures," *Revue d'histoire de l'Amérique française* 34, no. 1 (1980): 3–26.

13. On the French as reluctant colonizers, see Pritchard, *In Search of Empire*.

14. This policy, for the period under consideration here, is carefully outlined in W. J. Eccles, *Frontenac: The Courtier Governor* (with an introduction by Peter Moogk) (Lincoln: University of Nebraska Press, 2003); and in Yves F. Zoltvany, *Philippe de Rigaud de Vaudreuil, Governor of New France, 1703–1725*.

15. W. J. Eccles, "The Fur Trade and Eighteenth-Century Imperialism," in his *Essays on New France* (Toronto: Oxford University Press, 1987), 79–95.

16. Ibid.

17. Gratien Allaire, "Officiers et marchands: Les sociétés de commerce des fourrures, 1715–1760," *Revue d'histoire de l'Amérique française* 40, no. 3 (1987): 409–28.

18. See Eccles, *The Canadian Frontier*, 113, on the *congé* system. See documents 20 and 21 for examples of such partnership agreements.

19. See document 19 for one example of an *engagé* contract. See also Gratien Allaire, "Les engagements pour la traite des fourrures," *Revue d'histoire de l'Amérique française* 34, no. 1 (1980): 3–26.

20. Havard, *Empire et métissages*, 293–94, 339–40.

21. By the 1690s, the Company of the Farm held this monopoly. Eccles, *The Canadian Frontier*, 124–25.

22. Conrad E. Heidenreich and Françoise Noël, "The Fur Trade, ca. 1755," in *Historical Atlas*, ed. Harris, plate 40.

23. This breaks down as follows: Detroit, 900 packs (13.5 percent of total); Michilimackinac 650 packs (9.8 percent of total); Saint Joseph, 400 packs (6 percent of total). Conrad E. Heidenreich and Françoise Noël, "The Fur Trade, ca. 1755," in *Historical Atlas*, ed. Harris, plate 40.

24. The best full-length treatment of the history of the region, for the period covered by the documents in this collection, is Gilles Havard's *Empire et métissages*.

25. See, for example, Lyle M. Stone, *Fort Michilimackinac, 1715–1781* (East Lansing: Publications of the Michigan State University Museum, 1974); David A. Armour, *Colonial Michilimackinac* (Mackinac Island: Mackinac State Historic Parks, 2000). The latter publication lists the various archaeological reports from the excavations carried out at the post-1716 site since 1957.

26. Based on a map dated to around 1717 ([Anon.], Plan de Missilimakinak, Newberry Library, Chicago, Ayer Manuscript Collection, map 30, sheet no. 109, itself likely an updated version of a 1703 map by Baron de Lahontan), it seems likely that

the settlements at Michilimackinac were located near the shore of East Moran Bay, approximately between S. Airport Road on the north and W. Portage Rd. on the south, in modern day St. Ignace. Excavations within these boundaries, at Marquette Park, have revealed evidence of an occupation dating to the French period, but the work has been too preliminary to determine precisely who lived in the area of Marquette Park. Lyle M. Stone, *Archaeological Investigation of the Marquette Mission Site, St. Ignace, Michigan, 1971: A Preliminary Report* (Mackinac Island: Mackinac Island State Park Commission, Reports in Mackinac History and Archaeology, Number 1, 1972).

27. See, for example, the discussion in Virgil J. Vogel, *Indian Names in Michigan* (Ann Arbor: University of Michigan Press, 1986), 110–11.

28. Johanna E. Feest and Christian F. Feest, "Ottawa," in *Handbook of North American Indians*, vol. 15, *The Northeast*, ed. B. G. Trigger (Washington: Smithsonian Institution, 1978), 772–86; Conrad E. Heidenreich, "Huron," ibid., 368–88. On the demographic and locational changes produced by the Iroquois wars, see Lucien Campeau, *Catastrophe démographique sur les Grands Lacs* (Montreal: Éditions Bellarmin, 1983). On the Iroquois wars, their causes and effects, see José António Brandão, *"Your fyre shall burn no more": Iroquois Policy towards New France and Its Native Allies to 1701* (Lincoln: University of Nebraska Press, 1997).

29. The Jesuits left detailed records of their work in New France, and the bulk of their writings have been published in translation. See Reuben Gold Thwaites, ed., *The Jesuit Relations and Allied Documents, 1610–1791*, 73 vols. (Cleveland: Burrows Bros., 1896–1901) [hereafter cited as *JR*]. For an overview of the Society of Jesus, its work in North America, and the methods Jesuits used to try to convert Native peoples, see James Axtell, *The Invasion Within: The Contest of Cultures in Colonial North America* (New York: Oxford University Press, 1985), 23–127, 271–86. On the founding of the mission, see *JR*, 55:101, 161. See appendix 3 for a list of missionaries assigned to Michilimackinac.

30. *JR*, 57:249–51; ibid., 61:103–5; Havard, *Empire et métissages*, 126–34. In the early 1720s, after the Ottawas had relocated their village to the south side of the straits, they were said to number 1,500. Feest and Feest, "Ottawa," *Handbook*, 774. The growth in numbers of Ottawas may reflect a movement to Michilimackinac from the mission further north at Sault Ste. Marie.

31. See document 37 for this estimate. See appendix 3 for a full listing of commanders at Michilimackinac and the dates of their posting there.

32. Havard, *Empire et métissages*, 73.

33. See document 37 for this estimate.

34. Armour, *Colonial Michilimackinac*, 12–18, 40. Cadillac was prone to exaggeration to make himself look good. See his dramatic and self-serving account of his trip to take up his post at Michilimackinac in document 37.

35. [Anon.], Plan de Missilimakinak, Newberry Library, Chicago, Ayer Manuscript Collection, map 30, sheet no. 109.

36. Both Madame Cadillac and La Durantaye remained at Quebec and Montreal. See, for example, documents 33 and 38. La Porte de Louvigny's wife, Marie Nolan, does not appear in the following documents. However, the gap in the number of children born to her coincides with de Louvigny's posting to Michilimackinac, 1690–1694.

René Jetté, *Dictionnaire généalogique des familles du Québec des origines à 1730* (Montréal: Les Presses de l'Université de Montréal), 651 [hereafter cited as *DG*]. Havard records that three métis sisters, Madeleine, Isabelle, and Marguerite Couc, followed their husbands to Michilimackinac. Havard, *Empire et métissages*, 627.

37. Louis-Armand, Baron de Lahontan, *New Voyages to North America* [1703], ed. R. G. Thwaites, (Chicago: A. C. McClurg, 1905), 1:146. See also the map between pages 36 and 37.

38. [Anon.], Plan de Missilimakinak, Newberry Library, Chicago, Ayer Manuscript Collection, map 30, sheet no. 109. Portions of this map are clearly based on Lahontan's map, first produced for the 1703 English edition of his *Journal*, but based on his visit to Michilimackinac in 1688–89. The Plan de Missilimakinak shows the straits, bay, and islands in exactly the same shape and placement as does Lahontan's. Even the marked water depths between St. Ignace and Michilimacki-nac Island are identical. The only significant difference between the two maps regarding the St. Ignace area is that the Plan de Missilimakinak clearly shows a fort in the midst of the French settlement in St. Ignace.

39. The most recent writer to make this assertion is Timothy J. Kent in his *Rendezvous at the Straits: Fur Trade and Military Activities at Fort de Buade and Fort Michili-mackinac, 1669–1781*, 2 vols. (Ossineke, Mich: Silver Fox Enterprises, 2004), 1:56, 78.

40. [Louis-Antoine de Bougainville], "Mémoire de Bougainville sur l'état de la Nouvelle-France a l'époque de la guerre de sept ans (1757)," in *Relations et mémoires inédits pour servir à l'histoire de la France dans les pays d'outremer*, ed. Pierre Margry (Paris: Challamel Aimé, 1867), 58.

41. Pierre-François-Xavier Charlevoix, *Journal of a Voyage to North America* (London: R. and J. Dodsley, 1761), 2:93. See also Havard, "Postes français."

42. On Frontenac, see the note at document 31.

43. Estat de ce qui est deub pour les reduits . . . , 25 juillet 1689, Archives nationales de France [hereafter AN], Colonies, series C11A, 10: ff. 238r–241r. Louis XIV approved of this means of raising money for costly expenditures (see document 30). On the king's permission to Denonville, see Theodore Calvin Pease and Raymond C. Werner, eds. and trans., *The French Foundations, 1680–1693: Collections of the Illinois State Historical Library* (Springfield, Illinois State Historical Library, 1934), 23:99–100. Kent, *Rendezvous at the Straits*, 1:103–4, quotes at length from this source, but either ignores, or fails to see, its implications for his claim that Fort de Buade was built before 1687.

44. Frontenac et Champigny au ministre, 15 septembre 1692, AN, Colonies, C11A, 12: f. 6v.

45. Frontenac au ministre, 20 octobre 1691, *Rapporte de l'Archiviste de la Province de Québec, 1927–1928*, p. 69.

46. On La Durantaye as an honest and competent officer, see Champigny au minis-tre, 10 mai 1691, AN, Colonies, C11A, 11: f. 259v. Louvigny and Frontenac wasted little time in lining their pockets. By 1692 Champigny was reporting that Louvigny, with Frontenac's orders, was to charge a tax of one beaver pelt to all traders passing through Michilimackinac. Champigny au ministre, 10 novembre 1692, ibid., 12: f. 91r.

47. Gilles Havard dates the construction of Fort de Buade, in different places in his work, at 1690 and 1691. Havard, *Empire et métissages*, 606, 657.

48. Pease and Werner, eds., *The French Foundations*, 100. The translations are this author's.

49. Estat de ce qui est deub pour les reduits . . . , 25 juillet 1689, AN, Colonies, C11A, 10: ff. 238r–241r.

50. Lahontan, *New Voyages*, 1:135, 139–42.

51. See the description above by Charlevoix and Bougainville; and Havard, *Empire et métissages*, 301–3.

52. Etat de la depense faite pour les fortifications de Canada . . . , 1694, AN, Colonies, C11A, 13: f. 115v. Havard suggests, mistakenly, that the whole fort had to be rebuilt. Havard, *Empire et métissages*, 606.

53. *Relation du sieur De lamotte Cadillac* . . . (Versailles au Parc au Cerf, 1718), Newberry Library, Ayer Manuscript Collection, MS 130. This document was published in *Découvertes et établissements des Français dans l'ouest et dans le sud de l'Amérique septentrionale, 1614–1754*, ed. Pierre Margry (Paris: D. Jouaust, 1876–1886), 5:75–132. It was translated by Milo Milton Quaife in his *The Western Country in the 17th Century: The Memoirs of Lamothe Cadillac and Pierre Liette* (Chicago: Lakeside Press, 1947), 3–83. The transcription that Margry produced is filled with errors, and scholars have invariably relied upon it and his extremely limited discussion of the document's authorship since. All extant translations of the document, including Quaife's, are based on Margry's transcription. In what follows, for ease of reference (the original has no pagination), I cite Quaife, correcting the French as needed. A scholarly treatment of this important work is long overdue.

54. Quaife, "Memoirs of Cadillac," 4–5.

55. Ibid., 9–10.

56. Father Étienne Carheil to Louis Hector Callières, 30 August 1702, *JR*, 65:197–99.

57. Ibid., 65:189–253, but see especially 195, 197, 199, 205–9. Quote at 237.

58. See document 48. Documents 2–10 also reveal that many people engaged in the trade did not trust their partners, and that cheating, or attempted cheating, was very common.

59. Quaife, "Memoirs of Cadillac," 16–17.

60. Ibid., 13–14; Aigremont au ministre, 14 novembre 1708, AN, Colonies, C11A, 29: f. 69r.

61. Quaife, "Memoirs of Cadillac," 15.

62. Ibid., 14.

63. A visitor to Michilimackinac in 1749 chastised the inhabitants for their lack of industry in agriculture. [Michel Chartier de Lotbinière], *Fort Michilimackinac in 1749: Lotbinière's Plan and Map*, ed. and trans. Marie Gérin-Lajoie, volume 2, leaflet 5 of *Mackinac History* (Lansing, Mich.: Mackinac Island State Parks Commission, 1976), 9.

64. The lengthy dispute between the Jesuits and Cadillac, who opened up the post at Detroit and drew away most of the Wyandots and some Ottawas from Mich-

ilimackinac, can be found, in translation, in the *Michigan Pioneer and Historical Society Collections*, vol. 33 (1904): 102–60, and vol. 34 (1905): 285–91.

65. Pierre-François-Xavier Charlevoix, *History and General Description of New France*, 6 vols. [1744], trans. John Gilmary Shea (Chicago: Loyola University Press, 1870), 5:182.

66. Memoire du Roy au S[ieu]rs . . . de Vaudreuil . . . et Raudot, 9 juin 1706, AN, Colonies, series B, vol. 27: f. 218v; Vaudreuil et Raudot au ministre, 3 novembre 1706, AN, Colonies, C11A, 24: ff. 26r–26v.

67. Aigremont au ministre, 14 novembre 1708, AN, Colonies, C11A, 29: f. 74v.

68. Memoire de . . . Begon, 20 septembre 1713, AN, Colonies, C11A, 34: ff. 128r–128v.

69. Armour, *Colonial Michilimackinac*, 18–19.

70. Vaudreuil et Raudot au ministre, 2 novembre 1710, AN, Colonies, C11A, 31: f. 17v. Vaudreuil's efforts to reopen the fort, and his reasons, are discussed in Zoltvany, *Philippe de Rigaud de Vaudreuil, Governor of New France*, 116–29.

71. M. de Vaudreuil au ministre, 15 octobre 1712, *Rapporte de l'Archiviste de la Province de Québec, 1947–48*, p. 168.

72. Louvigny au ministre, 3 octobre 1715, AN, Colonies, C11A, 35: f. 220r.

73. On the war, see Edmunds and Peyser, *The Fox Wars*, 78–86. Kent, *Rendezvous at the Straits*, 1:186, also dates the construction of the new fort to this period.

74. Kent, in *Rendezvous at the Straits*, 1:180, has no doubt that Fort Buade was reoccupied from 1712 to 1715.

75. Armour, *Colonial Michilimackinac*, 17, dates the Ottawa move to 1710.

76. Aigremont au ministre, 14 novembre 1708, AN, Colonies, C11A, 29: f. 68v.

77. Father Gabriel Marest to Father Germon, November 9, 1712, *JR*, 66:283.

78. Thomas Wien and James Pritchard, "Canadian North Atlantic Trade," in *Historical Atlas*, ed. Harris, plate 48.

79. The summary provided here hardly does justice to the complexity of this topic or to the extant scholarship on the law and justice in New France. Rather, the aim has been to provide enough information to allow readers new to the history of New France to understand the documents in this collection. For two excellent surveys of the law in New France, see chapter 3 of Peter Moogk's *La Nouvelle France*, and John Dickinson's *Law in New France* (Winnipeg: University of Manitoba Canadian Legal History Project, Working Paper Series, 1992). For more detailed analyses, see John Dickinson, *Justice et justiciables: La procédure civile à la prévôté de Québec, 1667–1759* (Québec: Les Presses de l'Université Laval, 1982); André Lachance, *Crimes et criminels en Nouvelle-France* (Montreal: Boréal Express, 1984); Lachance, *La justice criminelle du roi au Canada au xviiie siècle* (Québec: Les Presses de L'Université Laval, 1978).

80. For an excellent, if brief, survey of the administrative structure of New France, see André Vachon, *The Administration of New France, 1627–1760* (Toronto: University of Toronto Press, 1970).

81. For a study of the intendants of New France and their roles, see Jean-Claude Dubé, *Les intendants de la Nouvelle-France* (Montréal: Fides, 1984). The most recent

monograph on the Sovereign Council is Elise Frêlon, *Les pouvoirs du Conseil Souverain de la Nouvelle-France dans l'Édiction de la Norme (1663–1760)* (Paris: L'Harmattan, 2002).

82. Dickinson, *Law in New France*, 11. See appendix 2 for the French terms and their translations as used here. The royal courts were created in Quebec in 1677, Three Rivers in 1667, and Montreal in 1693.

83. Ibid., 9.

84. Moogk, *La Nouvelle France*, 63. Moogk has explored this notion further in his "The Liturgy of Humiliation, Pain, and Death: The Execution of Criminals in New France," *The Canadian Historical Review* 88, 1 (March 2007): 89–112.

85. Moogk, *La Nouvelle France*, 208; Dickinson, *Law in New France*, 5, 13.

86. Moogk, *La Nouvelle France*, 63–64. Numerous documents in this collection reflect the limitations on women's legal status, while others show quite clearly that women such as Marie Carlié had a certain amount of freedom to proceed as they wished in matters of business.

87. Moogk, *La Nouvelle France*, 65.

88. Ibid., 73, 74.

89. Dickinson, *Law in New France*, 6. This provision accounts for the numerous instances in the documents of multiple witnesses recounting the same story.

90. Dickinson, *Law in New France*, 7. See documents 60–62, wherein many of these punishments, including "banishment" to Michilimackinac, were meted out. Of note in this instance is the fact that straws were drawn to see which of the accused was to serve any of the decreed punishments.

91. Moogk, *La Nouvelle France*, 74; Dickinson, *Law in New France*, 22. For a recent, detailed study of the role of a notary, see Louis Lavallée, "La vie et la pratique d'un notaire rural sous le régime français: Le cas de Guillaume Barette, notaire à La Prairie entre 1709–1744," *Revue d'histoire de l'Amérique française* 47, no. 4 (1994): 499–519.

92. Dickinson, *Law in New France*, 22.

93. The following is taken from Dickinson, *Law in New France*, 24–27.

Edge of Empire

Copy of Saint-Lusson's Act of possession of the Northern Territories

1671, May 16, Sault Ste-Marie[1]

Copy of the Act of possession by the sieur de St-Lusson,[2] May 16, 1671

We Jean Baptiste de St Lusson sent by the order of Monsieur Talon, Intendant of Canada, in order to take repeated possession of all the lands toward the North, having arrived at Ste. Marie of the Sault,[3] had caused to be assembled there on the 15th of May 1671 with the assistance of the Jesuit Fathers[4] who have a mission established there, all the nations to whom the aforesaid Jesuit Fathers have preached the gospel, who were represented there by their delegates in the number of seventeen, To Wit: all those [nations] from the Outaouacs[5] those from Lakes Huron and Lake Superior or Tracy, from the northern lands of Hudson Bay, those from La Baye des Puans[6] and from Le Lac des Illinois,[7] all of whom declared of their own free will that they were submitting to the sovereign authority of His Majesty, and having separated after several shouts of joy, vowed in the presence of the aforesaid Jesuit Fathers and with all the customary ceremonies among these Indians, that they wanted to live and die in that resolve. Thereupon we have drawn up the present act, at Sainte Marie of the Sault May sixteenth one thousand six hundred seventy-one.

St. Lusson

NOTES

1. National Archives of Canada, Manuscript group 5, B1, vol. 5, part 2, copy of St-Lusson's act of possession of the northern territories, at Sault Ste-Marie, May 16, 1671, pp. 13–14. Original in the Ministère des affaires étrangères, Paris, Mémoires et documents. The first name of the author of this document is Simon-François.

2. Simon-François Daumont de Saint-Lusson was appointed deputy commissioner to study systematically, along with his interpreter Nicolas Perrot, the northern country; to seek out a reported copper mine; and to discover a northwest passage. His long, detailed report of assembling fourteen Indian nations who swore

allegiance to the king of France at Sault Ste. Marie, and his taking possession of the region on June 14, 1671, are documented and well known. Pierre Margry, ed., *Découvertes et établissements des Français dans l'ouest et dans le sud de l'Amérique septentrionale, 1614–1754*, 6 vols. (Paris: D. Jouaust, 1876–1886), 1:96–99; E. B. O'Callaghan, ed., *Documents Relative to the Colonial History of the State of New York*, 15 vols. (Albany: Weed, Parsons and Co., 1856–1883), 9:803–4; *Collections of the Wisconsin Historical Society*, 20 vols. (Madison: State Historical Society of Wisconsin, 1855–1911), 11:26–29. The shorter official report translated here describes the assemblage and taking possession that occurred the preceding month. It is possible that the delegates at the May assemblage returned with larger numbers for the June ceremony.

3. Modern-day Sault Ste. Marie.

4. Father Claude Dablon, in charge of missions in the upper lakes, describes a June 4 ceremony, with Saint-Lusson present, to mark the French taking possession of the area. Father Allouez presided over the religious aspects of the ceremony. Reuben Gold Thwaites, ed., *The Jesuit Relations and Allied Documents, 1610–1791*, 73 vols. (Cleveland: Burrows Bros., 1896–1901), 55:105–15 [hereafter cited as *JR*].

5. "Outaouacs," or "Ottawa country," is a reference to the area around what came to be known as Michilimackinac, home to the Ottawa nation of Indians.

6. Modern-day Green Bay in western Lake Michigan, home of the Winnebago nation of Indians. A literal rendering of this expression is "the bay of the stinkards." The Jesuit missionaries explained that the name came to be attached to the Winnebagos because of odors associated with their place of origin, and thus they were called "people of the stinking water." The smell in question, first curiously identified as salt, was later said to be that of sulphur. *Relation of 1647–48, JR*, 33:151 and 45:219.

7. This expression, literally the Lake of the Illinois, is a reference to Lake Michigan. *Relation of 1670–71, JR*, 55:101. The Illinois were a group of independent nations living south of the lake along the Illinois and Mississippi rivers. One nation, living in northeast Arkansas, was called the Michigamea. Charles Callendar, "Illinois," in *Handbook of North American Indians*, vol. 15, *The Northeast*, ed. B. G. Trigger (Washington, D.C.: Smithsonian Institution, 1978), 673 [hereafter cited as *Handbook*]. The name of the lake, however, is generally thought to be derived from an Algonquian word, spelled various ways and meaning "great lake." The Michigamea, one spelling of the Algonquian word, were named after another lake. Virgil J. Vogel, *Indian Names in Michigan* (Ann Arbor: University of Michigan Press, 1986), 1.

Petition by Charles de Couagne against Marie Félix, Louis 8akouts, and other Indian associates for their alleged pilfering of Couagne's goods and embezzlement at Michilimackinac

1683, July 8, Montreal[1]

To the Montreal magistrate

Charles de Couagne,[2] merchant-entrepreneur of this town humbly beseeches [the court], saying that last year he furnished the Indians named Marie Felix, Louis 8akouts,[3] and Denis 8k8Outé with merchandise and money in the amount of three thousand three hundred four livres nineteen sols according to the bill attached herewith, payable in beaver at the current price of the king's office at Quebek, which amount they have not yet paid which they should have paid upon their arrival at Montreal which was last Saturday. But on the contrary they diverted without agreement and unbeknowst to the said supplicant the beaver they had obtained with his merchandise in order to siphon it off from his payment that even in the agreement that the said supplicant made with them for the satisfaction of the loan that he made to them of the said merchandise, they promised to provide him, after paying the bill, beaver for one thousand livres and money and at the current price as stated above at the time of delivery [. . .] of the said beaver, all of it without prejudice to each one's particular debt according to strict law and that they also promised to pay upon their arrival in beaver at the current price, which they have not done and have not paid the said amounts although they have since turned their merchandise into a great quantity of beavers that they left with several items of merchandise at the place to which they went for their business and dealings just as he [Couagne] learned from the man named Denis and his Indian wife and those themselves who diverted the greatest portion in every direction [. . .] in order to siphon off what is due the supplicant who is greatly suffering from it because of the bad faith of the said people which obliges him to have recourse to you [. . .].

In consideration of this, Sir, may it please you to permit the said supplicant to have furs, merchandise, canoes, and other things belonging to the above said persons seized and attached wherever they may be found and to have an investigation to find the said things, [and] at this time in case he finds more of his merchandise in kind, that the supplicant be permitted to take it to a limit of what is due him and is equitable.

Charles de Coaigne

The above petition having been considered, [the supplicant is] permitted to seize canoes, furs and other things that belong to the said debtors wherever they may be, with their right to legal recourse maintained, however, we order the witnesses to be summoned to testify truthfully about the diversion of the said things. We order etc. Done the sixth of July sixteen hundred eighty-three. Signed Migeon DeBranssat[4] with paraph[5] collated with the original which remains in the hands of the said sieur de Coaigne for him to use as he sees fit.

paraph

And at the bottom of another petition presented by sieur de Couaigne to Monsieur the [governor] general the ruling of my lord is written as follows:

Permission to carry out the order of the Montreal magistrate even in the judicial district of Quebek and elsewhere in taking [. . .] from the royal judge of the said place. Done at Montreal this eighth of July sixteen hundred eighty three.

Lefebvre de la Barre[6]

Collated with the original which is at the bottom of the said petition presented by sieur de Couaigne to my aforesaid lord [and] presented by the said sieur de Couaigne to me, the undersigned notary, to collate and given to him at this very instant. Done at Montreal this eighth of July sixteen hundred eighty-three.

Maugue[7] paraph

Notary

NOTES

1. Archives nationales du Québec à Montréal, Documents judiciaires de la juridiction seigneuriale de Montréal (1651–1695) [cote TL 2, feuilles détachées, 1681–1693].

2. Charles de Couagne was a highly placed Montreal fur trader, merchant, and entrepreneur, close to Governor Frontenac. George Brown et al., eds., *Dictionary of Canadian Biography*, 14 vols. to date (Toronto: University of Toronto Press, 1966–), 2:153–54 [hereafter *DCB*].

3. Seventeenth- and eighteenth-century French writers used a symbol, written like the number eight (8), to represent a sound in the Iroquoian languages that most closely resembles the *ou* sound in French. The "8" and the *ou* were used interchangeably.

4. Jean-Baptiste Migeon de Branssat came to New France in 1665 and served as seigneurial attorney, as subdelegate of the intendant, and as judge. In France he had earned the "titles of bachelor of laws and lawyer in the Parlement." In this period, he was the civil and criminal judge in the Montreal bailiff's court. *DCB*, 1:508–9.

5. A paraph is a flourish after a signature, originally used as a means to prevent forgery.

6. Governor-general of New France from 1682–1685. For more on La Barre, see document 16.

7. Claude Maugue was a notary and clerk of the court at Montreal from 1677 to 1684 and served as deputy to the attorney general until his death in 1696. *DCB*, 1:498.

Subpoena delivered to Louis Ouacuse to determine profit and expenses to arrive at a court order for payment to be made

1683, July 31, Montreal[1]

Summons delivered to Louis 8acouse to determine profits, costs and expenses in order to permit the judge to arrive at a judgment

In the year sixteen hundred eighty-three on the last day of July upon the petition of sieur Charles de Couagne merchant entrepreneur in this town and in accordance with the order of the magistrate of Montreal Island, I the undersigned sergeant registered in the bailiwick of Montreal Island, summoned Louis 8acouse called the Lame One, an Indian of La Montagne,[2] speaking to him personally [. . .] in this town to be and appear today at the present time in the hearing room before my said sieur magistrate to see definitely the profit among the said sieur de Couagne and the said 8acouse and the others in his partnership and see the expenses and expenditures and what the said 8acouse will be able to say to the said sieur de Couagne and his other partners and furthermore to be able to order payment jointly and severally of what will be found to be owed with expenses [. . .] I have given and left him a copy this day and year,

Lory[3] paraph.

NOTES

1. Archives nationales du Québec à Montréal, Documents judiciaires de la juridiction seigneuriale de Montréal (1651–1695) [cote TL 2, feuilles détachées, 1681–1693].

2. Literally, "the Mountain"; this is a reference to one of the Sulpician mission villages at Lake of the Two Mountains near Montreal. The Sulpicians, another missionary order in New France, had taken to creating native communities for the Indians they sought to convert. These villages, called "reserves," were located within areas controlled by the French, and far from what the missionaries considered the "corrupting" influences of the "pagan" Indians. James Axtell, *The Invasion Within: The Contest of Cultures in Colonial North America.* (New York: Oxford University Press, 1985).

3. François Lorit (Lory, Lerry, Lorris), *dit* Gargot. He arrived in New France in 1664. He became a process server and sergeant-at-law in the bailiff's court of Montreal. *DCB*, 2:446–47.

Interrogation of Louis Ouakouts, called the Lame One, a Huron to whom Couagne in 1682 gave trade goods, along with other Indians, to trade among the Ottawas at Michilimackinac

1683, July 16, Montreal[1]

Interrogation based upon the facts, conducted by us, Jean Baptiste Migeon etc. magistrate of Montreal island, of Louis Oakon [Ouakouts] of the Huron[2] nation, lame, debtor, and receiver of a considerable number of beaver whose value is that of the merchandise that sieur Charles de Couagne, a merchant in this town, had given to him last year [1682] jointly with the wife of Laurent Dubeau to go trade among the Ottawas, according to the facts and items placed in our hands of which no copy required by the ordinance was given to the said Oakon considering that he is an Indian and he is not able to either read or write, to which interrogation we proceeded as follows.

On the thirtieth and last day of July sixteen hundred eighty-three at four o'clock in the afternoon in our courtroom the said Louis Oakon appeared aided by sieur Lamarque,[3] who lives in this town, to serve as interpreter and receive the answers by [. . .] the said Oakon summoned by our order by sergeant Lory in order to be heard and interrogated based upon facts and items, and after swearing in both the said interpreter and the said Oakon, to answer and tell the truth about the said facts about which he was interrogated.

We asked him about the first fact, how long has he been back from the Oüattaoüas?
Answers around twenty-five days.

Asked what he had gone to do among the Oattaoas?
Answers that he had gone there to trade.

Asked who had provided him with merchandise for trading?
Answers that it is sieur Renauld.[4]

Asked what has become of the merchandise that he entrusted him with?
Answers that he traded them at the Ottattaoues' place commonly known as Missimakina.

Asked what he did with the proceeds from the said merchandise?
Answers that he brought the proceeds from the said merchandise to sieur Renauld his contractual partner.[5]

Asked how many beaver he obtained and how many packs he brought to this place?
Answers six packs of dry beaver and one of beaver in robes.[6]

Asked how many dry beaver there were in each pack since the arrival, and upon the admonition given to him by the said sieur Lamarque about the obligation he had to tell the truth and not lie, he stated that he carried eight packs of beaver just as he wrote and marked with carbon[7] on the floor of our courtroom five of which are of thirty dry beavers in each pack; the sixth pack contained twelve robes of which two were made of six beavers each, and the remainder [made] of seven beavers each with the exception of one [robe] that is made of nine beavers, the seventh pack contained twenty dry beavers, and the eighth and last [pack] contained around ten beavers all cut short[8] save two big ones, which pack he gave to the said sieur Renauld who gave him their value in money with the exception of the said two big ones that have been placed among the others.

Migeon de Branssat paraph.

Lamarque paraph.

Asked if he gave all the said packs stated above to the said sieur Renauld?
Answers that he brought them all to the said sieur Renauld.

Asked whether from all the merchandise that he carried to the above Ouattaouas some did not remain there to trade or whether from the said merchandise he did not lend some to some of his acquaintances?
Answers that he did not leave any merchandise in kind but he loaned a great deal to Indians who went trading as far as the Nadoecioux.[9]

Asked how many beavers' worth of merchandise he loaned the said Indians?
Answers that he loaned several people fifty-two beavers' worth according to their description that he made in our and the interpreter's presence.

Asked if he doesn't remember the name of the Indians to whom he loaned [the merchandise]?
Answers that he will call upon his memory and will enumerate them, to wit in the first place he loaned to the man named Oenkoachahé six beavers' worth [of trade goods] and a pair of stockings worth two beavers; to Oundeouahariac six beavers for an Iroquois-style blanket; to Ayaho six beavers for an Iroquois-style blanket, a pair of sleeves worth

two beavers, a small hooded coat and a small shirt worth one beaver; to Old Pike[10] 12 beavers for a present of tobacco that he gave to the elders; to The Heel[11] two pairs of stockings worth four beavers and six beavers for tobacco; to Ojahe the Just[12] four beavers, two for a shirt and two for vermilion; to The Rat[13] four beavers for tobacco, for which the number of beavers totals fifty-three.

Asked if he did not leave some merchandise at Missimakinna?
Answers no?

Asked why he is not declaring that he left ten pounds of powder in a canvas sack and 200 musket balls according to the Reverend Father Pierson's[14] statement?
Answers that it is true and that the powder is his own and the musket balls are part of the communal goods that he had with the said Dubeau's wife as well as twelve large rounds[15] of wampum.[16]

Asked if he did not divert some packs of beaver along the way?
Answers that he faithfully brought all the beaver that he acquired with the exception of one robe of seven beavers that he left in the hands of the Huron named Ouniahecha.

Asked if on the trails coming down or having arrived in this town he did not give any to his wife or relatives and friends unbeknownst to the said sieur Renauld and his partner?
Answers that he diverted only ten of them which were used to pay an Iroquois woman who had given him 20 rounds of wampum while leaving.

Migeon de Branssat paraph.

Asked if he did not eat or drink up beavers[17] that belonged to the partnership?
Answers that he drank up four that came from his nephew's hunting.

A reading was done to the said sieur de LaMarque, interpreter for the said Louis Oakin called the Lame One, who said that his replies were truthful and that he gave them and reported them faithfully just as the said Indian told him, which Indian stuck to his replies and declared that he did not know how to write or sign, having been asked this in conformity with the ordinance, and sieur LaMarque, the interpreter, signed with us and our assistant to the clerk of the court on the above said day and year.

J Lamarque paraph.

Migeon De Brannsat

Cabazie, assistant to the clerk of the court[18]

NOTES

1. Archives nationales du Québec à Montréal, Documents judiciaires de la juridiction seigneuriale de Montréal (1651–1695) [cote TL 2, feuilles détachées, 1681–1693]. The date of the document is as reported here, but the record of the proceeding mentions a hearing taking place on the 30th of the month.

2. The Hurons were a powerful confederacy of Iroquoian speakers who had lived around Lake Simcoe, Ontario. They had served as important allies of the French, and as key partners in the French fur trade. In this period, many of them lived at Michilimackinac.

3. Probably Charles-Paul Marin de La Malgue (La Margue, La Marque, La Marche). He was an officer in the colonial regular troops and was familiar with Iroquoian languages, the type spoken by the Huron Louis Ouakouts. *DCB*, 2:458.

4. It has proven impossible to conclusively identify this person. In this period, two unrelated men, Antoine Renaud *dit* Desmoulins (a miller) and Antoine Renaud *dit* le Tambour (a mason), lived in Montreal. Of the two, Renaud *dit* Desmoulins could sign his name. Yves Landry, ed., *Pour le Christ et le Roi: La vie au temps des premiers Montréalais* (Montreal: Éditions Libre Expression, 1992), 290.

5. Contractual partner, *sa partie.*

6. Dry beaver referred to beaver skins that were cleaned, stretched, and dried as individual pelts. Beaver robes referred to beaver skins sewn together, after undergoing the above process, to form a sort of cover used by Indians and which were later sold. The latter were also known as *castor gras*, "greasy beaver," which took its name from the way it was processed. For more on greasy beaver, see document 5.

7. Indians in northeastern North America did not have either a written language or a numerical system. Tallying of smaller amounts was done by direct representation (e.g., a stick or mark on a piece of bark or on the ground for each man in a war party, or beaver skin in a bundle), and large numbers were managed by metaphor (e.g., there were as many men in the war party as there are trees in the forest). In this case de Branssat reveals that Louis marked the number of pelts, etc., on the wooden floor with a bit of charcoal. The numbers mentioned in the rest of this document were most likely arrived at via the process that de Branssat describes here, but having once described the process, he simply provides the totals shown him by Louis.

8. Cut short, *babogis.*

9. These people, known to the French by the names of Nadouessioux and Sioux, are the Dakota. They lived in Wisconsin and north-central Minnesota and were often at war with the Ojibwas of the Upper Great Lakes, and thus were a threat to French interests in the region. Barry M. Pritzker, *A Native American Encyclopedia: History, Culture, and Peoples* (Oxford and New York: Oxford University Press, 2000), 316–19; Robert E. Ritzenhaler, "Southwestern Chippewa," in *Handbook*, 15:744.

10. Old Pike, *Le Vieux Brochet.*

11. The Heel, *Le Talon.*

12. Ojahe the Just, *Ojahe Le Juste.*

13. Known to the French by this name, he was known to other Natives as Kondiaronk or Sastaretsi. He was a Petun Huron chief from Michilimackinac. His people had

fled there after the Iroquois attacks against the Hurons. He was a staunch supporter of the French and harbored a deep loathing of the Iroquois. During the peace negotiations at Montreal in 1701, at which he was one of the few Indian leaders to stand up to the Iroquois, he contracted a fever and died. *DCB*, 2:320–23.

14. Father Philippe Pierson was sent to serve among the Hurons at Michilimackinac in 1673. He lived there until 1683, when he went to work among the Sioux. He died at Quebec in 1688. *JR*, 50:327 and 71:151.

15. Rounds, *ronds*.

16. Wampum refers to small beads, originally made from marine shells, used by Natives throughout northeastern North America. Wampum was used to decorate items, but more importantly it was used as a mnemonic device to "record" speeches made during treaties and other meetings among Natives and between Indians and Europeans. Wampum was strung in various sequences on strings, and in patterns on belts, which were then exchanged between the negotiating parties to serve as reminders of what had transpired and had been agreed upon. André Vachon, "Colliers et ceintures de porcelaine dans la diplomatie indienne," *Les Cahiers des Dix* 36 (1971): 179–92; Vachon, "Colliers et ceintures de porcelaine chez les indiens de la Nouvelle-France," *Les Cahiers des Dix* 35 (1970): 251–78.

17. That is, did he not trade beaver pelts for food or drink?

18. Pierre Cabazié also served as a notary and sergeant-at-arms. *DCB*, 2:111.

Testimony of Simone Côté and others on alleged embezzlement at Michilimackinac in the case of Couagne vs. Louis Ouakouts, Marie Félix, et al.

1683, July 16 and 27, Montreal[1]

There appeared before us Simonne Costé[2] a witness summoned to testify truthfully on the facts of the said complaint and possession of stolen beaver and on the summons that was given to her by Lory sergeant of this bailiwick that she showed us and after having taken her customary oath she said her name was Simonne Costé forty-seven years of age, a merchant[3] residing in this town and neither a relative of or related by marriage to the said Renaud nor to the said Indians of whom she has heard speak and testifies on the facts of the said complaint that having learned from her son Simon Soumandre that the man named Louis Boiteux[4] of the Huron nation ordinarily residing in the village of the mountain of this place and that he had eight packs of dry beaver in his canoe and some other packs of greasy beaver[5] whereupon the deponent went to see it at the water's edge in order to speak to the said Indian to whom she spoke asking him if he didn't have some letters for her, she saw several packs of dry beaver and several robes that were not in packs which packs and robes were carried to the seminary[6] by several Indians who were then on the water's edge whom the said Lame One had disembarked, and [in response to] the judicial inquiry whether there were no Frenchmen who arrived she learned that Marie Félix wife of Laurent Dubaux [Duboc, etc.], a habitant of the environs of Québek, was supposed to arrive soon having the responsibility for letters that were coming from the Outaouais, and as she had arrived and she brought the letters that she had to my lord the [superior] general, the deponent saw the said Lame One before his shop who was taking the road to the said sieur Renaud's place, having on his shoulder four or five [. . .] dry beavers and a pack, and the said Lame One's wife who was following him loaded with two packs of beaver who instead of following the said Lame One, her husband, took the mountain road via monsieur Perrot's street,[7] and two or three other Indians, women and boys who were loaded with the baggage from their canoe or with personal effects which is all that she said she knew and that she did not see the said Lame One nor his wife to pay her or to deal with her, and after the reading of her deposition persisted in it and signed it with us and the clerk of the court.

Simonne Costé

Migeon de Branssat paraph.

Maugue paraph.

Clerk of the Court

There appeared next sieur Jean Jacques Patron,[8] a witness summoned by Lory whose writ was shown to us, and after having taken from him the accustomed oath required in such a case said he was named Jean Jacques Patron, merchant-entrepreneur residing in this town and not a relative of nor related by marriage to the said plaintiff any more than the said parties, and testifies on the facts of the said complaint that around two weeks ago going to the said plaintiff at about two o'clock in the afternoon he saw four Indians who were carrying into this place's seminary house at least eight packs of dry beaver, and having increased his pace in order to join them before they entered the said house to recognize who they were, and having arrived at the door of the said seminary as he was observing them enter he noticed one of the ecclesiastics of this place with the reverend Father Beschefer[9] who was in an upstairs window which obligated the deponent to continue on his way without learning from where the said Indians were coming, which is what he said he knows and after the reading said it contained the truth and persisted in it and signed it with us and our clerk of the court.

five words crossed out null and void

Patron paraph.

Migeon de Branssat paraph.

Maugue paraph.

Clerk of the Court

There appeared before us Marie Felix to testify truthfully upon the summons that was given to her by Lory that she showed us, and after taking her oath that is required in such cases [she] said she was named Marie Felix, the wife of Lauret Dubaux, a habitant of Cap Rouge near Québek, having come down a little while ago from the Outaouais with the said accused Lame One [and said] she was neither a relative of nor related by marriage to the said plaintiff any more than the said accused, testified on the information in the said complaint that last year she went to trade among the Outaouais[10] accompanied by the said accused with whom she took merchandise at the said plaintiff's place on credit to be paid for by them upon their return this year, and in coming down the said Lame One had loaded into the canoe that they had brought down eight packs of dry beaver containing thirty beavers each and two packs of greasy beaver one of which is claimed by the female relative of the said Lame One who also came down with him and the deponent who said that she did not have complete knowledge about the beaver that he was able to obtain in the Outaouais country in view of the fact that during most of her stay there she was sick and that in spite of her the said Lame One took possession of all the merchandise without being willing to give her any information on the trading he conducted, which greatly disturbed her during her sickness as well as the news she heard that he was eating up and dissipating [the trade goods], having smoked most of the tobacco that they had brought there, of which the deponent had diverted eight fathoms[11] fearing that the said Lame One would smoke it, from which she obtained eight beavers that she placed among the packs that she loaded into his canoe and since delivered to the plaintiff. Furthermore she added that the said Lame One pulled out of one pack of those he had carried to the seminary ten beavers that he gave to an Iroquois woman who lives in the village of the mountain to pay her for some wampum that the said Lame One said he got from her before his departure, and yet the said Lame One told the deponent as they were among the Outaouais that he had given the said wampum to a woman with the intention [of being?] paid, the latter woman finding herself incapable of paying wanted to return it to the said Lame One [who refused to take it back] saying that it was his and that she should keep it [because] his [wife] had given it to him with the intention that he make a present of it for her relatives among the said Outaouais. Furthermore she declared that the said Lame One's wife carried off one pack from those that her husband brought from the said Outaouais country and that he even bragged about having left two hundred beavers there that he had recently traded and which took the merchandise of their partnership[12] and that he left debts to be collected whose numbers the partnership does not know and that as for the partnership, two beavers are owed to it by the Hurons and twelve beavers by the Outaouais called Le Talon which is all that she says she knows after the reading of her deposition that she says to be the truth and persisted and signed with us and the clerk of the court.

Migeon De Branssat paraph.

Marie Felix

Maugue paraph.

Clerk of the Court

On July 27, 1683 there appeared before us the witness named below summoned by sergeant Lory in accordance with our order at the bottom of the petition presented to us by sieur DeCouaigne, the plaintiff, and after having taken his customary oath and our having inquired as to his name, surname, age, position and residence he said he was named Jean Couture, thirty-three years of age, formerly a domestic servant of the Reverend Jesuit Fathers, only recently having come down from the Outaouais where he had gone to take care of his affairs who said he was neither a relative of nor related by marriage to Marie Felix, wife of Laurent Dubaux, a habitant of Quebec, any more than to the Indians with whom the said woman had gone into partnership. He said and testified as to the facts in the said complaint that he had no knowledge whatever that the said Dubos woman had diverted beavers or other furs any more than the said Indians, her partners, whom he saw last winter at Michilmakima, one of whom, a man named Louis Ouacont, The Lame One, who dissipated the better part of the merchandise that he had in partnership with the said Dubos woman, having made very poor use of it, having distributed it now to make himself esteemed, and at other times to corrupt the said [Indians], [Jean Couture] declaring that the said Dubos woman for her part did all she could to trade advantageously the merchandise that she took in partnership with the said Indians, that he learned that he [Louis] drank several beavers in coming down toward Sunken River,[13] declaring furthermore that the Jesuit Reverend Father Pierson gave him a packet of letters to deliver to the said Marie Felix with a statement of the merchandise she left at the said place Missilimakina in the house of the Jesuit Reverend Fathers that we took from the said deponent, at the bottom of which is also what the said Louis The Lame One left at the said place, to wit ten pounds of powder in a sack and 200 musketballs, all of the above said merchandise being in three cases entrusted to the said Father Pierson, knowing of nothing else at all that belongs to either the said Dubos woman or the said Indians her partners, and that all the French will be able to say, as he who is testifying, that the said Dubos woman did her duty to [. . .] the sale of the said merchandise while the said Indians consumed it without discretion, which is all he said he knew and after the reading of his deposition he said it contained the truth and persisted in it and declared that he did not know how to sign this investigation, in accordance with the ordinance.[14]

Migeon De Branssat paraph.

NOTES

1. Archives nationales du Québec à Montréal, Documents judiciaires de la juridiction seigneuriale de Montréal (1651–1695) [cote TL 2, feuilles détachées, 1681–1693].

2. Simone Côté. She was married to Pierre Soumande, a master edge-tool maker. In addition to the son mentioned below, the couple had a daughter, Louise Soumande, who became a nun and was the first superior of the Hôpital Général of Quebec. *DCB*, 2:613.

3. This is a clear example of the active role women played in the commercial life of the colony. This woman is not just said to be involved in a business activity, she is said to be a business person by occupation. The roles of women in New France is a topic of some debate. See, for example, Jan Noel, "New-France: Les femmes favorisées," in *Rethinking Canada: The Promise of Women's History*, ed. Veronica Strong-Boag and Anita Clair Fellman (Toronto: Copp Clark Pitman, 1986), 23–44; Noel, "Women in New France: Further Reflections," *Atlantis* 8, no. 1 (Fall/automne 1982): 125–30; Micheline Dumont, "Les femmes de la Nouvelle-France étaient-elles favorisées?" *Atlantis* 8, no. 1 (Fall/automne 1982): 118–24; Lilianne Plamondon, "A Businesswoman in New France: Marie-anne Barbel, the Widow Fornel," in *Rethinking Canada*, ed. Strong-Boag and Fellman, 45–58; Josette Brun, "Les femmes d'affaires en Nouvelle-France au 18e siècle: Le cas de l'île Royale," *Acadiensis* 27, no. 1 (Autumn 1997): 44–66. Part of the controversy comes, as Noel notes, from modern scholars projecting perceptions of women's roles, and the divisions in them, from a later period back into the 1600s and 1700s, where they did not obtain. Jan Noel, "'The Nagging Wife' Revisited: Women and the Fur Trade in New France," *French Colonial History* 7 (2006): 45–60.

4. This is Louis Ouakouts. *Boiteux* means "lame," and while other witnesses have, after using his proper names, used the word *boiteux* to describe his condition and/or to suggest that he is known as The Lame One because of it, she has erroneously used the word in place of his actual name.

5. Greasy beaver (*castor gras*) took its name from the way it was processed:

   the inner side [of the pelts was] scraped and rubbed with the marrow of certain animals [. . .] [and sewn into] robes which were worn by the Indians with the fur next to the body. The scraping of the inner side of the pelt loosened the deep roots of the long guard hair, and with wearing, this hair dropped out leaving the fur. With constant wearing [. . .] the skin became well greased, pliable, and yellow in colour and the fur downy or *cotonné*.

It was this soft underfur that was most desired for making the felt hats for which most beaver pelts were destined in this period. Harold A. Innis, *The Fur Trade in Canada*, rev. ed. (Toronto: University of Toronto Press, 1956), 14. That hat makers had less work to do to prepare the furs made them more desirable, and thus they were worth more. From 1677 to 1696, greasy beaver was worth 82s 6d a livre and dry beaver was worth 52s 6d. From 1696 to 1706, the prices were 78s 9d and 40s respectively. In the years 1706 to 1710, the price was 20s for greasy and 30s for dry beaver. From 1710 to 1714 the prices were 30–40s and 30s a livre, and from 1715 to 1719 they were 57–80s and 28–32s a livre. Louise Dechêne, *Habitants et marchands de Montréal au xviie siècle* (Montréal: Librairie Plon, 1974), tableaux 14, p. 141.

6. Probably a reference to the Sulpician residence near Mont Royal in the center of Montreal Island. In 1684 a new seminary and residence were constructed on Rue Notre-Dame, further back from the waterfront. Landry, ed., *Pour le Christ et le Roi*, 128–29, 152–53.

7. François-Marie Perrot was a highly controversial governor of Montreal from 1669 to 1684, when he was removed by Louis XIV. He engaged heavily in the fur trade, despite the king's prohibitions. *DCB*, 1:540–42. Perrot's house was located on Rue Saint-Paul, the street closest to the southeastern branch of the St. Lawrence River. Landry, ed., *Pour le Christ et le Roi*, 153.

8. Patron was the uncle of Daniel Greysolon Dulhut, an important explorer and colonial officer in New France. For more about Dulhut, see document 28.

9. Father Thierry Beschefer, a Jesuit priest. He resided in Quebec and was the superior of the order from 1680 to 1686. *DCB*, 2:61–62.

10. Marie Félix, as indicated in document 2, was a Native woman. This reference to a woman, Indian or otherwise, traveling specifically to engage in trade is rare in the documentary history of New France.

11. A *brasse* ("fathom" in English) was a measure of five French feet (*pieds*) in length. John Francis McDermott, *A Glossary of Mississippi Valley French, 1673–1850* (St. Louis: Washington University Studies, new series, 1941), 34. Tobacco was sold by length coiled in hard, rope-like rolls.

12. That is, for which beavers he used his partners' trade goods.

13. Sunken River, *la rivière creuse*. Nicolas Bellin, in his 1744 *Carte des lacs du Canada*, shows an "R. Creuse" on the Ottawa River, some distance north of modern day Ottawa, Ontario. This is possibly the river known today as Deep River.

14. The Civil Ordinance of 1667, which set out the process of civil law in New France.

Statement of trade goods belonging to Marie du Bocq

1683, Michilimackinac[1]

> *Statement of trade goods belonging to Marie Felix du Bocq Left with the Fathers at Missilimakina 1683:*

18 combs
Eleven dozen big knives
A packet of iron arrowheads
2 gross of awls
7 half large muskets[2]
21 leather knives[3]

[*Marginal note*: giving copy of the said statement to the said sieur Renaud and is at the said amount][4]

12 strike-a-lights[5]
Around 10 pounds of lead[6]
140 musket balls
7 to 8 pounds of powder
7 large double mirrors
a heap of blue beads
a half-fathom of transparent [beads]
6 fathoms of black
10 fathoms of red
20 fathoms of white
2 pounds of white cosmetic powder[7]
2 pounds of yellow in a heap

For Louis Dakont

Around 10 pounds of powder in a long sack
200 musket balls

[*Vertical note in the left margin*: All of it in 3 boxes]

NOTES

1. Archives nationales du Québec à Montréal, Documents judiciaires de la juridiction seigneuriale de Montréal (1651–1695) [cote TL 2, feuilles détachées, 1681–1693]. This document was attached to document 5.

2. Large muskets, *biscayennes*. A *biscäien* was a large caliber musket, used to fire from ramparts. *Grand Larousse en 5 volumes*.

3. *Trenches* is written here, but the correct spelling, in the singular, is *tranche*. The writer probably meant to write *tranchet*, a leather-cutting knife.

4. The note actually reads "donne coppie dudit memoire audit sieur Renaud est a ladite somme."

5. Strike-a-lights, *battes feu*.

6. The term used here is *plomb à tourtes*, which translated literally means "wild pigeon lead."

7. *Blanc d'Espagne*, the term used here, was a white lead pigment used as a cosmetic, and was also called *céruse* in French and "ceruse" in English today. See "blanc d'Espaigne" in Randle Cotgrave, *A Dictionarie of the French and English Tongues* (London: Adam Islip, 1611; repr. Columbia: University of South Carolina Press, 1968). Today, *blanc d'Espagne* refers to natural calcium carbonate. *Le Nouveau Petit Robert: Dictionnaire de la langue française* (Paris: Dictionnaires le Robert, 1993).

Petition by Charles de Couagne asking that Madame Soumande [Simone Côté], and others, be summoned to testify; and that permission be granted to seize Louis Ouakont's canoe

1683, July 16, Montreal[1]

Petition by Charles de Couagne asking that Madame Soumande [Simone Côté]; Jean Jacques Patron; the captain of the Indians at La Montagne; and Denis and his wife be summoned to testify; and that permission be granted to seize Louis 8akont's canoe.

I entreat Monsieur de Laury [Lory] to beg Madame Soumande to allow herself to be subpoenaed to give testimony about the pack of beaver that she saw carried off the same day that Louis Ouakonts arrived in Montreal and I would be obliged to her and also to Monsieur Patron to say how many packs he saw carried to the seminary and to subpoena the captain of the Indians of La Montagne with Denis and his wife to testify truthfully. Done in Montreal July 16, 1683.

Charles de Couagne paraph.

And to seize Louis Ouakont's canoe with the permission of Monsieur Dollier[2] or Monsieur Mariet.[3]

NOTES

1. Archives nationales du Québec à Montréal, Documents judiciaires de la juridiction seigneuriale de Montréal (1651–1695) [cote TL 2, feuilles détachées, 1681–1693].

2. François Dollier de Casson was superior of the Sulpician Order of priests in New France, and as such, seigneur of Montreal Island. *DCB*, 2:190.

3. Joseph Mariet was a Sulpician priest at the Montreal Seminary. He arrived at Montreal in 1668 and died there in 1704. René Jetté, ed., *Dictionnaire généalogique des familles du Québec des origines à 1730* (Montréal: Les Presses de l'Université de Montréal: 1983), 771 [hereafter Jetté, DG].

Petition of Charles de Couagne providing questions and facts justifying calling Jean Couture to be interrogated

1683, July 16, Montreal[1]

Facts upon which it will be necessary to question sieur Couture, firstly if anything had been placed in his hands at Meschielmaquilnak [Michili-mackinac] or other locations for Marie Felix or someone else, something belonging to the said Marie Felix or her partnership;

For the knowledge he may have of what happened in the said partnership concerning both her and her partners;

About the quantity of trade goods that they may have left among the Ottawas and other locations in the region, plus whether they made a cache[2] or gave furs to be taken to other people who could come down here or whether they saw any given to be taken to others or heard of who could have come down or could have stayed up there.

Plus through whom the said sieur Couture is to go down to Quebec and with whom, not having a canoe of his own, and whether he says that he wants to leave today or tomorrow.

Charles de Couagne paraph.

NOTES

1. Archives nationales du Québec à Montréal, Documents judiciaires de la juridiction seigneuriale de Montréal (1651–1695) [cote TL 2, feuilles détachées, 1681–1693]. This document was attached to document 5.
2. Cache, *quache*. Goods, furs, and food were sometimes stored—usually buried—at given locations along a travel route to be picked up at a later time. The common practice was to store food that need not be carried all the way to the end destination, but which would be needed on the return trip home.

Petition by Claude Tardy, a Montreal merchant who with a partner outfitted a canoe for, and provided goods to, some traders whom he accuses of having diverted most of the goods

1683, October 4, Montreal[1]

To the Montreal magistrate

Claude Tardy, a merchant in this town, humbly submits this petition saying that he had fitted out together with sieur Renaud, a merchant, whose authorization he presently has, a canoe for going to trade among the Ottawas in which there were the men named Guillory,[2] Loisel[3] and Villedieu[4] who having arrived several days ago with very few belongings and giving a very poor account of the goods placed in their hands leads the petitioner to suspect them and to believe that they have diverted most of the goods, which obliges him to appeal to you to be well informed about this.

Taking this into consideration, sir, please permit the said supplicant to have the diversion investigated and to this end to have all those whom the petitioner finds with knowledge of the said diversion called before you and during this [procedure] for security and the preservation of his rights let it please you to order the beaver that will at present be found belonging to the said Villedieu and Loisel which is in the hands of sieur Charron de La Barre[5] be seized and attached in his possession at the petitioner's risks and perils until the investigation is completed and decided by you and justice done.

Tardy paraph.

In view of the above petition and the written agreement made with the above named persons, the petitioner is permitted to seize in order to find out [. . .] the witnesses summoned to testify truthfully about the alleged possession of stolen goods. We so order etc. Done the 4th day of October 1683.

Migeon De Branssat paraph.

NOTES

1. Archives nationales du Québec à Montréal, Documents judiciaires de la juridiction seigneuriale de Montréal (1651–1695) [cote TL 2, feuilles détachées, 1681–1693].

2. Simon Guillory, a master armorer. His son, also named Simon, who was about five years old at this time, went on to become a prominent merchant in the fur trade. Jetté, *DG*, 544–45. Guillory, the father, had a house on Rue Saint-Paul in Montreal. Many of the people whose names appear in these documents, such as René Fezeret, Charles de Couagne, Jacques le Ber, Jean-Baptiste Migeon, and Daniel Greysolon Dulhut, also lived on Rue Saint-Paul. Landry, ed., *Pour le Christ et le Roi*, 152–53.

3. Joseph Loisel, who became an outfitter in the fur trade. He was the son of Louis Loisel, a master ironsmith. Jetté, *DG*, 740.

4. Probably Antoine Villedieu, who was married at Pointe-aux-Trembles, Montreal, in 1685. Jetté, *DG*, 1128.

5. François Charon de La Barre (1654–1719) was a Montreal merchant and, at this time, a moneylender to fur traders. In August 1683 Charon was one of four Montreal merchants who had Cavelier de La Salle's furs at Fort Frontenac seized. After a nearly fatal illness several years later, he devoted himself to major works of charity. He was the founder of the Brothers Hospitallers of the Cross, and of St. Joseph and the Hôpital Général (almshouse) of Montreal. *DCB*, 2:132–35.

Judicial investigation, based upon Tardy's petition, against the traders Loisel and Villedieu, including the testimony of eyewitnesses

1683, October 4–7, Montreal[1]

Inquiry undertaken upon the petition of sieur Claude Tardy and associates whose rights have been granted by us, magistrate of Montreal, over certain furs that he said were taken by the men named Joseph Loizel and Villedieu to whom he had entrusted a congé to trade among the Ottawas from whom they have been back for several days and whom he accuses of having diverted several furs coming from their trading. In order to verify this he has had summoned by sergeant Lory whose writ has been shown to me in accordance with our order dated this day the witnesses named below, the first of whom we have heard with our clerk of the court. After taking his oath, age, position, and residence he said he was named Jean Fillastreau twenty-three years of age,[2] having been back for several days from the said Ottawa country with the man named Jolicoeur[3] and company with the said Loizel and Villedieu, the accused, to whom he is not related nor related by marriage nor a servant any more than to the said plaintiff and testified on the fact of the said complaint that being at Missilmakina around the month of August he saw the said Villedieu and Loizel arrive as they came back from trading, the latter from the poux[4] Villedieu from Chagouamigon,[5] who having divided up their share with other partners from various companies had as their share eighteen packs of dry and greasy beaver each pack containing about thirty to forty beavers and the ones containing greasy ones around eight to ten robes not knowing in actual fact the quantity there could be of one or the other kind dry or greasy, and that they embarked at the said Missilimakina in the canoe in which they came down, and that the deponent accompanied the said Jolicoeur in another canoe all four having come down together and that the said Loizel and Villedieu having met a man named Grandmaison around the Calumets[6] and having no provisions at all they untied one of their packs and took out thirteen or fourteen dry beavers to buy some provisions from the said Grandmaison, and that they came down together as far as this town, and that the said Villedieu and Loizel unloaded there the number of packs that they carried to sieur Charron's, [. . .] he believes furthermore he added that the said Guito went down in place of Simon Guilory partner of the said accused who remained at the said Missilmakina and agreed with the said Guito for thirty dry beavers and to him the deponent one hundred francs in silver payable on his arrival and that their canoe was loaded with seven packs of dry beaver and two of robes containing sixteen robes and some pieces inside and five packs of dry beaver belonging to the partnership [word(s) crossed out] of the said Villedieu and Loizel with two packs of robes containing sixteen robes and some pieces inside of which he does not know the number, and that the said Guito left five packs of dry beaver in the house of Pierre Gaigné at Prairie de la Magdelaine[7] and the value of six robes both in the said packs and the one he used to sleep in belonging to the said Jollicoeur the said packs coming from the fur trading he had done with the children of sieur De Repentigny[8] at the time the king had forbidden going trading in the said Ottawa country[9] which is all he said he knew and that he did not see any of the said packs unloaded in this town other than what he learned from his brother, the deponent having gotten out of his canoe above this town's mill because he had been told that Monsieur Perrot the governor wanted to have him arrested and made a prisoner to find out from him how many packs the man named Cochois had brought and received from Monsieur de LaSalle[10] who was in debt to him, and after the reading of his deposition that he said contained the truth and persisted in it and stated he did not know how to write or make his mark for this inquiry according to the ordinance three words of no value crossed out, tax required of twenty sols granted to him.

Migeon De Branssat paraph.

Maugue paraph. *clerk of the court*

On the sixth day of October sixteen hundred eighty-three there appeared before us the below named witness summoned by sergeant Lory whose writ was shown to us and whose oath we took and having inquired as to his name he said his name was Pierre Gaigne thirty-eight years of age an habitant living at Prairie de la Magdelaine [etc.] He testified on the facts of the said complaint and those that were placed in our hands by the said Tardy, that Tuesday the twenty-eighth of the past month the men named Loizel, Villedieu, Guito, and Fillastreau arrived at the said La Prairie around three o'clock in the afternoon where they landed because of the bad weather, and the deponent having learned about their arrival went to the water's edge to join them the latter carried into the Jesuit Fathers' barn at the said location several packs of beaver whose number in actual fact he does not know and everything that was in their canoe except for five packs which were carried to his house belonging to the said Guito of which four were of dry beaver and the fifth of robes and dry beavers also that last Monday the fourth of this month the said Guito untied around two of the packs he brought into sieur François Hazeur's[11] house to pay his debts and buy his commodities the other three [packs] remained in his said house, and that he had heard the said Guito say that he and the said accused had brought the quantity of thirty-six packs of beaver of which five belonged to the said Guito and the remaining thirty-one belonged [to?] or had been brought by the said Loizel and Villedieu. Asked the said witness if he did not know that the said Villedieu and Loizel had diverted some of their beaver on the way or elsewhere in French houses. He said that he had no knowledge of this and that what they spent at his house where they stayed almost two days because of the bad weather was paid by the said Guito and that they did not unpack any of their said beavers, and that he had no knowledge of the quantity of robes they had obtained among the Ottawas from whom they are coming back, any more than other furs like raccoons, martins, otters, fishers, etc., and that he is not informed about it or trade goods any more than the debts they had incurred with the Indians not even knowing if the said Loizel and Villedieu sent any to their wives, relatives or friends nor whether they sold any for money, the deponent stating that he saw in the said Loizel and Villedieu's hands letters without his knowing to whom they were addressed except for two whose writing he saw, one of which the said Guito had brought for the widow and the other for Guillory's wife, not knowing if the said accused had delivered those [letters] that they had, nor the number of packs they delivered to sieur Charron except nine which were sent to him by Simon Guillory, which is all that he said he knew [etc.]

P. Ganier

Tax required forty-five sols granted

Migeon De Branssat paraph

Maugue paraph

On the said day there appeared the below named witness summoned by sergeant Lory whose writ was shown to us and having asked him for his name, age, position and residence he said his name was Jacques Guito dit Jolicoeur sixty years of age, a tailor[12] living at Prairie de la Magdelaine when he is not on a trip from which he came down a short while ago [etc. etc.] [said] that he arrived from the Ottawa country the day before St. Michael's Day[13] the twenty-eighth of last month at the said location of La Prairie where he was obliged to remain with Fillastreau who was in his canoe, Loizel and Villedieu who were in another and who came down together with him from Missilmakina from where they left on the thirteenth of last August, stating that he had five packs of his own beaver all dry except for six robes, which packs were given to him by the sons of sieur de Repentigny last year at Missilmakina where he remained because of a sickness that he caught, and that he came down from the said location in place of Guillory who was a member of the partnership of the said Loizel and Villedieu in exchange for thirty beavers and the sum of one hundred livres to the said Fillastreau payable by the said Tardy Loizel Guillory and Villedieu; and that he had in the canoe in which the said deponent was traveling besides the five packs belonging to him two packs belonging to the said Fillastreau, eleven packs belonging to Tardy and his associates' partnership that he delivered to sieur Charron nine of which belonged to the said Guillory and the two others to the said partnership of which four were of greasy and seven of dry beaver and the said Loizel and Villedieu brought to me in the canoe in which they were traveling sixteen belonging to the said partnership of which four were greasy and twelve were dry, and two others belonging to him [La Rue?] that he was sending to his wife residing on this island the other to the said Villedieu that he had received from sieur Perré from the remainder of the partnership that he had had with him three years ago the deponent stating that since they embarked together at Michyl-makina as far as Prairie de la Magdelaine and from the latter as far as the Petite Riviere of this town where the said Loizel and Villedieu disembarked with him, they untied no pack at all nor pulled out any beaver that was part of the said partnership but only the said Villedieu and the deponent having met on their way as they were coming down sieur d'Argenteuil,[14] Hertel,[15] and Grandmaison[16] they drank and the said Villedieu in order to pay for their expense pulled ten beavers out of the pack that was his own and they did not spend or divert anything else either on the way or at the top of the island or at the said Prairie which he affirms is true, and that they separated out even the goods that remained to them at Michilmakina from their partnership and the said Guillory retained the share of the partner in charge[17] with his that they also left entrusted to the man named Xaintes[18] at Michilmakina in the hope of coming back this spring according to the word given to them about it by sieur Dulhut,[19] the deponent adding that he did not learn from them the number of robes they were able to trade nor how many otters, martins, fishers, or raccoons of which he is not informed which is all that he said he knew [etc.] and declared that he did not know how to write or sign etc.

Tax required forty-five sols granted.

Migeon De Branssat paraph.

Maugue paraph.

Continuation of the above investigation [. . .] done by us the seventh day of October

Jean Obuchon[20] a witness summoned to testify on the facts of the said complaint and summoned by sergeant Lory whose writ was shown to us, and after having taken his oath asked etc. He said his name is Jean Obuchon fifty-four years of age a merchant living in this town etc., testified on the fact of certain packs of greasy and dry beaver [. . .] that he gave yesterday to sieur Renaud; he gave three packs of beavers of all kinds to sieur Renaud for goods that he bought from him jointly [with?] sieur Cuillerier,[21] a habitant of LaChine and on the same terms namely 40 percent and that it is beaver that he has had at his place since last year and that he did not receive one single [beaver] hair from the said Loizel and Villedieu nor any more than that from Guillory's wife and that he has no knowledge that they gave any to other people and that around a week ago crossing his path he saw them unload several packs and carry them to sieur Charron's which is what he said he knew and after the reading of his deposition that he said contained the truth he signed it with us and the said clerk of the court.

Required tax granted 20 sols.

Jean Obuchon

Migeon De Branssat paraph.

Maugue paraph.

Clerk of the court

Considering that there are no charges against the said defendants we have converted the said investigation into a trial. Ruling done this October 7th 1683, and the said plaintiff permitted to provide evidence. So ordered.

Migeon De Branssat paraph.

NOTES

1. Archives nationales du Québec à Montréal, Documents judiciaires de la juridiction seigneuriale de Montréal (1651–1695) [cote TL 2, feuilles détachées, 1681–1693].

2. One of four children of René Filiatrault and Jeanne Hérault. Jean was born in Montreal in 1660. Jetté, *DG*, 419.

3. Jacques Guitault (Guito) *dit* Jolicoeur was a sergeant in the Carignan Regiment who arrived in New France in 1665 and settled in the Montreal region. Jetté, *DG*, 547.

4. *Les poux*, the Potawatomis. The latter were Algonquian-speaking allies of New France. In this period they lived all around Lake Michigan and on the Door Peninsula in Wisconsin, and groups were making their way back to their homelands around the St. Joseph River area in lower Michigan. James A. Clifton, "Potawatomi," in *Handbook*, 15:725–26. Loisel had likely visited the groups in Wisconsin.

5. Near Ashland, Wisconsin.

6. Le Sault des Calumets (the Peacepipe Falls or Rapids) are on the Ottawa River at today's Ottawa, Ontario.

7. Pierre Gagné of Laprairie on the east shore of the St. Lawrence River, across from Montreal Island.

8. Jean-Baptiste Legardeur de Repentigny, councilor in the Conseil Souverain, had twenty-one children. His sons Pierre Legardeur de Repentigny, Jean-Paul de Legardeur de Saint-Pierre, and Pierre-Noël Legardeur de Tilly all served, at some point, in the Canadian military, and all engaged in the fur trade. *DCB*, 2:384–87.

9. Trade to the Ottawas had been prohibited in 1676 and 1678. In 1681 the king allowed twenty-five congés per year to trade. Joseph L. Peyser, ed. and trans., *Jacques Legardeur de Saint-Pierre: Officer, Gentleman, Entrepreneur* (East Lansing/Mackinac Island: Michigan State University Press/Mackinac State Historic Parks, 1996), 6.

10. René-Robert Cavelier de La Salle, a much-traveled explorer and fur trader who was closely connected to Governor Frontenac, and who encouraged La Salle's voyages of discovery and trade in the face of the king's prohibitions on extending the fur trade. In 1679 La Salle built the first ship to sail in the upper Great Lakes and sailed it through the Straits of Mackinac to Green Bay. Named the *Griffon* after the symbol on Frontenac's coat of arms, the ship was lost in a storm shortly after. In 1682 La Salle became the first Frenchman to travel down the Mississippi to where it emptied into the Gulf of Mexico. By 1684 La Salle had convinced the French Crown of the merits of establishing a colony at the mouth of the Mississippi. La Salle hoped to bring all the furs from the upper Great Lakes via that river and avoid the frozen St. Lawrence and all the portages it took to get materials to and from the river. Unfortunately for La Salle, the Mississippi splits up into many little

rivers at its delta mouth, and he got lost trying to find the main river to the Gulf of Mexico. Lost, starving, and tired of searching for the river for several years, some of La Salle's men shot him on the morning of March 19, 1687. *DCB*, 2:172–84.

11. François Hazeur was based at Quebec and was a leading merchant in New France, involved in the major companies that dominated the fur trade. He also served as councilor in the Conseil Supérieur. He married Anne Soumande, daughter of Simone Côté mentioned in document 5. Hazeur had a large house on Rue Saint-Paul in Montreal, which he probably used to store furs, as well as goods to be exchanged for furs. *DCB*, 2:275; Landry, ed., *Pour le Christ et le Roi*, 152.

12. A tailor, *tailleur dhabits*.

13. St. Michael's Day is September 29.

14. Pierre d'Ailleboust d'Argenteuil was an excellent officer who enjoyed good relations with a number of Indian nations. "Throughout the 1690s Argenteuil made many trips to the Michilimackinac region" having "led several fur trade convoys back to Montreal." *DCB*, 2:12–13.

15. Probably Joseph-François Hertel de La Fresnière, officer, interpreter and seigneur, but the reference might be to his son Jean-Baptiste Hertel de Rouville, who would have been about fifteen years old at this date. The latter was said to "have taken up soldiering at an early age," and thus may have been out voyaging with his older companions in this period. *DCB*, 2:282–86, quote at 284.

16. Probably Laurent Borry de Grandmaison, habitant and voyageur from Montreal. *DCB*, 2:295; Jetté, *DG*, 131.

17. Partner in charge, *la part du bourgeois*. See McDermott, *A Glossary of Mississippi Valley French, 1673–1850*, 34, for an explanation of the term *bourgeois* as used in the fur trade.

18. Probably Etienne Xaintes. Jetté identifies two brothers named Xaintes: Etienne Xaintes, a *harquebusier* (gunsmith) born c. 1635 and died in 1688, and Claude Xaintes, a cutler, born c. 1639 and died between January 21, 1682, and December 23, 1684. Jetté, *DG*, 1135. In 1688 Etienne was involved in an altercation in Montreal shortly after he was said to have returned from Michilimackinac. A *harquebus* or *arquebus* was a heavy matchlock musket invented in the fifteenth century. A *harquebusier* was a matchlock gunsmith. For more about Xaintes, see documents 23 and 26.

19. Daniel Greysolon Dulhut [Du Lhut, Du Luth], explorer, *coureur de bois*, officer in the Troupes de la Marine, founder of posts in the *pays d'en haut*. Early in 1683, Governor La Barre had sent him, with a convoy of fifteen canoes, to the *pays d'en haut* to secure the allegiance of the Indian nations of the region in preparation for La Barre's intended war against the Iroquois. While there, as was the wont of many officers in such circumstances, he engaged heavily in fur trading. *DCB*, 2:261–64.

20. Probably Jean Aubuchon *dit* l'Espérance, a Montreal merchant who was killed in his bed in 1685. He was said to have been forty-five years old in the 1681 census, and had a house on Rue St. Paul. Jetté, *DG*, 28; Landry, ed., *Pour le Christ et le Roi*, 153.

21. René Cuillerier, who came to Montreal in 1659 to work for the Sulpicians. He helped found the parish of La Chine on the island, and died there in 1712 after a long life as a trader and habitant. Cuillerier was captured by the Oneida Iroquois in 1661 and left an account of the society of his captors. See José António Brandão, ed. and trans. (with K. Janet Ritch), *Nation Iroquoise: A Seventeenth-Century Ethnography of the Iroquois* (Lincoln: University of Nebraska Press, 2003).

Petition by Claude Tardy for the Judge to interrogate witnesses named by Tardy and including questions which Tardy suggests be asked of the witnesses

1683, October 5, Montreal[1]

Claude Tardy a merchant in this place humbly entreats you, saying that yesterday he presented you with his petition with the goal of an inquiry into his being embezzled of the proceeds coming from the merchandise that he had placed in the hands of the men named Villedieu, Loisel and Guillory, and as an ample investigation is necessary, the supplicant is obliged to have recourse to you and calls for you to hear the witnesses to the facts attached here.

With this in mind, sir, please be willing to proceed to the location of Prairie de la Madelaine to examine the witnesses whom the supplicant will have summoned before you in accordance with your ruling of yesterday, and to carry out your said ruling order your necessary officers to be with you and administer justice.

Tardy paraph.

In view of the above petition and the facts attached thereto we order that [the hearing] be set up at the said location of Prairie de la Madelaine with our assistant to the clerk of the court, in the absence of our clerk of the court, and sergeant Lory to hear witnesses who will be produced for the supplicant at his expense to testify on the stated facts, subject to determining the tax at the end of the hearing. We order the said Lory to summon the said witnesses to appear before us tomorrow at eight o'clock in the morning at the said location of La Prairie against the said defendants and to accelerate the investigation begun by us yesterday . . . Done the fifth day of October 1683

Migeon De Branssat paraph.

Facts[2] *about which the judge will interrogate the witnesses that I shall point out to him*

Firstly ask them whether they do not have common knowledge of packs of beaver that the said Loisel and Villedieu and Guillory sent and brought from the Ottawas and of how many beavers were in each one, how many robes were in each of the packs of greasy beaver, and how many packs of greasy and dry beaver there were, whether they did not divert some on the way or left some in a cache or French houses, whether the said packs of beaver were not opened or untied during the whole trip from which they could have diverted a number of these, whether there had not been other furs like peaux passé,[3] martins, otters, raccoons, fishers and other small furs, and whether they did not divert some along the way, whether they did not hear how many robes and other furs had been traded to them, whether they do not have knowledge of the quantity and kinds of trade goods they left in the Ottawa country and elsewhere, and whether they did not bring back or trade any of the said beaver on the way, whether they sold any or left any at the said Prairie de la Magdelaine either in their own or neighbors' possession,[4] and whether they did not secretly send any home to their relatives or to their wives and whether they did not give or deliver any to Montreal merchants or other such people, namely whether the letters that were addressed to the interested parties and given to the said Villedieu and Loisel were not intercepted, and namely if all the beaver that sieur Guillory delivered to them up there was delivered into the hands of sieur Charron, having heard that he had delivered twenty packs to them and they only delivered nine packs to the said sieur Charron?

Have the furs that are at Pierre Gaigné's impounded until the man named Jolicoeur establishes to whom they belong.

Done at Montreal the fifth of October 1683.

Tardy paraph.

NOTES

1. Archives nationales du Québec à Montréal, Documents judiciaires de la juridiction seigneuriale de Montréal (1651–1695) [cote TL 2, feuilles détachées, 1681–1693].

2. The following list, written by Tardy, accompanies his petition of October 5, 1683, above.

3. The exact meaning of this phrase is not clear. *Peaux* means "skins," and *passé* can mean "past" and "last." The writer might have meant that skins from animals such as those listed next were *passé de mode*, or "out of fashion," or "last" in terms of volume of furs traded. Beaver skins represented the most commonly traded furs.

4. Either in their own or neighbors' possession, *soit entre leurs mains ou d'autres voisins*.

Loizel & Villedieu's petition asking for a record of the court proceedings which led to the unexpected seizure of their beaver skins

1683, October 7, Montreal[1]

Joseph Loisel and Anthoine Villedieu merchants in this town humbly entreat the court saying that upon returning from the trip to the Ottawas that they completed a short while ago both for themselves and their partners, sieurs Reynaud and Tardy, for the trip's fur trade and after having paid for all the trade goods out of the load of furs they had brought, it happened that yesterday the sixth of October of the present year 1683 they were notified about a certain seizure, carried out upon the petition of the said sieur Tardy, of the shares and portions that were coming to them. As it is evident from the attached seizure which appears to be authorized by your order, sir, which can only have been given upon a petition of which they have not been notified any more than of your said order which has resulted in their not being able until now to know upon what the said seizure can be based. The supplicants [Loisel and Villedieu] owing nothing at all to the said sieur Tardy that comes to light nevertheless have learned that yesterday before you the said sieur Tardy had caused an inquiry to be initiated about which the supplicants would desire to be informed, as well as the petition that he presented to you, which they are not taking without having your ruling on this.

Taking this into consideration, sir, would you please order sieur M [. . .], your clerk of the court, who must have possession of the evidence, to deliver to the supplicants [copies of] dispatches, petitions, and investigation; except his wages that they offer to pay him, in order to continue as they find it best and to do what is right for you.

Villedieu paraph.

Basset[2] paraph.

[. . .] Loisel

In view of the above petition and the seizure by sieur Tardy on the 4th of October we order our clerk of the court to provide copies in large letters of the proceedings initiated by the complaint of the said sieur Tardy as well as the investigation done by us and converted into an ordinary trial reserving the right to investigate more fully. So ordered and done the 7th of October 1683.

Migeon De Branssat paraph.

NOTES

1. Archives nationales du Québec à Montréal, Documents judiciaires de la juridiction seigneuriale de Montréal (1651–1695) [cote TL 2, feuilles détachées, 1681–1693].

2. Bénigne Basset *dit* Deslauriers, royal notary. Jetté, *DG*, 54; *DCB*, 1:79.

Petition by Anthoine Villedieu against Claude Tardy for false accusations of embezzlement

1683, October 11, Montreal [1]

To the Magistrate of Montreal Island

Anthoine Villedieu humbly entreats the court both in his name and representing Joseph Loisel a habitant of this island, saying that they have presented their petition to you with the purpose of being informed about a certain complaint made to you by sieur Tardy a merchant of this town in which he puts forward the claim that the supplicants misappropriated and embezzled at his expense and to his loss a number of pelts that they had brought a short time ago from the Ottawas, from which an inquiry ensued about which the supplicants have likewise been informed; that finding no charge against them you have converted it into an ordinary trial and ordered them to proceed if they see fit and as they are sufficiently vindicated by the said inquiry and by all the trips they have previously taken to the said Ottawas for a number of people of this region without any reproach whatsoever, having always been decent and honorable people, it is now greatly prejudicial to them that they find themselves publicly accused by the said sieur Tardy of embezzlement in their latest partnership in which everyone on this island and even in the surrounding regions is interested, deluged by this false accusation, which obliges them to appeal to you to provide help to them.

Taking into consideration, sir, in view of the foregoing, the fact that the supplicants are fully vindicated and innocent as a result of the said inquiry, please order the said sieur Tardy to be called exceptionally to appear before you to compensate them, in the presence of six people that the supplicants will choose to attend the hearing as is legitimate and sentence him to pay all expenses, damages and interest and such fine as it pleases you to determine, upon the brief of the fiscal agent of the bailiwick, whose addition they request to achieve his ends and do the right thing for you.

Villedieu

Considering the above petition we order the said sieur Tardy accuser and party against the supplicants to bring without delay the facts presented by him and desist from pursuing them. To this effect he will be summoned in order to respond to and defend against the points in the said petition, then be ordered to do what is just. Done this eleventh day of October 16 [sixteen] eighty-three. We order etc.

To our bailiff or sergeant draw up the necessary paperwork required for this etc.

Migeon De Branssat paraph.

NOTE

1. Archives nationales du Québec à Montréal, Documents judiciaires de la juridiction seigneuriale de Montréal (1651–1695) [cote TL 2, feuilles détachées, 1681–1693].

Judgment rendered by Migeon de Branssat against Tardy in favor of Loisel and Villedieu whose good reputations were harmed by Tardy's baseless accusations

1683, October 13, Montreal[1]

Enters sieur Claude Tardy merchant in this locale, plaintiff by petition for an inquiry and judicial investigation to be conducted of the embezzlement and receipt of stolen goods to his detriment by the men named Anthoine Villedieu and Joseph Loisel whom he had fitted out last year to go trading among the Ottawas from whom they were back, and the small number of furs they brought back had given reason to the said plaintiff based on false rumors to suspect them for disloyalty and bad faith which had served as grounds for the said plaintiff to accuse them in court in order to have the right to seize the effects that they could discover belonging to the said Villedieu and Loisel, having concluded from his said petition that he was permitted to effectuate a seizure and have an investigation made of the alleged facts, at the bottom of which [petition] is our order requiring the witnesses to be summoned and pending this he would be permitted to proceed to a seizure in order to secure the claims of the said plaintiff the investigation conducted by us on the 4th, 6th, and 7th of this month our judgment in consequence of the investigation requiring that the said plaintiff be received [in court] to provide more ample evidence and pending this the said investigation be made and converted into a trial, order dated the said seventh of this month, another petition by the said plaintiff for the purpose of having us go down to Prairie de la Magdelaine to hear the witnesses who would be named by him to testify truthfully about the facts that he had alleged in the statement he had produced together with the said petition at the bottom of which was our order directing us to repair to the said Prairie with our deputy clerk of the court and sergeant Lory which trip we had not taken seeing that the witnesses he had to be heard were in this location, on the one hand the said Anthoine Villedieu and companion for whom he is acting intervening in the case by petition appearing because of the rumor and news that they had heard that the said plaintiff had obtained permission to seize their effects notwithstanding the fact that they had in good faith brought back the unsold trade goods[2] that had been entrusted to them by the said plaintiff concluding from that in order to be informed about the demands and claims of the said plaintiff there was given to them a copy of the proceedings that had transpired, consequently at the bottom of their petition to intervene in the case is our order enjoining our clerk of the court to deliver a large copy of the investigation to them which had been carried out by us as an ordinary trial on the said dates another petition by the defendant [. . .] and plaintiff as damages against Tardy for having accused them without foundation and shocking and giving a pretext to many people for believing that they [Villedieu and Loisel] had engaged in embezzlement which damaged their honor and good reputation concluding that he should be sentenced to pay such damages as we find their costs and expenditures to be [. . .] requiring the annex[3] of this island's fiscal agent, and the said Tardy replied that based upon the false reports that were given to him and on the few furs that the said partners brought he had reason to believe that they had misappropriated, that he was ready however to recognize the said partners as honest people, we after having heard the said parties and the above stated documents, discharged for the present the said Loisel and Villedieu from the accusation which was made against them by the said plaintiff who recognized them in court as good and honorable people and ordered him to recognize them as such before three of their friends except their [. . .] and furthermore we have sentenced the said sieur Tardy to pay the costs of the investigation and of our present sentence that we have taxed and liquidated at the amount of [*blank space*].[4]

So ordered etc., done and given by us bailiff civil and criminal judge of the island of Montreal October thirteenth sixteen hundred eighty-three notwithstanding appeal [. . .]

Migeon De Branssat paraph.

NOTES

1. Archives nationales du Québec à Montréal, Documents judiciaires de la juridiction seigneuriale de Montréal (1651–1695) [cote TL 2, feuilles détachées, 1681–1693].

2. The unsold trade goods, *le retour des marchandises*.

3. The legal term used here is *adjonction*, referring to a supplementary statement added to a document, thus "annex," "appendix," or "addition" in English. See appendix 2, "French-English Glossary of Seventeenth- and Eighteenth-Century Legal Terms."

4. This copy leaves the amount blank pending the fiscal officer's calculations, which were added as an annex to document 15.

Statement of court expenses related to the Petition of Tardy

1683, October 13, Montreal[1]

Statement of the costs incurred in court before the bailiff of Montreal island in connection with the petition of sieur Claude Tardy a merchant against [Anthoine] Villedieu and Joseph Loisel

Firstly for drawing up a petition and complaint against the said Loisel and Villedieu	15 sols
For all the bailiff's [. . .] both for sieur Tardy's petition and for the said Villedieu and Loisel's	12 livres tournois[2]
To the clerk of the court without including the large copy of the proceedings upon the petition of the said Villedieu and Loisel	8 livres tournois
To sergeant Lory for the seizure carried out against sieur Charron, 4 summons in town, official notification of the said seizure, and presence at the three hearings	5 livres tournois
Drawing up the present statement	10 sols
To all [. . .]	1 livre tournois
	27 livres tournois 5 sols
In addition for two petitions presented by the said Villedieu and Loisel against the said sieur Tardy in order to obtain compensation	1 livre tournois 10 sols

For copying the large copies requested by the said Loisel and Villedieu	6 livres tournois 8 sols
To the bailiff for his order	2 livres tournois
	37 livres tournois 3 sols

The above fees total the sum of thirty-seven livres three sols which we have assessed this October 13, 1683.

Migeon De Branssat paraph.

NOTES

1. Archives nationales du Québec à Montréal, Documents judiciaires de la juridiction seigneuriale de Montréal (1651–1695) [cote TL 2, feuilles détachées, 1681–1693].
2. Up to 1717, the *livre* in New France was worth three quarters of that of France, which was known as the *livre tournois* or *argent de France.* After that date, the value was the same.

Statement of expenditures made by sieur de La Durantaye in the Ottawa Country on behalf of the King

1684, Ottawa country[1]

Statement of the expenditures made by Sieur de la Durantaye[2] *in the Ottawa country for the King's service and the execution of the orders of General de la Barre*[3] *in the years 1683–1684, To Wit:*

Gave to the 4 Missillimakinac nations[4] July 2, 6 lbs of tobacco[5] at 6 #[6] per lb.	36 #.
Gave to the poutouatamis August 5, 1683—2 lbs of tobacco at 6 # per lb.	12
Gave to the chiefs of the same nation on the 6th—3 jerkins[7] at 48 # each.	144
Gave to the same on the same day 3 shirts at 8 # each.	24
Gave to the same on the same day 3 pairs of stockings at 8 # each.	24
Gave to 8 men of the same nation whom I was obliged to take along in order to take me to the village of the outagamis[8] who wanted to flee with the mascoutins[9] and quicapous [Kickapoos] after the murder of 60 of the aforesaid mascoutins by the Iroquois about which I was notified by the Reverend Father Alloez[10] of the Company of Jesus on August 26, 8 shirts at 8 # each.	64
Gave to the Outagamis to keep them in their village promising them the protection of the French Governor against the Iroquois, 3 lbs of tobacco at 6 #.	18
Gave to the same, a flintlock musket at.	80
Gave to the same a jerkin for the chief's attire.	50

Gave to the same a shirt and a pair of stockings at 8 # each.	16
Gave to the same two Iroquois-style blankets at 20 # each.	40
Gave to the quicapous for the same purpose 2 lbs of tobacco.	12
Gave to the same a muskett at.	80
a jerkin to dress the chief.	50
a shirt and a pair of stockings 8 # each.	16
2 Iroquois-style blankets at 20 # each.	40
Gave to 3 sacs[11] whom I was obliged to take along to take me by land to the Illinois from whom I was at a distance of 60 leagues [145 miles] having been ordered to go there on September 25, 1683	
Gave one blanket at.	20
a hooded jacket[12] at.	24
powder and lead.	20
For the same had a musket repaired by sieur de Tonty's[13] gun-smiths, having arrived at Fort St. Louis on October 2, to wit, to have the aforesaid musket assembled, and to make a breech and a spring.[14]	
Gave eleven beavers at 5 # each.	55
For food to the same on October 5 gave.	25
To another Sac to guide me during my return in a canoe by a river to the Fox village from Quinelonan from where I had left, 50 musketballs and 50 charges of powder purchased from private parties at the aforesaid Fort St. Louis [for] 6 beavers worth 4 # each.	24
To the same one gave a blanket also purchased at the aforesaid Fort St. Louis.	24
Plus gave to the same one fathom of tobacco worth.	10

Sieur Nicolas Perrot[15] gave to the Winnebagos,[16] Sacs, Foxes and Menominees[17] on my behalf on November 20 in order to invite them to go down to Montreal, 11 lbs of tobacco at 8 # per lb.	88
For food for 2 men whom I am obliged to take along on November 20 to go from Green Bay to Missillimakinac having received orders from Monsieur de la Barre to defend the aforesaid place of Missillimakinac that he indicated to me was to be attacked [by] the Iroquois, [the two of whom] were fed at my expense for 6 months.	300
From July 14, 1684 having received orders from Monsieur de la Barre to assemble all the French and Indians to proceed to the Iroquois country and go to war against them I immediately sent a canoe of 5 men to Green Bay from Missillimakinac where I then was, to whom I gave orders to tell the French and Indians of that location to come join me, which they did a few days later and to whom I gave as food one and a half sacks of corn at 20 # per sack.	30
Some fat for.	15
Gave to the man called Martin Fouessy who had been plundered by the Iroquois in the month of March of the same year with 13 other Frenchmen in the Fratigny River eight beavers for mounting a musket barrel that he had and for putting a plate on the aforesaid musket to enable the aforesaid Fouessy to go to war, the aforesaid eight beavers being worth.	20
Gave to 3 men sent to Monsieur de la Barre to bring me the orders to march against the Iroquois, named Guillet, L'Orangé and Debrieux 3 sacks of corn at 20 s. per sack.	60
Purchased from the same individuals named above 20 lbs of tobacco given to the Indians while inviting them to join the French to go to war against the Iroquois by order of Monsieur de la Barre, for the payment of which tobacco I drew a promissory note on Monsieur de la Chenaye[18] which note was paid off by sieur du pré[19] as it appears in my accounts with the aforesaid sieur dupré.	
Gave to 5 men to enable them to go to the war on July 25 10 lbs of powder at 5 # per lb.	50

to the same men gave 7 sacks of corn at 20 # per sack.	140
to the same men gave 4 axes at 8 # each.	32
to the same men gave 50 lbs of fat costing.	150
The present statement amounting to a total of.	2240[20]

I certify the present statement to be accurate whose contents have been provided for the king's service by sieur de la Durantaye commander in chief in the Ottawa country in the years 1684 and 1685.

Done at Quebec April 20. 1685.

de Meulles[21]

NOTES

1. Archives nationales de France, Archives des Colonies, Series C11A, vol. 6: ff. 451r–452r. This material, once housed in Paris, is now at the Centre des Archives d'outre-mer, Aix-en-Provence.

2. Captain Olivier Morel de La Durantaye. La Durantaye was the name of his seigneury. As was the fashion at the time, he added "of La Durantaye" (*de La Durantaye*) to his name, which became Olivier Morel de La Durantaye. Like other seigneurs, he was usually referred to by the added portion of his name, La Durantaye. He arrived in New France in 1665 as a captain in the Carignan-Salières regiment and died in the colony in 1716. He served in numerous campaigns against the Iroquois Indians and was commandant at Michilimackinac from 1683 to 1690. In that year he was replaced by Louis La Porte Louvigny, who Governor Frontenac thought would be more accommodating of his designs. In 1703 La Durantaye was appointed to the Conseil Souverain in acknowledgment of his character and long years of service to the Crown. *DCB*, 2:488–89. For more on Frontenac, see document 31.

3. Joseph-Antoine Lefebvre de La Barre served as governor-general of New France from 1682 until he was recalled in 1685. La Barre had been sent to New France to bring to heel the Iroquois Indians who lived south of Lake Ontario. The Iroquois had long been foes of New France, and in the 1680s renewed their hostilities against the colony because of its efforts to expand its network of Indian allies. La Barre's ill-planned and half-hearted 1684 campaign against the Iroquois ended in a humiliating peace in which the French essentially abandoned their Native allies to the Iroquois. La Barre was recalled and replaced with Jacques-René de Brisay de Denonville. Brandão, "*Your fyre shall burn no more*," 117–29; W. J. Eccles, *Frontenac: The Courtier Governor* (1959; Toronto: McClelland and Stewart, 1965), 157–72; *DCB*, 1:442–46.

4. It is not clear what groups are being referred to here. The Ottawas had four tribal divisions and were the main nation in the area, but groups of Wendat (Huron/

Petun), Ojibwa, and Potawatomis also lived around Michilimackinac in this period. That the latter are mentioned separately in the next line as recipients of another gift of tobacco would suggest that this reference is to the Ottawa subgroups of Kiskakon, Sinago, Sable, and Nassauakueton.

5. Tobacco (*Nicotiana rustica*) was indigenous to northeastern North America and was a ubiquitous part of Indian cultures. Tobacco was grown by, and traded among, Native peoples and used to cure, to calm minds during periods of mourning, to initiate councils, and for the mere pleasure of smoking. J. F. Lafitau, *Moeurs des Sauvages Ameriquains Comparée Aux Moeurs des Premier Temps*, 2 vols. [1727]. Translated by E. L. Moore as *Customs of the American Indians Compared with the Customs of Primitive Times*, ed. W. N. Fenton, 2 vols. (Toronto: Champlain Society Publication 48–49, 1974 and 1977), 2:79–87, 304. The French quickly came to appreciate the role of tobacco in council processes with Indians and gave it as "presents" to show their goodwill towards their Native partners.

6. The written abbreviation for *livre* was similar to the "#" symbol.

7. Jerkins, *justaucorps*. A jerkin is a close-fitting man's sleeveless jacket, usually made of leather.

8. The Fox Indians, also known as the Mesquakie, were located in this period south and west of Green Bay, Wisconsin. The Fox had a troubled relationship with the French in that they accepted French trade but refused to let themselves be too closely tied to French plans and ambitions. Eventually, Fox resistance to French control led the French to try to annihilate the group. In this period, relations had not yet reached that level of hostility. R. David Edmunds and Joseph L. Peyser, *The Fox Wars: The Mesquakie Challenge to New France* (Norman, University of Oklahoma Press, 1993).

9. The Mascoutens, a sedentary Algonquian group, lived around southwestern and southeastern lower Lake Michigan. The Iroquois wars forced them to move often in the period before 1700. After 1800 the Mascoutens amalgamated with the Kickapoos. They too moved around a great deal in this period. Both the Mascouten and Kickapoo were heavily involved with the French as trading partners and military allies. Ives Goddard, "Mascouten," in *Handbook*, 15:668–72; Charles Callender, Richard K. Pope, and Susan M. Pope, "Kickapoo," ibid., 656–67.

10. Claude Allouez, early Jesuit missionary and explorer in Wisconsin and Michigan, active among the Miamis of the St. Joseph River from ca. 1683 to his death there in 1689. Dunning Idle, *The Post of the St. Joseph River during the French Régime, 1679–1761* [1946] (Niles: Support the Fort Inc., 2003), 5–6.

11. The Sauk Indians who lived in Green Bay. They were close allies of the Fox nation, with whom they shared many cultural features. Despite Sauk support of the Fox in their wars with the French, the Sauk remained, for the most part, on good terms with the French. Charles Callender, "Sauk," in *Handbook*, 15:648–55.

12. This sort of jacket would later be known as a "Mackinaw" jacket.

13. Henri de Tonty, La Salle's lieutenant, built Fort Saint-Louis at Starved Rock (*Le Rocher*), near Utica, Illinois, in 1682. In the spring of 1684, Tonty and Louis-Henri de Baugy repulsed an Iroquois attack at Starved Rock. Henri's younger brother, Alphonse de Tonty, was to serve as commander of Michilimackinac from 1697 to 1698, replacing Antoine Laumet *dit* Lamothe Cadillac. The Tontys were cousins of Daniel Greysolon Dulhut. *DCB*, 2:631, 634.

14. Breech and a spring, *resor de batrie*.

15. Nicolas Perrot was one of the earliest explorers, interpreters, and fur traders in the Upper Country. He was very influential with the various nations, and his written memoirs are one of the richest sources on the Indians of the Great Lakes during the last four decades of the seventeenth century. *DCB*, 2:516–20. Perrot donated a beautiful silver monstrance (a vessel for displaying the unconsecrated host used in Catholic religious services) to the mission at Green Bay. The monstrance was later used at St. Anne's church at Michilimackinac and is today in the Neville Museum in Green Bay, Wisconsin. Personal communication, David Armour to J. A. Brandão, October 2003.

16. The Winnebagos, a Siouan speaking group, lived in the Wisconsin area. In this period they were primarily located south of Green Bay, by the lake that bears their name. They were hostile towards the Fox and the Ottawas, but traded with the French. Population losses due to disease and warfare led the Winnebagos to intermarry with the Ojibwas, Potawatomis, and Menominees, among others. Nancy Oestrich Lurie, "Winnebago," in *Handbook*, 15:690–707.

17. The Menominees, an Algonquian group who lived west of Green Bay and south of Lake Superior. First contacted by the French explorer Nicolas Perrot in 1667, the Menominees accepted a Jesuit mission among them in 1671 and used their connections with the French to become a dominant group in the region by the early 1700s. Louise S. Spindler, "Menominee," in *Handbook*, 15:708–24.

18. Charles Aubert de La Chesnay was "New France's leading businessman of the 17th century." His furs and trade goods in the Upper Country in 1685 were valued at 100,000 livres. In 1693 he became one of the rare individuals from New France to be ennobled by the French king (Louis XIV). *DCB*, 2:26, 32.

19. Possibly Antoine Dupré *dit* Rochefort.

20. The correct total is 1,793 livres. The king either arrived at a lower amount, or simply refused to grant him more than 1,500 livres in payment. See document 46 for the king's response to La Durantaye's list of expenses.

21. Jacques de Meulles, intendant of New France 1682–1686.

Death and inventory of Jean Gay (or Laurent) dit Cascaret, a Michilimackinac resident, who came to Montreal to die

1684, May 19, Montreal[1]

In the year sixteen hundred eighty-four on the nineteenth day of May in the afternoon, we, the magistrate of Montreal Island, accompanied by the substitute magistrate, by the fiscal officer of this bailiwick, by our clerk of the court, and by sergeants-at-law Cabazié and Lory upon the news that we heard that a man named Cascaret had just died in the house of sieur Jean Martinet de Fonblanche, a surgeon living in this town where he had himself taken to be cared for and to receive medication for an abscess or ulcer in his throat which brought him from the Ottawas from where he arrived Wednesday night on the seventeenth of this month, from which abscess and ulcer he had been indisposed for eleven months at the place called Missilmakina from where he had himself taken to this place by two Ottawa Indians, we the magistrate of Montreal after having taken the said sieur Fonblanche's oath required in such cases, advised him to tell us the truth about the possessions the said deceased may have brought or have deposited with someone in order to have an inventory and a description made of these items to be kept for whomever it may concern.

The said sieur Fonblanche declared that he was aware that the said Cascaret had brought three packs of beaver, without knowing what kind of quality they were, which were carried into the house of Monsieur Perrot, governor of this island, who also learned through sieur Soumande's wife that she owed the said Cascaret from last year the sum of forty livres, in addition that the sieur de Coulonge told him 6 or 7 months ago that he owed Cascaret the value of forty pistoles[2] that he had deposited with him before embarking upon the voyage to the Ottawas, and that he had a part of it at his disposal but that as soon as he learned that the said Cascaret had arrived he would have his money ready, in addition to that, he had heard the said Cascaret say before he departed this life that he had left all his furs at the said place called Missilmakinak in the hands of sieur Jean Perré,[3] and that at the time that the said Cascaret arrived he had caused to be brought to my aforesaid sieur Perrot's place the packs of beaver that he had, [and] he arrived at the said sieur Fonblanche's house with a beaver robe which he was using as a blanket that he gave to him as a present, the latter gave him one of his jerkins until the time when he would be able to have himself dressed.

In the pockets of the jerkin we found two promissory notes in my said sieur Perrot's handwriting neither signed nor dated by him, in one of which he declares that he owes Charbonneau ninety-four [livres?] in silver, and the other is a declaration by which the said Charbonneau owes to the deceased Cascaret the sum of one hundred three livres fifteen sols, which [notes] we placed in the hands of our said clerk of the court, [he] additionally pointed out to us a pair of shoes and a pair of stockings that he was using yesterday and a worn-out medium-size jerkin of blue gro-gram[4] in which papers were found that we had sealed with our cachet and initialed by us, the said substitute magistrate, the said sieur Fonblanche and our clerk of the court to whom we gave them, furthermore [he] said that the said Cascaret brought a large canoe which cost him one hundred livres at Missilimakinak which is in front of my said sieur Perrot's mansion which is all that the said sieur Fonblanche declared, affirming his declaration to be true and that he saw no money since his arrival but six or seven sols marqués[5] and that he diverted nothing nor hidden what might belong to him and signed it with us, the substitute magistrate, and clerk of the court.

Migeon de Branssat

J Martinet paraph.

Jehan Gervaise

Maugue paraph.

Clerk of the court

Following the declaration we ordered before us Joseph Charbonneau whose oath we took who told us that he went up last autumn with Hervé the eldest son of Pierre Lorrain[6] and Jean LeGras[7] to go to the Ottawas and that they wintered at Ganetchitiagon[8] on Lake Ontario from which they left last April 6th to go to the Ottawas, that being with his said comrades at Chibounanain[9] on Lake Huron, the said deceased Cascaret arrived there with two Indians in a canoe on the second of this month who was having himself taken by them in order to get to this island to be medicated for the sickness from which he died, which said Cascaret entreated the respondent to help him in his need and help the said Indians to take him and that he would give him a pack of thirty beavers that he received upon his arrival in this place and the said Cascaret had two others in one of which there were twenty-six beavers, and in the other he did not know the number which he believes were brought to the house of monsieur Perrot, the governor of this island as well as the canoe in which they came down. The respondent declared that the said Cascaret told him along the way that before leaving Missilmakima he had written a will and that he had given half of what he might have to the Jesuit reverend fathers [and] the other [half] to sieur Peré and that he heard the said Cascaret say that sieur LaSalle owed him a great deal, and after having inquired of the said deponent if the said Cascaret since his arrival had received money from what could have been owed to him or for what he had brought to this island, said that he knew nothing about it and that the deceased told him nothing else and that he has no other knowledge that anyone diverted items that could have belonged to the said Cascaret and that he saw no money of his other than yesterday three coins of forty sols that he won at cards at a man named Lafontaine's place from a man named François Chesnier, a carpenter, that he does not believe the said Cascaret received any from anyone at all and that he did not see him with any, and after the reading of his declaration [he] said it contained the truth and stated that he did not know how to sign, questioned on this according to the ordinance and we signed with the substitute magistrate and our clerk of the court.

Migeon De Branssat paraph.

Jehan Gervaise

Maugue paraph.

On the said day in the afternoon

We then called for François Tardy,[10] surgeon's servant, living at sieur Fonblanche's from whom we took his oath in the presence of the said substitute magistrate and our clerk of the court, inquired if he didn't have knowledge of the said Cascaret's leaving some things money or otherwise, said that the deceased Cascaret arrived Wednesday night the seventeenth of this month and he came inside to have an ulcer dressed that had been bothering his throat for eleven months among the Ottawas from where he came down with Joseph Charbonneau and two Indians who brought him, that they landed at the Little River and that the deponent brought him into this house wearing only a miserable jerkin trimmed with braid, a sorry-looking hooded coat, a pair of stockings and a coarse shirt on him with miserable red breeches and a beaver robe which he used as a blanket which he gave as a present to the said sieur Fonblanche, and that there were some packs of beaver in his canoe of which three or four were carried away by the valets of governor Perrot into his mansion, furthermore testifies that he saw only seven or eight sols marqués with the said deceased Cascaret since his arrival and that he does not know if he borrowed any and that he saw nothing at all belonging to the said Cascaret diverted and after the reading of his deposition which he said contained the truth, signed it with us, substitute and clerk of the court, [he] added since that he went yesterday to sieur Soumande's wife to get a pair of shoes and a pair of stockings for the said Cascaret's use that we left deposited in the said sieur Fonblanche's hands and that the said Soumande woman declared that she owed the said Cascaret 30 or 40 livres tournois and [he] signed.

Migeon De Branssat paraph. *Tardif*

Jehan Gervaise

Maugue paraph.

Clerk of the court

On the said day in the afternoon [we] called Louis Charton whose oath we took, and inquired if he knew whether the said deceased Cascaret who had arrived two days ago from the Ottawa country received or borrowed any money. [He] said and declared that yesterday during the day he was with him from two o'clock in the afternoon until three at the innkeeper named Lafontaine's place, where he played cards with a man named Lescureuil[11] and borrowed from Lafontaine two little crowns[12] in order to gamble and having won four francs or one hundred sols[13] from the said Lescureuil he paid back the money that he had borrowed to the said Lafontaine and spent there what he had won, and after the reading of his testimony said it contained the truth and signed with us, the said substitute magistrate, and our clerk of the court.

Migeon De Branssat paraph.

L. Charton

Jehan Gervaise

Maugue paraph.

Clerk of the court

[We] called Marguerite Prud'homme wife of sieur Jean Martinet de Fon-blanche, surgeon, from whom we took her oath and asked her to tell us what she had in her possession belonging to the deceased Cascaret, who testified that the said Cascaret arrived the night before last from the Otta-was with two Indians and the man named Charbonneau who had brought him to this island to have an ulcer treated that he had in his throat for a long time among the Ottawas and that he arrived in their house with a miserable jerkin, a miserable shirt, dressed like those who come down from the said place, with a beaver robe which he used as a blanket which he gave to her husband as a present upon arriving, that the said Cascaret told her before dying that he had two or three packs of beaver at the home of Monsieur Perrot, the governor, and a large canoe that he said cost him one hundred francs in the said Ottawa country, and that out of the packs he was [. . .] to pay forty beavers to the Indians who brought him, and that sieur Coulonge owed him and that the Soumande lady also owed him around forty livres out of which he received a pair of stockings and a pair of shoes, declaring that he had no money at all other than eighteen sols marqués which had come from one hundred sols that he had won gambling with a man named LesCureuil having given the rest to Lafontaine's wife at whose house he had gambled and drunk yesterday, and that he had bor-rowed from the said Lafontaine two forty-sol coins that he returned to him on the spot, furthermore declared that yesterday at around 7 pm the said Cascaret showed her two promissory notes from Monsieur Perrot that we inventoried above, the lady who is testifying affirming that she found noth-ing nor saw anything diverted that belonged to the said Cascaret who told her that he had drawn up a will and given all that he had in case he died in the Ottawa country to sieur Peré with instructions to pay his debts and that there were six score robes at Michilimakinac, this having been done in the presence of Charles Lessard's wife,[14] and after the reading she signed with us, the substitute magistrate, and our clerk of the court.

three words crossed out with no value

Migeon De Branssat

M Prudhomme

Jehan Gervaise

Maugue paraph.

Clerk of the court

In the year sixteen hundred eighty-four and the fourth day of the month of July based on what has been represented to us by the deputy fiscal officer of this bailiwick, that it would be good to open a certain package that we had sealed when we worked on the inventory of the succession of the deceased Jean Gay dit Cascaret[15] in the presence of the said deputy and of sieur Jean Martinet de Fonblanche, surgeon in this town at whose house the said Cascaret died, for which reason we ordered the said deputy and the said sieur Fonblanche and sergeant Cabazié to come to our examination so as to be present at the opening of the said seal which in their presence we found signed and sealed as it was then having been recognized by the said above named people in the same condition and sealed with the same cachet that he put on it then.

Firstly, there was found in the said package of papers the envelope which is a congé that Monsieur de Frontenac was giving to Monsieur Mariette [Mariet] a priest and curate at La Montagne and initialed by us and classified ne varietur.[16] The 2nd paper was a letter wrapped in a paper and sealed with a thimble addressed to sieur Dupré, a merchant. The 3rd paper is a statement of merchandise that Pierre Chartyer left in the hands of the said Cascaret initialed and classified as B. The 4th is an agreement drawn up in the form of a partnership among the said Cascaret, the men named Martin, Chartyer, Cascaret, Mongeot and Turquot signed by 4 crosses at the bottom, signed Pierre Chartyer as eye witness the said agreement dated June [?] 16th 1681 initialed and classified as C. The 5th is a note on which Auk8sik8an is written three beavers for a small kettle and that the said Auk8sik8an is an Indian who owes 10 beavers for merchandise unsigned, initialed, and classified D. The 6th is a note signed Ch [. . .] which asks Cascaret to have him paid for something that was due him initialed and classified as E. The 7th is a letter signed by sieur Abraham Bouat[17] in which he notifies the said Cascaret that Vital had paid and was given a receipt for the amount of eighty [. . .] livres that he owed him initialed and classified as F. The 8th is an attestation from the said Chaunière saying that he has knowledge of an affair between Pierre Chartyer and the said Cascaret initialed and classified as G Second sheet.

The 9th is a statement of the beaver robes [. . .] merchandise that the said Cascaret said he provided to Pierre Chartyer, initialed and classified as H. The 10th is a statement of the merchandise that the said Pierre Chartyer gave to Kascaret initialed and classified as H. The 11th is a letter addressed to sieur LeMoyne de Ste-Anne[18] and sealed, given to sieur DuPré to transmit to Ste-Anne. The 12th is a statement signed Sainte Croix in which names of Indians are written who owe him initialed and classified as L. The items and papers indicated above were inventoried, initialed, and classified and signed by us, our deputy, our clerk of the court, Cabazier and by Jean Martinet de Fonblanche, [all] present on the said day and year written above.

Migeon De Branssat paraph.

Jehan Gervaise

Martinet paraph.

Cabazier paraph.

Maugue paraph.

Clerk of the court

Cascaret gave Charboneau one hundred twenty livres fifteen sols. I owe Charboneau ninety-four livres in silver.

NOTES

1. Archives nationales du Québec à Montréal, Documents judiciaires de la juridiction seigneuriale de Montréal (1651–1695) [cote TL 2, feuilles détachées, 1681–1693].

2. A *pistole* was an accounting term referring to 10 *livres.*

3. Jean Peré was a merchant from La Rochelle who became an "explorer, prospector, *coureur de bois*, interpreter, guide [. . .] apparently interested in the furs which he collected from among the Ottawa Indians." *DCB*, 1:536 (emphasis in original).

4. Grogram, *baraquan*. The latter was a coarse, loosely woven fabric of silk, silk and mohair, or silk and wool. See "Baragant," in Cotgrave, *Dictionarie*, and "grogram" in *Oxford Dictionary of English*, 2nd ed. (Oxford: Oxford University Press, 2003).

5. The *sol marqué* was a coin made of a copper-silver alloy. It was worth more than the sol that was made of copper. Marcel Trudel, *Initiation à la Nouvelle-France* (Montreal: Les Éditions HRW, 1971), 198.

6. Pierre Lorrain *dit* LaChappelle (a pit sawyer) had no sons by that name. Possibly Charbonneau meant that he went west "with Hervé *and* Pierre Lorrain's oldest son." The latter, born in 1660, was also called Pierre. It is not possible to more fully identify Hervé. *DG*, 743, 567–68.

7. Jean LeGras was a farmer and merchant-entrepreneur who understood Iroquoian speakers and served as an interpreter. Jetté, *DG*, 700.

8. This appears to be a phonetic rendering of Ganestiquiagon, the name of a Seneca Iroquois village located near the mouth of the Rouge River on the north shore of Lake Ontario, east of modern-day Toronto, Ontario. The location was a well-known stopping point for Ottawa fur brigades who were traveling to take their furs to the English in Albany, New York. Victor Konrad, "An Iroquois Frontier: The North Shore of Lake Ontario during the Late Seventeenth Century," *Journal of Historical Geography* 7, no. 2 (April 1981): 129–44; see especially 133–36.

9. Cheboygan, Michigan, on the lower northeastern Michigan peninsula, across from Mackinac and Bois Blanc islands.

10. Possibly François Tardif, who, in the 1681 census, was said to have been a servant of the Sulpicians in Montreal. In 1688 he went to the west as an engagé. Jetté, *DG*, 1062.

11. *Lescureuil* means "squirrel" in French. This was undoubtedly the man's nickname.

12. *escus blancs*: a *petit écu* ("little crown") was sometimes known as an *écu blanc* ("white crown"), a silver coin worth 3 livres, 6 sols.

13. The franc was a coin struck in France worth, at that time, 20 sols. Trudel, *Initiation*, 197–98. Charton could have said that Cascaret had won four livres tournois, meaning the same thing as four francs or 100 sols.

14. Marie-Anne Caron, whom he married in 1684 and with whom he had eleven children. Jetté, *DG*, 724.

15. We have here for the first time Cascaret's full name. His family name is spelled "Gay" in this document; while this may be a correct spelling, phonetically the name could also be "Guay."

16. *(Ne) varietur* is a Latin expression used to declare the state of a document and prevent changes that might be made to it. See appendix 2.

17. Abraham Bouat was an innkeeper and merchant-entrepreneur based in Montreal. His inn, located on Rue Notre-Dame near the church of the same name, was one of the few in early Montreal. Jetté, *DG*, 132; Landry, ed., *Pour le Christ et le Roi*, 152, 232. His son, François-Marie Bouat, became a judge of the royal court for Montreal and was also heavily involved in the fur trade. *DCB*, 2:81–82.

18. Standard biographical dictionaries do not identify anyone with the name LeMoyne (Lemoine) de Ste.-Anne. The Lemoine family, with numerous brothers who served in the military and were involved in the fur trade, included a number of men with last names of Lemoine de Sainte-Hélène. Either the notary erred in writing the name of the person here, or sieur Lemoyne de Ste.-Anne is not connected with the better-known family.

Court record of the death of Mathurin Normandin dit Beausoleil who had accompanied Cascaret on his trip from Michilimackinac

1684, May 20, Montreal[1]

Report of the visit of the magistrate and [court] officer to Beausoleil's deathbed

In the year sixteen hundred eighty-four on the 20th of May in the afternoon, we the magistrate of Montreal Island accompanied by the substitute magistrate of this jurisdiction, our clerk of the court, and sergeant Cabazié proceeded to the house of sieur Anthoine Forestier surgeon living in this town upon the news that we learned that Mathurin Normand,[2] having come back but a little while ago from the Ottawa country and a habitant of Cap de la Magdelaine where his family is and who has died, and after having administered the oath to Marie Magdelaine Le Cavalier wife of the said sieur Forestier in his absence, we inquired if the said deceased has been in her house for a long time, how he came there, and what he brought in order for a description to be made of it and to be kept for whomever it may concern. [She] said and declared that he arrived last Thursday night with the man named Cascaret who has been dead since yesterday, being ill and complaining of extreme pain in his side which had been tormenting him for eight months and having difficulty breathing, his lungs being dry and impaired from the strain he endured, who while he was alive after his arrival was looked after, medicated and treated in the same way that her husband would have done,[3] and despite her care God took him after about an hour and a half, and [she] affirmed that the said deceased brought upon his arrival but a miserable blanket, a feather pillow, an old gray cloak, a pair of old stockings, a waistcoat, a braided linden bark bag[4] and a beaver robe that he had borrowed from sieur Dulhut to whom he sent it back by the Indians who brought him, affirming that she did not divert or misappropriate anything, which old clothes we left in her care to keep them for whomever it concerns, from which and the above we drew up the present report, immediately thereafter we withdrew in view of the absence of the said sieur Forestier whom we are waiting to hear at the right time and place it now being almost nine o'clock in the evening, the lady signed with us, the said substitute magistrate, and our said clerk of the court.

Migeon De Branssat

M. Le Cavelier

Jehan Gervaise

Maugue paraph.

NOTES

1. Archives nationales du Québec à Montréal, Documents judiciaires de la juridiction seigneuriale de Montréal (1651–1695) [cote TL 2, feuilles détachées, 1681–1693].

2. The deceased's correct full name was Mathurin Normandin *dit* Beausoleil. Jetté, *DG*, 855.

3. Another example of the range of women's work.

4. A braided linden-bark bag, *un sacq descorce de bois blanc tressé.*

Service contract of Claude Guichard, Carpenter, and La Durantaye

1684, December 31, Quebec[1]

Before françois Genaple,[2] king's notary in the Quebec jurisdiction in New France, undersigned, appeared Claude Guichard, carpenter, living at the little St. Charles River, who has acknowledged on his side hiring himself out as in fact he does commit himself to Olivier Morel, Esquire, seigneur of la Durantaye residing in this town, to serve him during all the time that he will be on a journey that he is ready to go on and undertake next spring in order to go to the Ottawa country and during all of the aforesaid time of the aforesaid journey do everything that he will be directed and ordered to do by the aforesaid sieur de la Durantaye, until his return without his being able to leave or abandon him during the aforesaid journey subject to the penalties prescribed by the regulations of the Sovereign Council, and in case the aforesaid gentleman were to be summoned to war as he was this August[3] and in case he were obliged to take the aforesaid Guichard with him, his time will not count from the day that the aforesaid sieur de la durantaye has received his orders from My Lord the general for the King's service, until he goes back into the service of the aforesaid sieur de la Durantaye; but also in the event that this Guichard were to fall ill during the time of his aforesaid commitment to the service of the aforesaid gentleman nothing will be diminished or taken out of his wages and his time will not stop running or being counted. This present agreement is made for the sum of one hundred fifty livres for the first year, and two hundred livres for the following years if he is on the aforesaid journey that long, the aforesaid time to begin running on the twentieth of next coming April and to be paid in silver coins,[4] in addition to two used deerskins that the aforesaid sieur De la Durantaye promises to give to the aforesaid Guichard to clothe him at the end of the aforesaid journey after the latter's return. For thus etc., promising etc., obligating etc., renouncing etc. Done and drawn up at the aforesaid Quebec in the office of the aforesaid notary in the afternoon of the last day of December sixteen hundred eighty-four in the presence of sieur Lucian Boutteville, merchant, sieur René Senard, master baker in this upper town [of Quebec], witnesses who have signed with the aforesaid sieur de la durantaye and notary. And the aforesaid Guichard declares that he does not know how to sign, having been questioned on this.

La durantaye

Boutteville paraph.

R. Senard

Genaple paraph.

NOTES

1. Archives nationales du Québec à Québec, Greffe de Genaple.

2. François Genaple de Bellefonds, who in addition to being a notary, was a legal practitioner, process server, subdelegate for the intendant, and a seigneur. *DCB*, 2:241–3.

3. On July 19, 1684, La Durantaye left Michilimackinac with 500 men to join Governor-General La Barre's unsuccessful expedition against the Iroquois. *DCB*, 2:488.

4. In silver coins, *en argent monnoyer*.

Partnership agreement between Laurent Baudet and sieur de La Durantaye

1685, January 11, Quebec[1]

Before François Genaple, king's notary in his Quebec jurisdiction in New France, there appeared Laurent Baudet, a habitant from Saint François presently in this town staying at sieur Nolan's[2] house, who acknowledged and declared that he promised and does promise Ollivier Morel, esquire, seigneur of La Durantaye living in this aforesaid town, present at this proceeding and agreeing to undertake with him the trip to the Ottawas for which he will leave at the beginning of next spring upon the first navigation,[3] and this [agreement] is according to the following clauses and conditions: it is to be known that the aforesaid Baudet being in the aforesaid Ottawa country and locations for fur trading will go where stipulated and ordered by the aforesaid sieur de La Durantaye to trade among the six Indian nations the trade goods that he will put in his hands, and will bring back the produce from them, out of which will be taken the total and price of the aforesaid merchandise by the aforesaid sieur de La Durantaye on the basis of the bills that will be written for them of which the aforesaid Baudet will have copies; and the profit from the excess will be shared, to wit, one half to the aforesaid sieur de La Durantaye and the other half for the aforesaid Baudet and those who will be with him from his canoe, in return for which the aforesaid Baudet—as well as his aforesaid canoe companions—will for his share jointly run the risks of the aforesaid trade goods with them that will be placed in their hands, and this [is] with the aforesaid sieur de La Durantaye also jointly [running the risks] in proportion to his share which he is to have of the profits of the aforesaid trading that he will do.

[*Marginal note*: And it has been agreed that the aforesaid Baudet will be able to trade for his private profit in addition to his above mentioned share of the aforesaid profits, the blanket that he will take for his service on the trip with two shirts; on condition that all the partnership's merchandise be completely traded previously and the Indian's debts paid, coming from the aforesaid merchandise.]

For thus etc., promising etc., obligating etc., renouncing etc. Done and drawn up in the office of the aforesaid notary in the forenoon of the eleventh day of January one thousand six hundred eighty-five and the presence of sieur Lucian Boutteville, merchant, and René Senard, master baker living in this upper town, witnesses who have with the aforesaid sieur de La Durantaye and notary signed these presents; and the aforesaid Baudet declares that he does not know how to write or sign, having been questioned on this.

La durantaye

R. Senard

Boutteville paraph.

Genaple paraph.

NOTES

1. Archives nationales du Québec à Québec, Greffe de Genaple.

2. Pierre Nolan, innkeeper, merchant, and, in this period, artillery captain. His son Jean Nolan, born on board ship when his parents emigrated to New France, and who was about nineteen years old at this time, also became a merchant-entrepreneur in the fur trade. Jetté, DG, 851.

3. That is, when enough ice has melted on the rivers to permit navigation.

Partnership agreement between Jean Morneau & Jean Lariou & sieur de La Durantaye

1685, May 15, Montreal[1]

Before Claude Maugue, royal notary in New France residing in Montreal and the undersigned witnesses there appeared in person the honorable Ol-livier Morel, esquire, seigneur of La Durantaye on the one hand, and Jean Morneau and Jean Lariou, habitants of Batiscan[2] on the other hand, which parties have drawn up the following agreements, to wit: that the aforesaid Morneau and Lariou promise and obligate themselves to embark on the trip to the 8ta8ats, [Ottawa] in a canoe that the said sieur de La Durantaye will provide to them to trade the merchandise that they will take there according to the conditions stated below, to wit, that the said Morneau will have one third of the profit that he will make from the proceeds of both the trade goods and his work as gunsmith and edge-toolmaker, and will assume the risk in proportion to the profits he will take out of the said partnership; in regard to the aforesaid Lariou, he will have the ordinary voyageur's share of the profits less the merchandise and other expenses paid with what he was able to draw in advance according to what is written in the bills concerning him; in addition [he] will be able to trade for his own profit one musket, one blanket, and two shirts; the aforesaid sieur de La Durantaye recognizing furthermore that the aforesaid Morneau is provid-ing the aforesaid association with fifty-two livres' worth of tools used for edge-toolmaking for which he will be paid and which he will get back. For thus etc., promising etc., obligating etc., renouncing etc. Done and drawn up at the aforesaid Montreal in one of the shops of sieur Lemoyne[3] in the afternoon of the fifteenth of May sixteen hundred eighty-five, in the pres-ence of Daniel Denevers[4] and Anthoine Baillargeon[5] witnesses present in this place undersigned with my aforesaid sieur de La Durantaye and Mor-neau, the aforesaid Lariou declaring that he does not know how to write or sign according to the inquiry in conformity with the ordinance, no more than the aforesaid witnesses [who were] also questioned.

La durantaye

Jean Morneau

Maugue paraph.

And furthermore after the signing of the agreement on the preceding page, the said morneau and lariou have agreed to what follows, to wit that if one or the other were to be unwell, or if something untoward happened to him that prevented him from acting, the one who is well will take care to convert the trade goods into pelts and will take a man to replace the indisposed or deceased one, all to the advantage of the said deceased as much as can be done, in order for him to retain, upon his return, the rights and distribution of his estate to his heirs and to those appertaining. Executed this said day 15 May, 1685 in the presence of the above said witnesses who, with the said Lariou, declared they did not know how to sign, with the inquiry made according to the ordinance.

Jean Morneau

Maugue, royal notary

True copy.

NOTES

1. Archives nationales du Québec à Montréal, Greffe de Claude Maugue.
2. Jean Morneau died before July 6, 1693, in Batiscan. Jetté, *DG*, 840. Jean Lariou *dit* LaFontaine died in Batiscan in 1715 at either 75 or 85 years of age. Ibid., 655. Batiscan is located near the mouth of the river of the same name where it empties into the St. Lawrence River. It is between Trois-Rivières and Quebec.
3. Possibly Jacques Lemoyne (or Lemoine), a Montreal grocery merchant, or one of his sons. Jetté, *DG*, 711.
4. Daniel Denevers *dit* Brantigny or Brentigny was born December 17, 1656, at Sillery parish and died October 9, 1729, at Lotbinière parish. Jetté, *DG*, 329–30.
5. Antoine Baillargeon *dit* Durivage was a "voyageur to the Ottawas" who, around 1697, married an Indian woman named Marie Choupingua in Kaskaskia. They had three daughters and two sons. Jetté, *DG*, 41.

Summary of Governor Denonville's letters

1686, Versailles[1]

The Year 1686 [Summary of] Letters received from Canada from Monsieur de Denonville[2]

He sends copies of the letters that he wrote to sieurs Du Luth[3] and de La Durantaye[4] to tell them to fortify themselves on two routes leading to Missilimaquinak, in order to block the way to the English[5] and to provide a retreat for the Indians allied with the French.

Sieur de Tonty[6] took charge of assembling the Illinois and he [Denonville] had him leave to do that after having had 150 light muskets provided to him which is all that he was able to collect in the country. If the 500 light muskets that we sent had arrived earlier he would have taken them with him.

He praises highly the conduct of the aforesaid sieur de Tonty who is a very brave man and very enterprising.

He believes that he must give an account of the extreme poverty of several families who are reduced to begging and who all live like nobles. The family of sieur de St. Ours[7] who is a nobleman from [the French province of] Dauphiné is composed of ten children. The father is asking for permission to withdraw to France in order to seek the wherewithal to survive and to place his children in service in the homes of those who will be willing to feed them.

Sieur de Linctot[8] and his wife also have 10 Children and two from one of their daughters and do not have the means to do anything whatever, one of the oldest families of the country.

There is nothing more important than forbidding the governors and the intendants to participate in any trading whatever directly or indirectly.

He thought it necessary to make a choice of the most honest merchants of Canada in order to turn to good account the 25 congés granted on behalf of the settlers of the country and sends a list of their distribution.

The reason which obliged him to do this is that in the past those to whom they were distributed would sell them to those who gave them the most for them, from which practice several unpleasant consequences developed:

1st. In that some small merchants with nasty misconduct had made a common practice of making three congés out of two.

2nd. In that instead of sending the appropriate clothes and merchandise for the Indians, the canoes had been loaded only with brandy in spite of the prohibitions.[9]

3rd. In that they sent into the woods only rogues and vagabonds.

4th. In that the majority of these little merchants used them to trade with the English.[10]

NOTES

1. National Archives of Canada, Manuscript group 5 (transcriptions from Archives nationales de France), series B1, volume 5, part 3, Summary of Governor Denonville's letters in 1686, excerpts from transcribed pp. 373–74, 391–92, and 399–401. Original in Ministère des Affaires étrangères, Paris, Mémoires et documents.

2. Jacques-René Brisay de Denonville, governor-general of New France from 1685–89.

3. Daniel Greysolon Dulhut fortified Michilimackinac in 1683.

4. Olivier Morel de La Durantaye, Michilimackinac commander 1683–1690.

5. The traders in Albany, New York, had long sought to expand their fur-trade connections west, and under Governor Thomas Dongan they found someone who shared their ambitions. He sanctioned fur-trade trips into what the French considered their territory. Helen Broshar, "The First Push Westward of the Albany Traders," *Mississippi Valley Historical Review* 7, no. 3 (December 1920): 228–41; A. H. Buffinton, "The Policy of Albany and English Westward Expansion," *Mississippi Valley Historical Review* 8, no. 4 (March 1922): 327–66. In 1685 Johannes Roseboom traveled to Michilimackinac and traded there on behalf of the English. The French were worried about the threat this posed to their trade network and to the military connections with Native groups that the trade fostered. When they learned that the English would attempt another trip to Michilimackinac, French officials sent a large contingent of soldiers and Indian allies to intercept them. In 1687 Roseboom, attempting his second trip to the Ottawas, and Patrick Magregory, on his first voyage, were captured by a group led by Olivier Morel de La Durantaye. David A. Armour, *The Merchants of Albany, New York: 1686–1760* (New York and London: Garland Publishing, 1986), 1–17.

6. Henri de Tonty.

7. Pierre de Saint-Ours.

8. Michel Godefroy de Lintot (Linctot).

9. Alcohol caused much havoc among Indian societies in the Northeast. Indians, because they had no socially prescribed rules for limiting alcohol intake, usually drank to get drunk. The altered alcohol-induced state allowed them to break

normal social taboos with little punishment. The result of excessive drinking was often violence committed by one Native against another, and traders often took advantage of inebriated Indians to defraud them of their trade goods. Such situations created social disorder in Native societies and tensions between Indians and Europeans. French, and English, authorities had limited success controlling traders who wanted to sell alcohol to Natives, and Indians often worked as hard as the traders to counteract the various colonial prohibitions against alcohol sales. Peter Mancall, *Deadly Medicine: Indians and Alcohol in Early America* (Ithaca: Cornell University Press, 1995), especially 137–54 for the situation in New France.

10. There had long been a problem with illegal trade to Albany, where French traders often obtained better prices for their furs than those paid at the royal warehouses, where by law, the French had to take the furs they obtained from the Indians. Jean Lunn, "The Illegal Fur Trade out of New France, 1713–1760," *Canadian Historical Association Report* (1939): 61–76; Thomas E. Norton, *The Fur Trade in Colonial New York, 1686–1776* (Madison: University of Wisconsin Press, 1974), 121–51.

René Fezeret's complaint against Etienne de Sainte for attacking Marie Carlié, Fezeret's wife

1686, September 24, Montreal[1]

To the Montreal magistrate

René Fezeret[2] humbly beseeches you and pleads and protests to you that the man named Estienne de Sainte[3] is lodging free of cost at the said Fezeret's and that the said de Sainte has under his own authority broken the two doors of the shop that he is occupying in order to make 2 cat-flaps in them and because this is of consequence in that one of these doors opens up on the street and the other on the common that would cause great harm to the said lodging because of the access it would give both to thieves and to the great spring flooding and it is necessary for the said Fezeret to put these said doors back in good condition for Monsieur de Ste Helesne[4] to whom the house belongs, which damage Marie Carlié, the wife of the supplicant, noticed and gently pointed out to the said de Sainte that he had not done well to have made this opening and that furthermore he was not in his own home, that he knew well that the supplicant had to repair these doors to put them back in good condition, and that they ought to do things in cooperation with each other without acting thus in great conflict, to which the said de Sainte replied saying to her "mort Dieu[5] I want to," to which the said supplicant's wife said to him again very quietly, "But my dear sir if you had said the slightest thing to me I would have closed up 2 or 3 cats with food that would have been of use to you." De Sainte replied the same way as above and said very brusquely that neither cats or women were worth anything locked up and took the arm of the said supplicant's wife, seated as she was, with one hand in order to push her outside and with the other hand hit her several times in the back[6] and on the breast, who, filled with confusion and manhandled thus without letup, was constrained to call for help. The supplicant ran up and knew by the said openings that his said wife was very right to speak and while the said wife of the said supplicant was making her complaint about the said de Sainte's bad treatment, the said de Sainte struck her in the face and on her breast three times in the presence of her husband, the said supplicant, and the said supplicant asked him who gave him the liberty of thus hitting his wife and the said de Sainte took the supplicant by the throat with the man named Jean LeMoyne[7] and having overwhelmed the said supplicant struck him and tore his shirt and hit him several times, the said LeMoyne saying "Your wife had my beaver seized a month ago; to take my vengeance I've got to beat you even more gladly for her sake,"[8] which he would have done at will with the said de Sainte and would have killed him if the sieurs Beaubien[9] and Plattier had not come to pull the said supplicant from above and separate them, the said de Sainte held by the said Lachapelle[10] could not refrain from punching the face of the wife of the said supplicant, the latter being all covered with bruises and left very injured and the said supplicant with his throat all skinned and bruised from several blows, which is causing him great harm not being able to complete work begun for voyageurs besides the ignominy of seeing good family people thus mistreated by a headstrong man filled with ingratitude.

Considering this, sir, may it please you to permit the said supplicant to bring in the report of the surgeon and to have the facts made known [. . .] and to summon the witnesses by requiring the first bailiff or court sergeant to do this, and do justice and order him [de Sainte] to put the said doors completely back into shape and to pay all expenses, damages and interest.

Fezeret

Permission granted to open an inquiry before us; let the witnesses be summoned and brought in; ordered and done the 24th of September 1686.

Migeon De Branssat paraph.

NOTES

1. Archives nationales du Québec à Montréal, Documents judiciaires de la juridiction seigneuriale de Montréal (1651–1695) [cote TL 2, feuilles détachées, 1681–1693].

2. René Fezeret (c. 1642–1720) was likely the first gunsmith (*arquebusier*) and master armorer to ply his trade in New France. A fascinating individual, he had an extraordinary career, rising from tradesman to bourgeois entrepreneur in the fur trade to seigneur whose daughter married into the nobility. *DCB*, 2:221; Jetté, *DG*, 419. The events that follow all took place on Rue Saint-Paul, where Fezeret had a house.

3. Etienne Xaintes, a gunsmith. Either he or his brother were said to be living at Michilimackinac in 1683. *DG*, 1135; document 10.

4. Possibly Jacques Le Moyne de Sainte-Hélène, "one of the famous Le Moyne brothers." *DCB*, 1:465–67; Jetté, *DG*, 712.

5. Literally, "dead God." The expression can only be viewed as blasphemous, and thus cast de Sainte in a bad light.

6. The words in the original appear to be *dans les daus*. *Daus* is phonetically the equivalent of *dos*, meaning "back."

7. Jean-Baptiste Le Moyne (Lemoine), is said to be a twenty-two-year-old who had recently returned from Michilimackinac (see document 26). Among the famous Le Moyne family, there was a Jean-Baptiste Le Moyne de Martigny et de La Trinité. He was said, however, to have been baptized in April 1662. Assuming he was baptized in the same year that he was born (not always the case in this period), he would be at least twenty-four years old in 1686. Moreover, his biographer has him serving in an expedition against the English in Hudson's Bay at this time. *DCB*, 2:405. The fact that the Le Moyne mentioned in this document is rarely addressed as "sieur" by anyone other than de Sainte (who needed to make all his witnesses appear to be of "respectable society") would suggest he did not have the social standing of the better-known Le Moynes, who are almost always addressed that way or as "monsieur."

8. This phrasing bears comment. Le Moyne's reasoning suggests that he viewed the actions taken against him as the work of Fezeret's wife. That is, Marie Carlié did not act on behalf of her husband, according to Lemoyne, but rather she was the driving force in the business decision to have his furs taken.

9. Possibly Michel Trottier, sieur des Ruisseaux et de Beaubien. Jetté, *DG*, 1093.

10. Pierre Janot *dit* Lachappelle. See document 25 and Jetté, *DG*, 591.

Etienne de Sainte's statement denying Fezeret's complaint

1686, September 25, Montreal[1]

To the Montreal magistrate

Etienne de Sainte humbly beseeches you saying that he learned that about three days ago Madame Fezeret presented a petition to have the said supplicant investigated, saying that she and her husband had been manhandled by the said supplicant, which the said supplicant will prove to the contrary with good and irreproachable witnesses, that is to say that the said Madame Fezeret came to his place deliberately to forbid him to make a cat-flap in the door, to which the supplicant replied that he had in no way anything to do with her, that she should leave without delay, that she wanted to compel him to say foolish things and that she was asking for nothing else, to which the said Fezeret woman answered that if he were capable of talking to her about it attacking her honor she would reply to him with a slap in the face, and [also said] that he was a little rascal, a [piddling] little doctor,[2] and a drunkard and other foolish things that she repeated several times intending to provoke the said supplicant into ill-treating her. [She] called [. . .] her husband and upon his arrival the said Fezeret woman was at his [de Sainte's] place and had struck him twice in the stomach with a closed fist and at the same instant the said Fezeret her husband threw himself on him and turned him with a hold and bear hug grabbing him by his tie as if to strangle him which he would have carried out without the help given him [de Sainte] by sieur LeMoyne who found that the said supplicant was floored by the said Fezeret and his wife held him [de Sainte] in his house and mistreated him with punches and this is what the said supplicant will prove both by the said sieur Le Moyne and by other witnesses who saw the said supplicant manhandled by the said Fezeret and his wife at his [de Sainte's] home and the stubborn determination of the said Fezeret woman not to leave in spite of the admonitions addressed to her by several people who were present.

Considering this, Monsieur, please permit the said supplicant to have sieur LeMoyne informed and subpoenaed to testify and tell the truth [. . .]

what he knows about it [. . .] other witnesses that he will find who have seen and heard the said quarrel.

De Sainte

In view of the above petition, permission [is granted] to conduct an investigation; to that end let the witnesses be subpoenaed in order to testify truthfully about the deed and the circumstances. So ordered and done the 25th day of September 1686.

Migeon De Branssat paraph.

NOTES

1. Archives nationales du Québec à Montréal, Documents judiciaires de la juridiction seigneuriale de Montréal (1651–1695) [cote TL 2, feuilles détachées, 1681–1693].

2. The French term used here is *un petit docteur*. Marie Carlié's use of *petit* here is both diminutive and pejorative as applied to the term *docteur*, which basically meant "learned man" in the sixteenth and seventeenth centuries, and which Carlié used sarcastically.

Testimony of Fezeret's witnesses against de Sainte

1686, September 26, Montreal[1]

> *Investigation done by us the bailiff, civil and criminal judge of the island of Montreal upon the petition of René Fezeret and his wife living in this town plaintiffs and complainants against Etienne de Sainte, gunsmith, defendant and accused and his accomplices to which investigation we have proceeded as follows with our clerk of the court*

On the 24th day of September 1686 in the afternoon there appeared Joseph Loizel thirty-one years of age a habitant of Pointe aux Trembles on the said island presently staying in this town who, after taking his oath to tell the truth [etc.]

Testifies on the facts contained in the sieur Fezeret and his wife's complaint that we caused to be read to him that at about five in the evening going toward Pierre Gadois's house on rue Saint Paul with the men named Jean LeMoyne and Pierre Jannot dit Lachapelle he heard some noise in the house where the said de Sainte lives, facing the said plaintiff's, which they have sublet to him. He went there with the named men and saw the said Fezeret and his wife who were fighting hand-to-hand with the said de Sainte, the said Fezeret with his shirt completely ripped, [and the three passers-by] separated them after which he [Loizel] went away not knowing who was the aggressor of one or the other which is everything that he said he knew. His deposition was read to him [etc.] [he] requested a recompense of twenty sols [etc.].

Migeon De Branssat paraph.

Bourgine[2] paraph.

On this day and year in the afternoon at our hearing there appeared sieur Jean Jerosme Legay dit de Beaulieu, a merchant staying in this town twenty-four years of age who, after taking his oath [etc.] presented us with the summons given to him to testify upon being petitioned by the said Fezeret and his wife.

He testifies on the facts contained in the complaint of the said Fezeret and his wife, which we had read to him, that yesterday at about three to four o'clock in the afternoon being in his house next to the said de Sainte's and opposite the house of the said plaintiffs, the wife of the plaintiff seeing the said de Sainte making cat-flaps in the doors of her said house without their permission reproached him for making them without speaking to them. He answered her that [since] the rats and mice were eating his beaver he did not feel obligated to ask for their permission and that he was housed in this place by his sister Beaulieu a Quebec entrepreneur had rented it from the said Fezeret woman[3] for the whole summer and that a part of his trade goods that he had left him was still there[4] to which the said woman plaintiff replied it is I who am housing you and not she I am the mistress here which infuriated the said de Sainte who told her, gesturing with his arm, I do not recognize you in any way; you are not my mistress get out of here and at the same time the said Fezeret woman answered him you are acting like a [piddling] little doctor proclaiming your dogma[5] and [he] tried to put her outside but resisting him she reentered the said house threatening to make him leave, and the said de Sainte repeated leave Madame Fezeret [or] you will oblige me to say foolish things to you, to which she said if you were capable of saying anything to me that could harm my good reputation I would give you a slap and you are acting so proud because you have some beaver, and immediately she called Bellegarde her valet to tell her husband Fezeret to come, and at the very moment the said de Sainte said if Bellegarde comes I shall break his ass[6] the said Fezeret her husband came in after the said de Sainte and no sooner than he had entered, the deponent who is the neighbor separated only by a small shop heard a great clamor from people who were fighting and as he was preparing to go into the said house to separate them, the man named Jean LeMoine went in before him, inquiring from sieur Cochois's residence, and as the deponent went in he saw the said Le Moine grappling with the said Fezeret grabbing each other's hair and the said Fezeret woman with the said de Sainte and having separated all four of them he recognized that the said LeMoine instead of separating them had taken the side of the said de Sainte upon the Fezeret woman's reproaching him you are beating my husband like a gladiator[7] I had your furs seized for what you owed me, and heard him say if I can catch your husband elsewhere we'll be worth seeing, threatening her, to which the said Fezeret replied I'll fight you whenever you want I am not afraid of you and since they were out of reach of one another the deponent's wife having come to get him he went out, and a little while later he heard noise because they had started up again and all were fighting again in great disorder all four covered with blood and the said Fezeret's shirt completely torn, then a second time the men named Paul Bouchard, Loisel and one other separated them again a third time, which he saw having retraced his steps, the said LeMoine telling them that the said de Sainte being his friend and having seen him being murdered by the said Fezeret and his wife and that he had defended him by continuing to restrain the said Fezeret with his hand, and the deponent then advised the said Fezeret to remove his wife who had been the cause of the dispute and who was irritating them more and more and the said Fezeret withdrew, and his wife still remained in de Sainte's house seated on a pack saddle[?][8] the said de Sainte and LeMoine having left the said house which obliged the deponent to go find the said Fezeret to take his wife away to his house which he could not do as long as she still obstinately persisted in staying there, the said de Sainte seeing this and everyone futilely exhorting her to leave and go home and that she could cause more regrettable consequences, the said de Sainte took a bucket of water and threw it on her feet and at once the said Fezeret woman left quite ashamed of being reproached for having attracted this disorder nevertheless staying on the doorsill, she left because her said husband Fezeret came to take her by the arm, after which the said de Sainte began to jeer at her and came to see the said Fezeret woman at her door and said to her let us be reconciled Madame Fezeret[9] and let us bless a drink of wine together for it is what you are asking for, to which the said Fezeret woman replied since you made me leave your house leave mine, then the said de Sainte closed the door that opens on the said Saint-Paul Street which is all he had to say [etc.]. Approved reimbursement of forty sols to him [Le Gay].

Le Gay paraph.

Migeon De Branssat paraph.

Bourgine paraph.

On the said day and year in the afternoon in our hearing room appeared Laurant Rodier fourteen years six months of age domestic servant of Madame Perrot where he lives who after oath [etc.] testifies as to the facts mentioned in the said complaint whose reading was done that yesterday after lunch in the afternoon on Saint Paul Street he saw Fezeret's said wife in the house where Estienne de Sainte is presently living and who slapped the face of the said Fezeret woman as he heard without having seen it, the latter having been struck called her husband crying out that she was being murdered and he entered the said house upon his wife's cries with the said de Sainte continuing to abuse her calling a loose woman and a whore in the presence of the said Fezeret her husband she too was insulting him calling him a good-for-nothing and a blackguard the said de Sainte slapped her a second time and [. . .] the said de Sainte was still trying to [hit?] her in the [. . .] elsewhere, the said Fezeret seeing this threw himself onto him and [they] came to blows then Jean LeMoine arrived because of the noise they were making and threw himself onto the said Fezeret and manhandled him while saying if I had not come[10] to the assistance of de Sainte they would have murdered him and then several people ran up to separate them and put an end to it nevertheless the said LeMoine and de Sainte resisted them and tried to continue to beat the said Fezeret and his wife who defended themselves being attacked by the said De Sainte and LeMoine who said to them because you had my beaver seized it is necessary that I beat him at my pleasure and tried to start up again on two different occasions after which the said Fezeret went off his wife refusing to leave stubbornly persisting in remaining at the said De Sainte's in spite of his trying to put her outside and as he saw that she did not want to leave he went to get a bucket of water and threw it on her feet after which she withdrew, her husband having come to get her, and the said De Sainte, having been invited by some people who were drinking at the said Fezeret woman's house to come drink with them, he went in there and the said Fezeret woman put him out whom he seized by the throat and leaving her without hitting her he went off which is all he [the witness] said he knew [etc . . .] adding that the said De Sainte is more in the wrong than the said Fezeret [. . .] that the second son of the man named LeBoeuf, a habitant, was present as he was and stated that he did not know how to write or sign his name, having been asked this according to the ordinance and requested reimbursement, granted to him at fifteen sols.

On the said day and year in the afternoon in our hearing chamber

Migeon De Branssat paraph.

Bourgine paraph.

There appeared Pierre Jannot dit LaChapelle twenty-six years of age also a habitant of this island living on his concession at Pointe au Tremble who after taking the oath [etc.] to testify upon the petition of the said Fezeret and his wife this day is testifying on the facts contained in the said complaint which we had read to him that yesterday after lunch having gone to drink a bottle of wine at sieur Cachois's house with Joseph Loizel and LeMoine they heard noise in the house in which Estienne De Sainte is staying opposite Fezeret's, LeMoine slipped away from their company without their knowing it and came to the said De Sainte's house and since the noise continued the said Loisel ran there having had a lot to drink which obligated the deponent [Janot dit LaChapelle] to run after him and the two of them having arrived in the said De Sainte's house he saw the said LeMoyne hanging onto the said Fezeret by his hair and vice versa pummeling each other and the said De Sainte with them, all three of them fighting confusedly and not realizing that the said De Sainte was beating the wife of the said Fezeret whose shirt was completely torn, the latter went out after they had been separated, his wife not having wanted to leave and stubbornly staying there against the pleas of the people who came running to put an end to it and as the said De Sainte saw that she was persisting in staying there and not wanting to withdraw he went to get a bucket of water and threw it across the legs of the said Fezeret woman who was seated and whose husband took her away then saying as an excuse that she was in her house and that they could not make her leave so long as she had rented it out with a lease to the sister-in-law of the said De Sainte who said he had the right to rent it from her and [she] had entrusted him with the [. . .] that she had left there upon her departure for Quebec, which was all that he said he knew, that he does not know who started the quarrel or which one was most in the wrong. The reading of the testimony was done for him [etc.] Our clerk of the court requested reimbursement for him, approved at twenty-five sols.

Pierre Jannot

Migeon De Branssat paraph.

Bourgine paraph.

NOTES

1. Archives nationales du Québec à Montréal, Documents judiciaires de la juridiction seigneuriale de Montréal (1651–1695) [cote TL 2, feuilles détachées, 1681–1693].

2. Hilaire Bourgine, clerk and notary in Montreal. *DG*, 153.

3. Fezeret's wife is consistently referred to in this deposition as "ladite Fezeret," a less respectful manner of address than what one usually finds in court documents.

4. This portion of the original manuscript is not entirely clear. The original reads as follows, with its marginal additions shown by boldface type inserted where indicated into the text: *par sa soeur Beaulieu bourgeois de Québec **et lavoit louée de lad(it)e Fezeret pour tout leste et qune partye de ses marchandises en estoient encore** qui len avoit laissé.* Note that this testimony was given by de Sainte's next-door neighbor, also named Beaulieu, who, when being sworn in, stated that he was not related to the parties in this case. Below, the clerk of the court wrote that Fezeret's wife had leased the property to de Sainte's *sister-in-law*. It appears that it was de Sainte's *sister*, the wife of a Quebec merchant or entrepreneur named Beaulieu, who, acting for her husband, had leased the house from Fezeret's wife for Beaulieu and had permitted her brother, de Sainte, to stay there.

5. *Vous faicte le petit docteur avec vostre doctrine.* Marie Carlié's use of *petit* here is both diminutive and pejorative as applied to the term *docteur*, which basically meant "learned man" in the sixteenth and seventeenth centuries, and which Carlié used sarcastically. She is accusing de Sainte of being petty and dogmatic.

6. I shall break his ass, *je luy casseray le cul.*

7. Like a gladiator, *en home de cirque.*

8. The term used here, *bastre*, is likely a misspelling of *basté*, which Cotgrave (*Dictionarie*) translates as "pack saddle."

9. The polite term of address, "Madame Fezeret," used here mockingly by de Sainte, contrasts sharply with how the clerk of the court (and witness?) refer to her in this record.

10. The clerk of the court wrote here *sy tu nestois point venu*, "if you had not come," but it would appear logical that he meant to write *sy je nestois pas venu*, "if I had not come."

Judicial inquiry regarding the petition of Estienne de Sainte against Fezeret

1686, September 26–27, Montreal[1]

Judicial inquiry made by me bailiff civil and criminal judge of the island of Montreal upon the petition of Estienne de Sainte, a gunsmith recently back from the Ottawas presently in this town plaintiff against René Fezeret and his wife defendants and accused, to which inquiry we have proceeded as follows with our clerk of the court

On September 26, 1686 in the afternoon Jean Baptiste LeMoine appeared, twenty-two years of age living in the house of sieur Tarpin, an innkeeper and carrier recently back from the Ottawas, who after taking the oath to tell the truth [etc.] testifies regarding the facts contained in the said complaint that we had read to him that having heard some noise several days ago in the house of the said plaintiff [de Sainte] as he was at his relative sieur Cachois's door he asked the neighbor sieur Beaulieu who was causing that noise and he said that it was Fezeret and his wife who were quarreling, and then he entered the said house where he saw the said Fezeret who was having words with the said DeSainte who took her by the sleeve and tried to put her out of the said house who, finding herself treated like that turned around and gave it to him with both hands in his stomach and made him fall onto a chest and the two of them grabbed each other's arms and the said Fezeret her husband also wanted to throw himself upon the said De Sainte and seeing this the deponent in order to prevent them from fighting took him by the sleeve and at that very moment sieur de Beaulieu who [also] separated them and the said deponent withdrew without threatening anyone and not having taken anyone's side which is all that he said he knew [etc.] and our clerk of the court called for reimbursement for him approved at thirty sols.

Jean Baptiste Le Moyne

Migeon De Branssat paraph.

Bourgine paraph.

I hope, monsieur the judge, to be good enough to come to a friendly arrangement with Fezeret and his wife over the dispute we created and [. . .] I am offering personally to pay the expenses determined by the court. Your very humble servant will [thus] be obliged this 27th of September 1686.

De Saincte

Tell me, monsieur, I entreat you, your last thoughts on this affair in order for me to pursue or finish it according to its forestallment or continuance. I thank you for your charity and pray God that he be your reward.

Fezeret

Madame, Monsieur De Sainte submits to paying the court-ordered expenses provided that you live as good friends and I will have monsieur Migeon [the judge] render a judgment that I shall keep among my papers in case you might need it and I will give it to you.

E Guyotte [2]

For Madame Fezeret
For Monsieur the Priest's Hands

I consent willingly and for the love of God to the agreement that Monsieur the Priest worked out for you to the advantage of the man named De Sainte and to the conciliatory sentence that Monsieur the Judge is willing to render upon my entreaty in order to terminate any pursuit against him in the clauses that my said sieur the Judge is reading and will deem appropriate to be attached to the damages listed below:

Firstly

Make new doors to replace those he broke without any such order because the lodging is not mine and it is necessary for me to return it in good condition, which is the cause of all the clamor, [pay] all the expenses of the trial which will be if you please awarded by your ruling after the exact statement of them has been shown to you, such as the surgeon's fees in accordance with his statement; also the reimbursement for a shirt violently torn into twenty pieces on my body; as for the blows, bruises, abrasions and pains that we received and which my wife and I are suffering from even now, we leave that to your fairness and discretion as we do the fine for the

Church either now or in case of recidivism of the least offensive word as is his custom to say continuously to me, without any concern for the fact that he has eaten my father's bread and consequently for the respect that he owes me and my wife whom he shocks incessantly, about which I am bringing you my complaint and I give you everything with his consent to your merit and conscience. Done at Montreal this 28th of September 1686.

Fezeret

Marie Carlié

NOTES

1. Archives nationales du Québec à Montréal, Documents judiciaires de la juridiction seigneuriale de Montréal (1651–1695) [cote TL 2, feuilles détachées, 1681–1693].

2. Étienne Guyotte, parish priest of Notre-Dame de Montréal.

Verdict in favor of Fezeret against de Sainte with a list of court costs attached

1686, September 30, Montreal [1]

To all persons to whom these presents may come, greeting. We Jean Baptiste Migeon sieur DeBranssat, lawyer in parliament, civil and criminal judge in the bailiff's court of the island of Montreal, let it be known that in view of the judicial inquiry made by us upon the petition of René Fezeret, a gunsmith,[2] and his wife Marie Cavellier [Marie Carlié], living in this town, on the twenty-fourth of this month, against Estienne De Sainte, also a gunsmith, on the one hand, and the judicial inquiry done upon the petition of the said De Sainte against the said Fezeret and his wife, on the twenty-sixth of the said month, on the respective complaints at the bottom of which are our orders granting permission to summon the witnesses, that they have to dispose of the surgeon's report on the date of their consent in writing signed by the said parties who are waiting to settle their differences amicably with the greatest exactitude just as they could have done if they had not agreed to come together and reach an arrangement. Taking everything into consideration, we the undersigned bailiff [judge] have prohibited and do prohibit the said parties from offending, speaking ill of, or insulting each other on pain of a fine of fifty livres and we admonish them to live henceforth as good friends and furthermore we sentence the said De Sainte to pay one hundred sols for the said Fezeret's shirt and to the expenses of one and the other proceedings that we have awarded and liquidated jointly in the amount of one hundred livres thirteen sols, to payment of which sums he [De Sainte] submits, including the report of the said sieur Anthoine Forestier, a surgeon in this town, and to repair at his own expense the two cat flaps in the said doors which sum the said De Sainte will be compelled to pay by all just and reasonable means [. . .] and without prejudice. Done and given by us the undersigned bailiff on the thirtieth and last day of September one thousand six hundred eighty-six.

Migeon De-Branssat paraph.

Bourgine paraph.

[verdict:]

Statement of the expenses coming from both the petition of René[3] and his wife regarding their complaint and from Estienne de Sainte's petition and complaint

Firstly,

For the order to deliver summons regarding the complaint of sieur Fezeret and his wife.	12 livres tournois
For four summons delivered in town.	1 livre tournois 12 sols
For the hearing of the witnesses.	41.t.
To our clerk of the court for the two.	21.t. 13 sols
For the court sergeant.	21.t.
For the order on the bottom of the said de Sainte's complaint.	01.t. 12 sols
For the summons delivered to Jean LeMoine above the Saint-Pierre River, 8 sols.	01.t. [8 sols?]
For the investigation.	40 sols
To our clerk of the court.	11.t. 6 sols
For considering the pleadings and the conciliatory sentence.	41.t.
To our clerk of the court.	11.t. 5 sols
For the surgeon's report.	41.t.
	251.t. 13 sols
For the reimbursement of the witnesses.	51.t.

The above expenses were listed by us	301.t. 13 sols

Liquidated in the amount of thirty livres thirteen sols[4]

Carried out September 30, 1686

NOTES

1. Archives nationales du Québec à Montréal, Documents judiciaires de la juridiction seigneuriale de Montréal (1651–1695) [cote TL 2, feuilles détachées, 1681–1693].
2. Gunsmith, *harquebusier*.
3. The clerk of the court failed to write "Fezeret" here.
4. The correct amount, depending on how one counts the amount given to Jean Lemoine, is closer to 41 l.t., 16s.

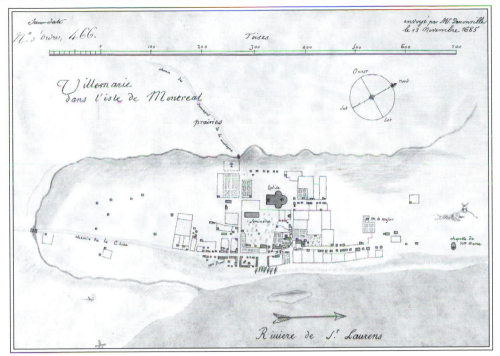

Montreal circa 1685. Rue Saint-Paul, the site of numerous activities mentioned in these documents, is the long street that runs across the bottom of the sketch. Library and Archives Canada, H3/340/Montréal/1685 Record No. 2300.

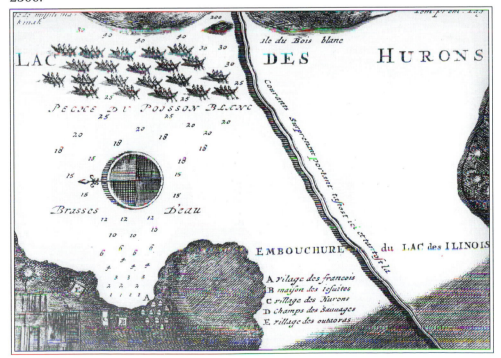

Map by Baron de Lahontan (1703) showing the community of Michilimackinac around 1688. The map is oriented with North at the left of the map and South at the right. Courtesy Mackinac State Historic Parks.

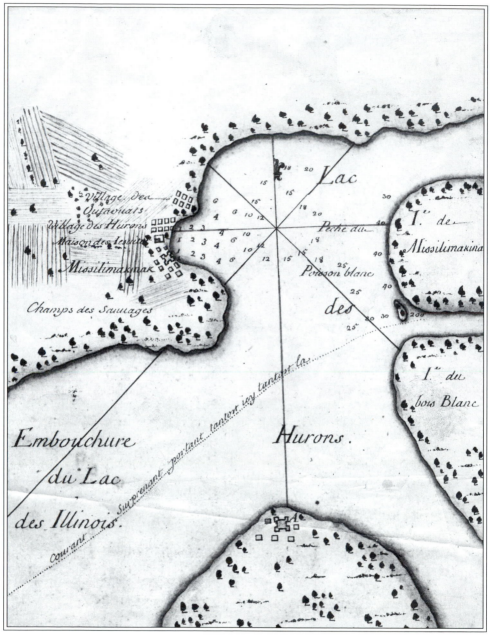

Anonymous map of Michilimackinac circa 1716 showing the new fort on the south side of the straits and the community at Fort du Buade on the north side of the straits. The latter was no longer there by this date. Courtesy Edward E. Ayer Collection, The Newberry Library, Chicago.

Beaver furs were a staple of New France's export trade throughout the colony's history, and the activities of the animal attracted the interest, and appealed to the imagination, of the French. "Beaver Hunting in Canada," engraved for *Middleton's Complete System of Geography*, (London, 1782). Courtesy Mackinac State Historic Parks.

Image of daily activities of Huron Indians. There was a community of Hurons at Michilimackinac before 1701. From Allain Mallet, *Description de l'univers,* vol. v (Paris: n.p., 1683). Courtesy Mackinac State Historic Parks.

A highly stylized portrayal of an Ojibwa family group. The Ojibwa Indians occupied the region north, west, and east of Michilimackinac. From the Reverend Thomas Bankes, *Bankes's New System of Geography, A New Royal Authentic and Complete System of Universal Geography Antient [sic] and Modern* (printed for J. Cooke, No. 17 Pater-noster-Row, London, 1787–1790). Courtesy Mackinac State Historic Parks.

Crucifix corpora from St. Ignace site. Statuettes of Christ, such as these, which could be affixed to crosses on rosaries, were used by Jesuit missionaries as part of their devotions and to help convert Indians to Catholicism. Courtesy of the Michigan State University Department of Anthropology.

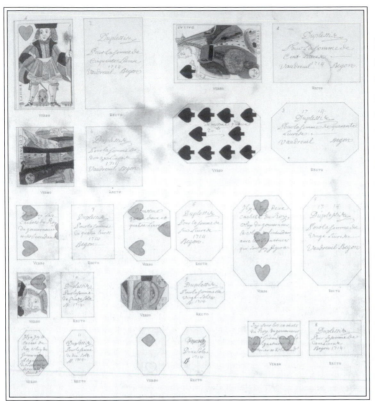

Due to a chronic shortage of currency, officials in New France often used playing cards instead. The cards were signed by the intendant of the colony, assigned a value, and could be redeemed when funds arrived from France. Library and Archives Canada, reference number C17059.

Image of a heavily tattooed Ottawa warrior, circa 1675. The Ottawas had villages near the French on both sides of the straits and were ready allies of the French in their wars against the various other Native groups and the English. By Fr. Louis Nicolas, 1675. Courtesy of Clements Library, University of Michigan.

Memoire des marchandises appartenan-
tes à Marie Felix du Bocq
laissées chez les Peres à Missilimaxinac
1683.

18. peignes.

onze douzaines de grands couteau.
un pacquet de fer de flesches.
2. grosses d'Alaisnes.
7. demy biscayennes.
21. Tranches   donné coppie des memoire
                aud s envaudt à sala [?]brunes
12. battes feu
enuiron 10. liures de plomb à Tourtes.
140. balds.
37. à 8. liures de poudre.
7. grands miroirs doubles.
une masse de Rassade bleüe.
une demy brasse de transparante.
6. brasses de noir
10. brasses de rouge.
20. brasses de blanches
2. liures de blan d'Espagne &
2. liures de jaune In masse.
        Pour Louis Oakont
enuiron 10. liures de poudre dans un
long sac &   le tout de 3. queuill
200. balds.

Statement of trade goods belonging to Marie du Bocq. Courtesy of
Bibliothèque et Archives Nationales du Québec.

The first pages of the enquiry in the case of Fezeret v. Boudor, June 5, 1700. Courtesy of Bibliothèque et Archives Nationales du Québec.

Judgment to the benefit of sieur Patron against sieur Dulhut

1687, March 3, Montreal [1]

Mathieu Gaillard, King's Councilor, Commissary in ordinary of the Marine and Subdelegate of Monsieur the Intendant of New France, by order of his Majesty, upon the petition presented to us the nineteenth of February last, by sieur Jean Jacques Patron, merchant-entrepreneur of the town of Montreal, requesting that sieur Louis le Conte Dupré, also a merchant-entrepreneur of the said place, in the name, and as agent, of the said sieur Dul'hut (nephew of Sieur Patron) be summoned before us to see and identify the signature and handwriting of three promissory notes signed by dul'hut, made in favor of the said sieur Patron. To wit, the first in the amount of eight thousand eight hundred five livres and ten sols dated the twelfth of May, 1683, signed Dulhut, the second in the amount of two thousand livres of the said day by which the said sieur Dul'hut declares that the said sieur Patron underwrote [for Dulhut] two bills of exchange, payable to sieur Mars,[2] also a merchant, in the said amount of two thousand livres, in two payments, each of one thousand livres, and that the said sieur Patron did that only to please him [Duluth], and the third and last [note] for the sum of eleven hundred livres, by which the said sieur dulhut declares, as well, that the said sieur Patron underwrote two bills of exchange payable to sieur Peloquin, also a merchant, dated the said day, the twelfth of May, 1683, and that the said sieur Patron did that only to please the said sieur Dulhut. Totalled together, the said three sums add up to eleven thousand, nine hundred five livres, ten sols. Our order, being at the end of the said petition of the said nineteenth day of the said month of February, requesting that the said sieur Dupré be summoned before us to identify the said promissory notes, and the writ of Sergeant Cabazié of the first day of the current month made out to the said sieur Dupré, to appear [in court] on the third, following the petitioner, one of the parties, and concluding with the payment of the said sum along with the interest due, in accordance with the judgment. And the said sieur le Conte Dupré appearing as representative and defendant in the said name of the other party, the parties having been heard, and after the said three promissory notes mentioned above were shown to the said sieur Dupré in the said name by the said sieur Patron, before us, and being recognized by the said sieur Dupré as having been written and signed by the said sieur Dulhut, [Dupré] said that he was familiar with all of them and had nothing to which to object, we have ordered the sieur Dulhut to pay the said sieur Patron, his uncle, the said sum of eleven thousand, nine hundred five livres, ten sols in cash, promissory notes, statements of accounts and receipts, and the latter amount with interest in accordance with the judgment, counting from this day, without court expenses, given the standing of the parties involved. And, as it was represented to us by the said sieur Dupré, in the said name, that sieur Duluth was on a lengthy trip in this country in the king's service, in which the said sieur Patron concurred, and with his consent, our present judgment is suspended until next autumn, which is the time that the said sieur Dupré asked for in order to have news of the said sieur Dulhut, and after that time expires the said sieur Patron is permitted to put it [the judgment] into execution and, nevertheless, he is allowed to proceed to a seizure as security for the debt owed to the said Patron. We Order, etc., done at Montreal, the third of March, 1687.

[Mathieu] Gaillard

By Monsieur the Subdelegate

Basset

Clerk of the Court

NOTES

1. Archives nationales du Québec à Montréal, Documents judiciaires de la juridiction seigneuriale de Montréal (1651–1695) [cote TL 2, feuilles détachées, 1681–1693]. This document was translated by José António Brandão with Joseph L. Peyser.
2. Possibly Simon Mars, a merchant-entrepreneur from the Quebec area. Jetté, *DG*, 774.

Marie Morin's sworn statement that she is pregnant by Alphonse de Tonty

1688, January 20, Montreal[1]

In the year one thousand six hundred eighty-eight on the twentieth day of January at nine o'clock in the morning there appeared before us in our mansion Marie Morin, the wife of Jacques Galoppe [Viger dit Galop], absent and a deserter from this colony who abandoned her and even took her abroad where she lived for several years; without the company of the said Galoppe who repudiated her and incestuously took as his wife and concubine Louise Prichard [Pichard] his half-sister and previously the wife of Jean Mardor[2] whom she abandoned and with whom the said Galoppe is on the run, the said Marie Morin, twenty-one years old, after giving her oath to tell the truth declared that this past summer she was employed in the service of Mistress de Blainville[3] to whose home sieur [Alphonse] de Tonty lieutenant in the Troupes de la Marine used to go very often, who timing himself to meet the deponent as she would leave in order to induce her to have his carnal company and after having resisted him several times finally one evening when she was leaving at night [*sic*] he pursued her so closely and begged her so strongly that she could not prevent herself from succumbing to his supplications and having placed her on the ground he took his pleasure with her and three days later at the same time he again had her carnal company from which she became pregnant and seven months gone or thereabouts affirming that she knew no one other than the said sieur Tonty, declaring that he is the father of the child[4] and that she received nothing from him but four livres for the two times that he knew her, whom we ordered to withdraw to her father and mother's house and live there properly, take care of her fruit, and answer to us for this on pain of the rope,[5] forbidding her to remain in this town on pain of prison and the whip if she relapses into poor self-control and prostitution as she has done, [we] have from all of the foregoing drawn up the present statement to be used and be valid for legitimate purposes after the said Marie declared that she did not know how to write or make her mark on this inquiry according to the ordinance, done on the above said day and year.

Migeon De Branssat

Adhemar[6] paraph.

NOTES

1. Archives nationales du Québec à Montréal, Documents judiciaires de la juridiction seigneuriale de Montréal (1651–1695) [cote TL 2, feuilles détachées, 1681–1693].

2. Jean Mardor married Louise Pichard in 1672 when she was thirteen years old. Jetté, *DG*, 913.

3. Hélène Picoté, wife of Jean-Baptiste Céloron, sieur de Blainville. Jetté, *DG*, 213.

4. The child, Louis, was born on April 11, 1688. Jetté, *DG*, 1083.

5. The sentence "take care of her fruit, and answer to us for this on pain of the rope" seems to be a warning to the young woman that should she terminate the pregnancy, she will be sent to the gallows. If this is the case, the warning against an abortion suggests that it was not unheard of for unwed women to have abortions.

6. Antoine Adhémar de Saint-Martin, royal notary, clerk of the court, and prison keeper. He took up his commission in the Montreal area in 1687. *DCB*, 2:10–11.

King to Denonville and Champigny

1688, March 8, Versailles[1]

The King to Denonville and Champigny[2]

His Majesty has had the clothing and other things needed for the soldiers who are in Canada purchased this year in accordance with the memorandum that they [Denonville and Champigny] will find enclosed, and He is pleased to have it pointed out to them that upon the notification that they gave that the clothing which was sent last year was not of good quality, He had the best fabrics that could be found in Paris selected in order to make these and that He is counting on the clothing, at least the jerkins, lasting two years, in order for them to take the necessary steps to have them kept in good condition, thus next year, He will not send any jerkins at all, but He will continue to send them the other things, and this order will be observed in the future. That is to say that jerkins will be sent every other year and all the other things every year [. . .]

His Majesty approves their not having included in the expense statements the one that was made for a redoubt at the strait of Lake Erie and for another at Missilimakinak and that they are having the cost paid out of the congés. It is quite important for the reasons that His Majesty has explained above to them that they find such expedients often in order to reduce the expenses that His Majesty is making for this country, and He is convinced that they will succeed in this by giving the needed attention to it.

NOTES

1. National Archives of Canada, manuscript group 1 (transcriptions from Archives des Colonies), series B, volume 15: 19–20v, excerpts of King to Denonville and Champigny.

2. Jean Bochart de Champigny, intendant of New France 1686–1702.

Instructions to Frontenac upon his being named Governor-General of New France

1689, June 7, Versailles[1]

He[2] must place himself in a position to travel as soon as he can to all the points occupied by the French in order to be informed of the condition they are in and to provide for their needs according to the circumstances. And since Missilimakinac is of the greatest importance for the good of the trade, His Majesty wants him, since he is not able to go there, to give all the orders that he deems necessary for the preservation of that post.

NOTES

1. Archives nationales de France, Archives des Colonies, series B, 15: 92v. Excerpt from Minister to Frontenac.

2. Louis de Buade, Count de Frontenac, was the controversial governor-general of New France from 1672 to 1682, when he was recalled by Louis XIV, and again from 1689 until his death in 1698. Frontenac was arrogant, venal, and had a penchant for ignoring the king's orders if they hindered his desires to assert his status or add to his coffers. He pursued expansionist policies in the fur trade against direct orders, appointed colonial officials who would obey his wishes, and caused no end of turmoil within the colony and with New France's Native allies. He was very well connected at court, and this led to his reappointment after he had already been removed from office for his disruptive behavior. W. J. Eccles, *Frontenac: The Courtier Governor.*

Agreement between Nicolas Perrot and Pierre Le Sueur

1690, May 14, Montreal[1]

I, the undersigned, being fully informed about the competence, honesty and skill of sieur pierre Le sueur,[2] and trusting entirely in his good conduct for the care of my interests in the handling and management of my merchandise, I have chosen the aforesaid sieur Lesueur to this end to whom I give full & complete power to dispose of as he deems appropriate and of my men whom he will need for the fur trade, building, hunting and generally every purpose for the good of my business without my knowledge as if I had delivered to him a general and unlimited power of attorney written by a notary, and since it is right to recognize the care that he will take I have agreed with him and I obligate myself to pay him or have paid to his order wherever it seems appropriate to him for his pay, wages or salary the sum of twelve hundred livres in beaver at the quebek warehouse price upon his return to montreal which will be around October of the year one thousand six hundred ninety-one. If the aforesaid sieur Le Sueur finds it appropriate to take his payment at mischelimaquina or other locations where I would have beaver he will be permitted to pay himself or have himself paid in preference to any others. In that case I obligate myself to have his beaver brought down in my canoes on condition that the aforesaid sieur Lesueur will take care and keep his eye on the beaver that I will send as if on his very own without his being obliged however to assume any risk. If the case were to occur that he and I decided together for the good of my business that he should not come down at all next year in that case I obligate myself to pay him another twelve hundred livres at the quebek office price for a second year and we will make a new written agreement subject to the reciprocal satisfaction of both. He will live smoke and be clothed at my expense and if there is still something to be explained we will do it at any time and whenever he wishes. These presents made up in duplicate at Ville marie [Montreal], this 14th of May one thousand six hundred ninety.

Le Sueur

N Perrot

There appeared [here] the aforesaid sieurs perrot and Le Sueur presently in this city who have recognized and avowed having signed in their hand and ordinary signature which they are accustomed to doing in their affairs the agreements and transaction written above that they said and affirmed contain the truth and caused to be written by another hand, promising the aforesaid parties reciprocally each of them in his own right to maintain, satisfy, and fulfill according to its form and substance without contravening it in any manner whatever directly or indirectly on pain of all expenses, damages and interest, for thus, et cetera promising, etc., renouncing etc. Done and drawn up at the aforesaid city of Ville Marie, office of the aforementioned notary in the year one thousand six hundred ninety, the fourteenth day of May in the afternoon in the presence of Georges pruneau[3] and Jean Quesnevillé[4] practitioners witnesses residing in the aforementioned Villemarie. Undersigned with the aforementioned sieurs perrot and LeSueur and notary after being read in conformity with the ordinance.

N Nicolas

pierre

Approved five words of no value crossed out

N Perrot

J. Quesnevillé

Le Sueur

G. Pruneau Adhémar

NOTES

1. National Archives of Canada, Manuscript group 18, B10, original 2pp. and transcription 2pp.

2. Pierre Le Sueur, explorer and trader. Le Sueur, who had come to New France as a servant of the Jesuits, traded and traveled widely. He was an adventurer in the true sense of the word. He traded at Michilimackinac in the early 1680s, accompanied Nicolas Perrot when the latter claimed the upper Mississippi region on behalf of the French Crown, and petitioned to command a fort among the Sioux. He died in 1704 in Havana, Cuba, of fever while en route to the French settlement in Louisiana. *DCB*, 2:427–28.

3. Georges Pruneau was a royal bailiff at Montreal. Jetté, *DG*, 952.

4. Quesneville was a master tailor, royal-court officer, and jail keeper in Montreal. *DCB*, 2:534.

Protest by Françoise Duquet against completion of sale of her house and lot to the Bishop of Quebec on grounds of misrepresentation

1690, September 1, Quebec[1]

Today, the first day of September in the year 1690 in the forenoon Madame françoise Duquet, wife of Monsieur Ollivier Morel, Knight [and] Seigneur of La Durantaye, commanding for the king at missilimackinac living in this town on rue St. Louis, appeared before us and requested the recording of her declaration that she is opposing the proceeding with and completion of her sale that Monsieur de Villeray,[2] First Councilor of the Sovereign Council of this country drew up and transmitted to Monseigneur [the Bishop] of Quebec,[3] in the name of and as attorney for the said sieur de la durantaje her husband, of the lot and house belonging to her[4] situated on rue Ste. anne and rue des Jardins by the contract drawn up before us February 25, 1689; this lady protesting the invalidity of the said contract and consent that she gave it, due to her having been induced and pushed by the said sieur de Villeray by his persuasion and given to understand that the said sieur de la durantaje intended to sell his said possessions in order to have her taken to and settled in France with him, about which she now knows the opposite, for which reason she is formally preventing anything being added or done to [?] any expense or increase to the said site and house to the offers to conclude the contract that she is having returned and that she may have received from the said Lord Bishop of quebec save the assessment of the rents during the time of possession since the said contract [. . .] agreement and of her protestation abounding against all that could be done to the contrary. Done and drawn up in the office of the said notary, in the forenoon on the said day and year in the presence of sieurs Estienne Marandeau[5] and Bouteville, the son,[6] a merchant living on rue Ste. Anne, witnesses who signed with the said lady and us.

F. duquet

Bouteville

Marandeau paraph.

Genaple paraph.

NOTES

1. Archives nationales du Québec à Québec, Greffe de Genaple.

2. Louis Rouer de Villeray, who held the office of first councilor for over thirty years, was an honest high official of New France on excellent terms with the bishops of Quebec. *DCB*, 1:579–83.

3. Jean-Baptiste de La Croix de Chevrières de Saint-Vallier, the second bishop of Quebec, arrived in New France in July, 1688.

4. House belonging to her, *à elle appartenante*.

5. Étienne Maranda (Marandeau) was a bailiff in the Quebec court. Jetté, *DG*, 761.

6. Nearly five years earlier, Lucian Boutteville, a Quebec merchant, served as a witness to a partnership agreement between Lurent Baudet and La Durantaye. ANQ-Q, Greffe de Genaple, January 11, 1685.

Summary investigation of the beaver trade

1692, September 16, Montreal[1]

Summary investigation made by Jacques Alexis de Fleury, esquire, sieur Deschambault, bachelor of law, counsel at the parliament of Paris, bailiff [and] civil and criminal judge of the island of Montreal, upon the petition of sieur Alphonse de Tonty, esquire, half-pay captain in the Troupes de la Marine in the name of and holding a power of attorney from sieur Henry de Tonty, esquire, his brother, seigneur and king's governor of Fort Saint Louis of the Illinois in accordance with our order of yesterday placed at the bottom of the petition presented to us by the said sieur [Alphonse] de Tonty in the said name to which inquiry we have proceeded as follows:

On the sixteenth day of September one thousand six hundred ninety-two before nine o'clock in the morning in our mansion at Villemarie.

There appeared Pierre Dailleboust esquire, sieur Dargenteuil, half-pay lieutenant in the Troupes de la Marine staying in this town on Notre Dame street thirty-three years of age who took the oath to tell the truth, stating to us that he was not related by marriage to, nor a servant or domestic of the said parties and showed us the written summons given to him by the sergeant who obtained it yesterday upon the petition of the said sieur de Tonty in the said name, testifies upon the facts contained in the said petition and other facts that the said sieur Tonty placed in our hands and to whom [i.e., to Argenteuil] we had it read by our clerk of the court, that being at Missilimakinac last spring monsieur de Laforest[2] who was at the said place of Missilimakinac asked him [i.e., Tonty] if through his intervention he could arrange to have the Espissines [Nipissing] Indians and others who were going down to this town take down four packs of beaver whereupon he [Tonty] answered that he would do whatever he could but he had his own to send down, and then the said sieur de LaForest replied while smiling that the aforesaid four packs belonged to Monsieur de Callieres[3] and that if he did not have them sent down, he would write to my aforesaid sieur de Callieres that he [Tonty] had not wanted to [?], whereupon the deponent took three of the said packs that he sent down with the Indians who brought them here and being of a mind then not to go down he made out the address upon the request of Monsieur de La Forest in the hands of sieur Juchereau in order to be brought to his address, and that subsequently, having arrived in this town, he saw the letter address "D" on four packs of beaver that the said sieur de La Forest was writing to Monsieur de Callieres for the Reaumes, and Madame Perrot,[4] and the said deponent said that sieur de La Forest had delivered three packs of beavers to him that he said were for Monsieur de Callieres and Monsieur de Callieres told him not to let them out of his hands, and that Monsieur de La Forest did not tell him that the said beaver belonged to Madame Perrot but rather to Monsieur de Callieres, testifies that when the said deponent came down from the Ottawas for La Prairie, the said sieur de La Forest did not let him know at all that the said beaver belonged to the said sieur de Tonty in any way, that far from that he told him to act as if it were his very own and that if he made a cache for his [beaver] to put it there as well; and that in truth being here he would not have created any difficulty giving it back to sieur de Tonty in view of the partnership that he [Tonty] has with the said sieur de La Forest, if Monsieur de Callieres had not opposed it, and even in coming down said to sieur de Tonty that he would put the said beaver in his hands, that it is true that the said sieur de Tonty asked the said deponent for the said beaver having arrived at Lachine, he answered him once the said Indians were set up in camp he would give them [the beavers] to him without giving any details to whom it might concern, which is all that he said he knew, the reading of his deposition being done for him [he] said the latter was the truth and persisted in it and signed it with us and our clerk of the court and no reimbursement was required.

P. D. Dargenteuil

Deschambault paraph.

Adhemar paraph.

There appeared Pierre Le Febvre living in La Prairie de la Magdeleine forty-eight years of age who after the oath taken by him to tell the truth and that he was not related, related by marriage, a servant or domestic of either one or the other of the parties, presented to us the summons given to him by sergeant Pruneau on the fifteenth of this month to testify truthfully upon the petition of the said sieur de Tonty in the said name.

[Lefebvre] testifies on the facts contained in the said petition placed in our hands by the said sieur de Tonty that on the twenty-fourth of last month, Monsieur de Callieres ordered him to come to this town with Biscornet[5] and Charles Diel[6] and having arrived in this town Monsieur de Callieres asked them whether he might know about the payment they had made to Monsieur de La Durantaye on behalf of Ignace Hébert,[7] a debtor of Madame Perrot, they replied that they had paid for it all in beaver [. . .] and that it was difficult for them to be able to recognize the said beavers with the exception of those from a nation called the Ayougas and some Sioux, which the said payment included, and then three packs having been shown to them they recognized two of them that were part of the payment they had made and delivered and the other they recognized as not being part of the said payment made by them, which he assures is true with all his soul; and then the said sieur Dargenteuil who was present asked what they recognized they said that it was the letter A that was on the packs, and then he treated them like treacherous rogues telling them that it was he who had put on the said letter, and immediately the deponent [Lefebvre] asked that the said packs be opened and by the beavers that were in them which he knew perfectly as being among those with which he had made the said payment, confirmed what he had assured were from those with which they had paid and from there they betook themselves to Monsieur LeBer's[8] place where they also showed them a pack that was untied which they recognized as being among those with which they had made the above said payment for Ignace Hebert to Monsieur de La Durantaye acting for the said Madame Perrot, which is all that he said he knew, the reading of the deposition done for him [and he] said the latter contained the truth persisted in it and stated he did not know how to write or make his mark on this investigation in accordance with the ordinance.

Remuneration required for him set at three livres. Approved [*blank space*] words of no value [which were] crossed out.

Deschambault paraph.

Adhemar paraph.

There appeared Charles Diel a habitant living at La Prairie St. Lambert thirty-five years of age or thereabouts who after the oath taken by him to tell the truth declared he was not related or related by marriage to, or a servant or domestic of the parties and showed us the summons given to him by sergeant Pruneau yesterday to testify truthfully at the petition of the said sieur de Tonty in the said name.

Testifies on the facts contained in the said petition and others placed in our hands, which we had read by our clerk of the court, that on the twenty-fourth of last month, he was shown at Monsieur Dargenteuil's house two packs of beaver and one at Monsieur LeBer's house untied which he recognized perfectly well due to having handled them several times and due to some having been prepared by him and his company as a payment for Ignace Hebert to Monsieur de La Durantaye acting for Madame Perrot at Missilimakinac, which he now again certifies as pure truth, which is all he said he knew, reading done for him of his deposition said the latter contained the truth and persisted in it and signed with us and our clerk of the court and required reimbursement to him set by us at three livres.

Deschambault paraph.

Charl Diel

Adhemar paraph.

There appeared Anthoine Cailler dit Biscornet living at La Prairie de St. Lambert forty-two years of age who after the oath etc, etc.

Testifies on the facts contained in the said petition and others placed in our hands, that on the twenty-fourth of last month, he was shown three packs of beaver, two at Monsieur Dargenteuil's house one untied that was at Monsieur LeBer's house, which packs after having inspected and handled them the said deponent recognized as the same beaver with which they had made the payment for Leger Hebert[9] to Monsieur de La Durantaye acting for madame Perrot at Missilimakinac, which he affirms is true in his heart so as to be very certain for having handled it in their company more than a hundred times before the said payment, having brought it and traded it among the Sioux and hoyo8la which is all he said he knew, reading of his deposition having been done [he] said it contained the truth and persisted in it and signed it with us and our clerk of the court, remuneration required for him set at three livres.

Deschambault paraph.

Anthoine Caillez

Adhemar paraph.

There appeared Simon Guilhory[10] living at the said Villemarie on rue St.-Paul twenty-two years of age who after he took the oath to tell the truth and stated to us that he was not a relative of, related through marriage to, or servant or domestic of the parties but merely one of the engagés of sieurs Tonty and de La Forest, showed us the summons given to him by sergeant Pruneau yesterday upon the petition of the said sieur de Tonty in the said name, testifies on the facts mentioned in the said petition and on the facts placed in our hands by the said sieur de Tonty which we had our clerk of the court read to him, that being ready to leave Missilimakinac to take sieurs de Tonty and La Forest down to this town delivered to his canoe, in which a man named de Chatellet was with him, three packs of dry beaver marked with an M and a P which letters and marks having been seen by the deponent, he asked them to whom this beaver belonged, they told him that it belonged to Madame Perrot just as the said letters M P indicated, and having been obliged to postpone the trip due to reports of the enemy[11] he himself with his comrade de Chatellet had added it [i.e., the beaver] to the sieurs de La Forest and Tonty's pile [of beaver]; and then sometime afterwards came down empty without the said beaver, which is all that he said he knew, the reading of his deposition being done for him, [he] said it contained the truth and persisted in it and signed it with us, our clerk of the court, and required reimbursement to him set by us at thirty sols.

Deschambault paraph.

Simon Guillory

Adhemar paraph.

Assessed to us 2 livres tournois

To the clerk of the court [. . .] 1 livre tournois 6 sols 8 deniers or his engrossment.

Done by us the above bailiff the above year and day.

Adhemar paraph.

NOTES

1. Archives nationales du Québec à Montréal, Documents judiciaires de la juridiction seigneuriale de Montréal (1651–1695) [cote TL 2, feuilles détachées, 1681–1693].

2. François Dauphin de La Forest, captain, holder of the trade at Fort Saint-Louis-des-Illinois in partnership first with Henri de Tonty, then with Alphonse de Tonty. *DCB*, 2:169–70.

3. Louis-Hector de Callière(s), governor of Montreal at this time. He became governor-general of New France in 1698 after the death of Frontenac. *DCB*, 2:114.

4. This may be Madeleine Raclos (Raclot), the wife of explorer Nicolas Perrot who was commandant at Green Bay from 1683 to 1695. Jetté, *DG*, 898; *DCB*, 2:517.

5. Antoine Cailler (Caillé, Caillez) *dit* Brulefer or Biscornet was a blacksmith. Jetté, *DG*, 191. Brulefer means "iron burner."

6. He is identified below as a thirty-five-year-old resident of La Prairie St. Lambert.

7. Ignace Hébert *dit* Deslauriers was an outfitter for the western fur trade. Jetté, *DG*, 562.

8. Jacques LeBer, merchant-entrepreneur, had one of the largest houses on Rue Saint-Paul. Landry, ed., *Pour le Christ et le Roi*, 153.

9. Léger Hébert was the older brother of Ignace Hébert. Jetté, *DG*, 562.

10. Simon Guillory (Guilory, Guilhory) was a recruiter for the west and a fur merchant. Jetté, *DG*, 545.

11. The Iroquois were at war with the French at this time and had made incursions into the region.

Service contract between sieurs Louis Duquet Duverdier, etc., and sieur de La Durantaye

1693, August 31, Montreal[1]

Before Claude Maugue, royal notary of the island of Montreal, residing there, and the undersigned witnesses, there appeared sieurs Louis Duquet Duverdier and Anthoine Duquet Madry and Estienne Benoit Livernois[2] who have promised and obligated themselves to go up to the Ottawas this year and to pick up and bring to this place thirty bales of beaver that are at Michilimackinac belonging to Ollivier Morel, esquire, seigneur of La Durantaye, at the place that will be indicated at Villemarie, next year where they will proceed during the customary season for coming down, helping one another to be sure that the said thirty bales will be faithfully transported.

This agreement executed in return for my aforesaid sieur de La Durantaye providing them with a permit to trade there for their own profit the goods that will be granted to them by him and subject to the conditions set by him in the aforesaid permit without his being able to take any of their aforesaid profits, for thus etc. promising etc. obligating etc. to wit the aforesaid Duquets and Benoit jointly and severally one for the other, as it is said, on pain of all expenses, damages, and interest. Done at Villemarie in the notary's office in the forenoon of the last day of August 16 hundred ninety-three in the presence of sieurs François Marie Renaudavelle esquire and sieur Desmeloize, captain in the Troupe de la Marine in this country,[3] and of François Guillory,[4] witnesses [who] have signed with the aforesaid sieur Madry and notary. The aforesaid Duverdier and Benoit upon inquiry declare that they do not know how to write.

De Desmeloizes

de la Durantaye

Madri

S. Francois Guillory

Maugue paraph.

NOTES

1. Archives nationales du Québec à Montréal, Greffe de Claude Maugue.

2. The wife of Olivier Morel de La Durantaye was Françoise Duquet, who was born in 1645 in Quebec and died there in 1719. In 1660 she had married Jean Madry, king's surgeon in New France, who drowned in 1669. They had no children. In 1670 the young widow married La Durantaye, subsequently bearing him nine children. Françoise Duquet had a brother named Antoine Duquet *dit* Madry, born in 1660, who was an engagé in the western trade, as was another of her brothers, Louis Duquet, sieur Duverdier, born in 1657. Note that Etienne Benoît *dit* Nivernois or Livernois, born in 1662 in Montreal, was also an engagé, unrelated to La Durantaye. Jetté, *DG*, 82, 392, 393, 749, 832.

3. These two names appear to refer to the same person, François-Marie Renaud d'Avène de Desmeloizes, captain in the Troupes de la Marine. He was born around 1655 and died in 1699. *DCB*, 1:572–73. He signed his name here as "De Desmeloizes."

4. This may be François Guillory, born in Montreal on March 18, 1676. Jetté, *DG*, 544.

Agreement between Monsieur Lamothe Cadillac and Moreau

1694, September 9, Montreal[1]

Before Ant. adhemar, royal notary of the island of Montreal residing at ville marie and witnesses named in addition, were personally present Anthoine de La Motte, Esquire, sieur de Cadillac,[2] Captain in the Troupes de la Marine on the one hand and Joseph moreau and Jean baptiste marest, voyageur presently in this town on the other hand, which parties have in good faith made the agreements and partnerships which follow.

To wit: that the aforesaid sieur de Lamotte promises to put very shortly into the hands of the aforesaid Moreau and marest a congé for three men and a canoe to go trade among the Ottawas and neighboring nations in the customary manner; plus the aforesaid parties will take trade goods and other things needed to fit out the aforesaid canoe, which goods the aforesaid Morreau and marest will be bound to take with an engagé whom they will take to the aforesaid ottawa country, which they will trade as promptly and faithfully and profitably as he [*sic*] can and to bring down to this town the beaver or pelts which will come from the aforesaid trade goods, and having arrived in this town will have to pay out of their pelts for the goods and other things that they will have taken for their equipment and what is left over will be divided into two equal shares of which one will belong to the aforesaid sieur de la Motte and the other will belong to the aforesaid morreau and marest, out of which the aforesaid morreau and marest will pay the engagé whom they will take and in case of loss, either of trade goods on going up or furs on coming down, [the loss] will be shared by halves between sieur de la Mothe and the aforesaid Moreau and marest. For thus etc., promises etc., renounces etc.

Done and signed at the aforesaid villemarie in the office of the aforesaid notary in the year one thousand six hundred ninety-four the ninth day of September in the afternoon in the presence of Mathurin Guillet and George Pruneau witnesses living at the aforesaid ville marie undersigned with sieurs de lamotte moreau and notary. The aforesaid marest declared that he does not know how to write or sign after being called upon 6 times after the reading done in conformity with the ordinance.

Lamothe Cadillac

Joseph Moreau

Mathurin Guillet

G. Pruneau

Adhémar

NOTES

1. Archives nationales du Québec à Montréal, Greffe d'Antoine Adhémar de Saint-Martin.

2. Antoine Laumet *dit* Lamothe Cadillac. He commanded Michilimackinac from 1694 to 1697 and went on to establish the post and colony at Detroit in 1701. He was cut from much the same cloth as Frontenac, who supported him in his ambitions. Cadillac was a schemer who appears to have had little regard for the long-term consequences of his actions on others and on the colony if he could somehow gain from them. *DCB*, 2:351–56.

Lamothe Cadillac to the Minister

1695, August 3, Fort de Buade on Michilimackinac Island[1]

Sieur Lamotte Cadillac at Fort de Buade, on the island of Missilimakina August 3, 1695

You have no doubt learned that Count de Frontenac designated me last year to come and take command of the Ottawa country in sieur de Louvigny's place and that the convoy that I was leading came to a stop, the season being very bad and too advanced. My departure was on September 24 and I could only go 25 leagues[2] in 12 days in the incessant rain or the adverse winds which prevailed at that time. I did what I could to encourage the voyageurs to continue this trip, but seeing no way out of the situation, I resolved to send them back in good order, foreseeing that they would not fail to withdraw on their own and I was not sorry to have made that decision.

However frightful they made the undertaking for me to proceed to that location due to the difficulty of the sheets of ice and the lakes to be crossed, I simply determined that either it was necessary to die on the way or give up, and to that end, I selected five of the most vigorous men who were in my convoy and two Indians, and having taken provisions only for two months, I continued on my way with these men. I finally arrived at my post and it seemed to me that upon this occasion the King's service needed the same zeal that I have always had in all of those that have occurred.

It is therefore important that you be informed in case you are not, that this village is one of the strongest that there is in all of Canada. There is a fine palisaded fort, a highly disciplined garrison of élite soldiers, sixty houses[3] which form a street in a straight line, and in addition to those who presently reside there for two or three months of the year, there are around two hundred men who are selected people, the best built and the best looking that there are in this new world.

The houses are lined up on the edge of this great lake huron and they eat only fish there and some smoked meat[4] so that a drink of brandy after the meal seems necessary to settle the bilious meats and the heartburn they leave in the stomach. The air is penetrating and corrosive and without the brandy that they have in the morning, sicknesses would be more frequent.[5]

The Indians' villages in which there are six or seven thousand souls[6] are at a distance of a pistol shot from ours. All the land is cleared for three leagues in the vicinity and perfectly well cultivated, and it produces sufficient corn for the subsistence of the French and the Indians who live here.

NOTES

1. Archives nationales de France, Archives des Colonies, series C11E, vol. 14: ff. 10r–12v. Note that the heading places Fort de Buade on "Michilimackinac Island" rather than on the upper peninsula of Michigan, where it was located.

2. A league was 2.42 miles in length.

3. For more on the number of houses, see the discussion in the introduction.

4. Smoked meat, *viande bouquanée*.

5. It is hard to imagine why air from a body of fresh water would be "corrosive." It is likely that Cadillac was trying to make a case for the need to keep brandy flowing into the region, because it was a very profitable trade item with Indians and because the priests in the region had long advocated for an end to the sale of brandy. See Father Étienne de Carheil to Monsieur Louis Hector Callières, 30 August, 1702, in *JR*, 65: 189–253.

6. This is an exaggeration. See the discussion of this topic in the introduction.

Agreement regarding the purchase, via credit, of trade goods by Marie Guyon

1696, April 23, Montreal[1]

Obligation of Marie-Thérèse Guyon, wife of Antoine de Lamothe to Antoine Pascaud,[2] Montreal

Before Anthoine Adhémar, royal notary of the island of montreal residing at ville marie, undersigned, and witnesses named below, appeared Madame Marie Thérèse Guyon, wife of Anthoine de la Mothe, Esquire, sieur de Cadillac, Captain of a company of the Troupes de la Marine and in command for the King at Missillimakinac and the ottawa country, acting for and in the name of the aforesaid sieur delamothe, by virtue of the power that she has from him through the missive from him signed at Missillimakinac on August 16, 1695, specifically for buying merchandise from a given merchant and the aforesaid lady will observe that she has represented and this very moment obtained [credit], acknowledged and declared that she rightly and honestly is in debt to sieur Anthoine pascaud, a merchant of this town, [who is] absent, sieur Jean Ardouin, his clerk present here agreeing to the sum of three thousand one hundred fourteen livres seven sols six deniers for good trade goods to the aforesaid Madame delamothe having delivered a little while ago his present letter by the aforesaid sieur Lardouin for the outfit that she is sending to the aforesaid sieur de la Mothe her husband with which she was and is satisfied.

The aforesaid Madame de Lamothe in the aforesaid name has promised to give and pay to the aforesaid sieur pascaud or to the bearer in this town the aforesaid sum of three thousand one hundred fourteen livres seven sols six deniers in the month of September of next year one thousand six hundred ninety-seven or rather if the aforesaid sieur de lamothe's things come down in the aforesaid year of 1697, under penalty of all expenses, damages and interest under the mortgage obligation of all the present and future real and movable property of the aforesaid lady and of the aforesaid sieur delamothe her husband that she has submitted to the utmost rigor of the law, and [as to the place] for [satisfying] the present agreement the aforesaid lady has Selected her residence, the house where she presently resides at sixteen Rue Notre Dame at the aforesaid place and notwithstanding and promising and renouncing and done and signed at the aforesaid ville marie at the house of the aforesaid Madame dela Mothe in the year one thousand six hundred ninety-six on the twenty-third day of April in the forenoon in the presence of witnesses sieurs pierre Cabazie and Charles Varin, practitioners living in the aforesaid ville marie, undersigned with the aforesaid Madame de Lamothe, the aforesaid sieur Ardouin and the notary in conformity with the ordinance.

Marie Thérèse Guyon

Ardouin

Cabazié

C. Varin

Adhémar

Before the aforesaid undersigned notary and witnesses named below appeared sieur Anthoine pascaud, merchant and bourgeois of ville marie, who has acknowledged and declares that he has been paid by Monsieur de Lamothe the sum contained in the obligation on the other page of which he is clear, and in case other receipts should be found since the aforesaid wife of the aforesaid sieur de Lamothe [has done business with?] the aforesaid sieur Pascaud before a notary or in a private agreement [those receipts?] will not serve with the present receipt as one and the same receipt.

Done and signed at the aforesaid ville marie in the office of the aforesaid notary in the year one thousand seven hundred six on the seventh day of July in the afternoon in the presence of sieur Jacques Brisset, Senior,[3] and Jacques Aubuchon[4] witnesses living at the aforesaid ville marie undersigned with the aforesaid pascaud and notary after the reading done in conformity with the ordinance.

A Pascaud

Jacques Aubuchon

J. Brisset

Adhémar

NOTES

1. Archives nationales du Québec à Montréal, Greffe d'Antoine Adhémar de Saint-Martin.

2. Antoine Pascaud was a prominent merchant-entrepreneur based in Montreal. He supplied, in addition to Cadillac, the Tonty brothers and Pierre le Sueur. *DCB*, 2:508–9.

3. Probably Jacques Brisset *dit* Courchesne, a fur-trade outfitter and seigneur of île Dupas. The islands, at the northwestern end of Lac St. Pierre, put the seigneury at the border of the Montreal and Trois-Rivières governmental jurisdictions. Jetté, *DG*, 172; Louise Dechêne, plate 51, in *The Historical Atlas of Canada*, vol. 1, *From the Beginning to 1800*, ed. R. C. Harris (Toronto: University of Toronto Press, 1987).

4. Jacques Aubuchon *dit* Lespérance, a merchant. Jetté, *DG*, 28.

Service contract of Jean Lalonde with Cadillac

1696, September 2, Montreal [1]

Jean Lalonde dit L'Espérance was present, living in ville marie, who voluntarily offered and committed himself to Antoine de Lamothe, Esquire, sieur de Cadillac, Captain in the Troupes de la Marine and commandant in the ottawa country, absent; Madame Thérèse Guyon, his wife, present at this [meeting] and accepting for one year in order [for Lalonde] to go to the ottawas commencing from the day of his departure from this town during which time the aforesaid Lalonde will do everything honest and legal that he will be ordered to do conforming to the common practice of voyageurs, will work for the profit of the aforesaid sieur delamothe and will advise him as to his damage if it comes to his knowledge, without being able to leave the service of the aforesaid sieur de Lamothe without his consent.

This agreement is made on condition that the aforesaid lady promises to furnish him with his food and canoe during the aforesaid time in accordance with the common practice of voyageurs, [the foregoing] in addition to paying him the sum of three hundred livres in the money of this country for his wages and salary for the aforesaid year to be paid upon his return.

The aforesaid Lalonde will be permitted to take along for his use two hooded coats, six shirts, two pairs of leggings, and twelve pounds of tobacco and if he does not use them, he will be at liberty to trade them, as he will also be permitted to trade his musket and his blanket. For thus etc., promises etc., renounces etc. Done and signed at the aforesaid ville marie in the office of the aforesaid notary the second day of September one thousand six hundred ninety-six in the afternoon in the presence of sieurs françois Lory and George Pruneau, witnesses living in the aforesaid ville marie undersigned with the aforesaid Madame de lamothe and notary. The aforesaid Lalonde declared that he does not know how to write or sign after being called upon 6 times in conformity with the ordinance.

Lory

G. Pruneau

Marie Therese Guyon

Adhémar

NOTE

1. Archives nationales du Québec à Montréal, Greffe d'Antoine Adhémar de Saint-Martin.

House-rental lease from sieur Petit to Mme Cadillac

1696, September 24, Montreal[1]

Jean petit[2] came before the notary in the name of and as attorney for pierre Lussaud des Ruisseaux[3] and marguerite Sédillot his wife, who in the name of the aforesaid has acknowledged and declared that he has given and yielded possession by these presents by reason of rent and payment in money to commence on the fifteenth of next October until one year has been completed and culminated, and promises during the aforesaid time to allow Madame thérèse Guyon, spouse of Ant. de Lamothe Cadillac, a Captain in the Troupes de la Marine in this post [*sic*], and agreeing and reserving for her on the aforesaid basis during the aforesaid time a house and courtyard that Messrs de Crisafy[4] formerly occupied, situated in this town on Rue St.-Paul and thus all of it is taken such as it is and the aforesaid Madame de Lamothe said that she indeed knows this having seen and inspected it all, with which she was and is satisfied.

The present lease is drawn up with the costs and conditions stated immediately hereafter in consideration of the sum of one hundred twenty livres in the currency of this country[5] which the aforesaid Madame de lamothe promises and obligates herself to give and pay at the end of the year and in addition on condition that the aforesaid lady sees to the upkeep of the aforesaid house and premises and takes care of any minor repairs, the aforesaid sieur petit taking care of the major ones according to common practice. The aforesaid Madame de Lamothe will not be able to give up her right to the present lease to anyone whomsoever without the consent of the aforesaid lessor in the aforesaid name, Agreeing to this, promises and binds and relinquishes and draws up at the aforesaid ville marie in the office of the aforesaid notary in the year one thousand six hundred ninety-six on the twenty-fourth day of September in the afternoon in the presence of Messrs Jean quesneville and George pruneau witnesses living in the aforesaid ville marie undersigned with the parties and notary in conformity with the ordinance.

marie thérèse Guyon

J. Petit

G. Pruneau

J. Quesneville

Adhémar

NOTES

1. Archives nationales du Québec à Montréal, Greffe d'Antoine Adhémar de Saint-Martin.

2. Probably Jean Petit, sieur de Boismorel. He served in various capacities in the Montreal bailiwick. Jetté, *DG*, 905.

3. Pierre Lusseau *dit* Desruisseaux, a sergeant in the Dorvilliers company. Jetté, *DG*, 746. His wife, Marguerite Sédilot, was the widow of Jean Aubuchon, and the mother of Jacques Aubuchon mentioned in document 38.

4. Antoine and Thomas de Crisafy, both of Sicilian birth and nobility, became distinguished officers of New France. Thomas, the younger of the two, died in February 1696. Antoine was appointed governor of Trois-Rivières and died in office there in 1709. *DCB*, 1:239–40 and 2:162–63.

5. Up to 1717, the *livre* in New France was worth three quarters of that of France, which was known as the *livre tournois* or *argent de France*.

Champigny to the Minister re: Alphonse de Tonty's illegal trade at Michilimackinac

1697, early September[1]

Record of those who went up to Missillimaquinac Ottawa Indian country with sieur de Tonty half-pay Captain at the beginning of September 1697[2]

To Wit
   In the canoe with him
   sieurs
   Arnault the elder[3]
   Boudor[4]
   Charly[5]
   Blondeau the elder[6]
   La Rose the elder[7]

   In other canoes
   Joseph[8]
   Barthelmy grenier   } for the said Sr de Tonty
   Duhagon dit La Croix
   Blondeau the younger[9]
   La Rose the younger
   Montour[10]
   Pierrot Ramezay
   fillatrau[11]
   DuClos brother-in-law of Sr. Chérin lieutenant
   Lagrave[12]
   Augencourt soldier

Approved on October 23(?) 1697

Champigny

NOTES

1. Archives nationales de France, Archives des Colonies, series C11A, 15: 143r–143v.

2. The king's edict of May 28, 1696, reiterated in his ordinance of April 28, 1697, decreed that no fur trading was to take place at Forts Frontenac (Kingston, Ont.), Michilimackinac, or St. Joseph (Niles, Mich.). The king "formally and expressly prohibited the aforesaid officers and soldiers from trading in any form whatever with the Indians on these posts or in the vicinity directly or indirectly or under any pretext Whatever on pain of loss of rank and being dismissed from the service for the officers and the galleys for the soldiers and others." See Joseph L. Peyser, editor and translator, *Letters from New France: The Upper Country, 1686–1783* (Urbana and Chicago: University of Illinois Press, 1992), 61–62, for the translation of Louis XIV's complete ordinance.

3. Arnauld was a "contraband trader" staying at Michilimackinac from before 1701. One source identifies him as "Sieur de Lotbinière's son-in-law." *Wisconsin Historical Society Collections* (hereafter *WHC*), 16: 207–8, 229, 235–36, 244. He may be Bertrand Arnaud, a fur merchant and the elder brother of Jean Arnaud, also a fur merchant. Jetté, *DG*, 20.

4. Jean Boudor was a Montreal merchant-entrepreneur known to have dealt in contraband. He was born around 1661. *WHC* 16:240, 244, 249; *DCB* 2:160, 453; Jetté, *DG*, 142. See also documents 47 and 48.

5. Probably either Pierre Charly *dit* de Saint-Ange, born in 1672 and an employer of voyageurs for the West in the 1690s, or Jean-Baptiste Charly Saint-Ange (who signed "Charly"), born in 1668 and a fur trader and merchant since 1691. Jetté, *DG*, 231; *DCB*, 2:131.

6. Probably Maurice Blondeau, born in 1662, who was an employer of engagés for the West from 1693 to 1728, a merchant-entrepreneur, and an important merchant of furs. His younger brother, Thomas Blondeau *dit* Lafranchise, was born in 1674. Jetté, *DG*, 116–17.

7. La Rose is identified as a merchant by Intendant Champigny, citing Sieur Dupré in the former's remarks on Callières's September 6, 1697, orders to Le Verrier. AN Col., C11A 15: 144–46v.

8. Joseph Lorrain, born in 1677, was an engagé to the West from 1696 to 1712. Jetté, *DG*, 743.

9. See note above regarding Blondeau the elder.

10. Louis Couc *dit* Montour was an employee and recruiter in the fur trade. Jetté, *DG*, 278; *DCB*, 3:147.

11. This may be a misspelling of Filteau or Feuilleteau. Among the sons of Pierre Filteau and Gillette Savard were Nicolas, born in 1673, and Gabriel, born in 1678. Jetté, *DG*, 420.

12. Possibly Pierre Lagrave, born around 1674, reported to have been an engagé for the West in 1701. Jetté, *DG*, 630.

Callières's orders to Le Verrier to stop the French from going to the Ottawa country, and Champigny's remarks

1697, September, Montreal[1]

Copy of an order by Monsieur de Callière, governor of Montreal,[2] *to the said Le Verrier*[3] *to stop the french who are going to the Ottawas*

Sieur Le Verrier, captain in the marine detachment, is ordered to leave this town without delay with the detachment that will be given to him by sieur de Langloiserie[4] to go to the foot of the long sault[5] of the grand Rivière[6] to station himself at a place that he will deem most suitable for guarding its two banks, in order to prevent any Frenchmen from being able to go up either in canoes belonging to them or among the Indians, trying with every kind of skill and force to take them and bring them to me in this town under heavy guard with the merchandise, drinks and things that belong to them, except those who are authorized by sieur de Tonty[7] whom he will allow to pass according to the permit that was granted him by Count de Frontenac.

He will likewise seize all those he encounters in the Ottawa River, both going and coming notwithstanding all the congés they may display, And in case he were to find any caches of merchandise in the woods or elsewhere along his route going up from laChine[8] he will take them away in order to bring them into this town upon his return, making a report on everything he was able to find.

He will find out at la Chine and the end of the island if some French canoes had not been seen going up and when; and if on arriving at the Long Sault he were to see from fresh tracks that some had recently gone up who could be none other than Frenchmen, he will detach one or two canoes with an officer in each to pursue them with all possible dispatch as far as the falls of the Chaudière[9] in order to try to catch them.

It will be in order, in the place that he has found suitable to position himself, to have a small fort built of stakes Indian fashion, or at least an abatis[10] for safety against enemies, in which he will have such a good guard

posted that he will not be taken by surprise. And in order for no Frenchmen to be able to conceal himself from his view during the night, he will
detach one canoe every night that he will send to be on the lookout toward
the South bank of the North River in order to seize those who would like to
pass through, trusting moreover in his good conduct to successfully carry
out the mission on which I am sending him. Done at Montreal this 6th of
September 1697. The original signed Le Chevalier de Callière.

Remarks made by sieur de Champigny[11] on the order alongside [above][12]
here, with violations of the said order and of the King's edict suppressing
congés.

One sees that sieur le Verrier is to allow all those authorized by sieur
de Tonty to go up, and consequently the latter was free to have anyone he
pleased go through.

It is good to note that the said sieur de Tonty, who in 7 or 8 years did not
come one single time from Montreal to Quebec, took two trips there last
summer, in which nothing was noticed but a close relationship between
him and Count Frontenac and Monsieur de Callières whose outcome was
a secret order from Monsieur de Frontenac to go up to Missilimakinac, the
Ottawa country, without even the Intendant knowing about it until after
his departure, although he [the Intendant] was to have visaed the order
according to what His Majesty ordered by his dispatch of May 8, 1694.

What did sieur de Tonty do in accordance with this order? He left without waiting for those who were to go up with permits to go get their furs
and he took in his canoe instead of soldiers or voyageurs five Montreal
merchants. To be honest, they embarked with him in one single canoe in
which no trade goods were observed, but common sense precludes 5 or 6
merchants thus leaving their normal business and their families to take a
half-pay Captain into the woods more than 300 leagues from their homes
without some significant purpose. Indeed, at the time of their departure,
sieur de la Touche,[13] who is precise in his duty and in charge of surveil-
lance, having gone up three leagues above Montreal, found out what follows which is the excerpt of the letter he wrote me about it on September
17, 1697.

Being at la Chine at the departure of Monsieur de Tonty, he [Tonty]
showed me [la Touche][14] one canoe in which there were only provisions,
manned by sieurs Boudor, Arnault, Blondeau, Charly, and la Rose. However, having been informed at the same place about what had happened
and how many men and canoes were going up before Monsieur de Tonty,

Monsieur Rané, who can be participating in this, said openly that a good six days ago five or six canoes of four or five men each went through by day to the South of la Chine and that they were going in the direction of Monsieur Le Verrier whom Monsieur de Callière sent to the Long Sault, as you will see from the copy that I took of the order that he gave to the said sieur Le Verrier who entrusted me with it. But all that is in writing, besides Monsieur de Callière having permitted the carters to go out with their harnessed animals at night, according to what I have learned, having the gates of Montreal opened, [with] merchandise for la Chine under the pretext that it belonged to the Indians who could not take it up in their canoes because of the little water and the strands[15] in the river, as if that had ever been the practice.[16]

There is nothing more true than what this letter contains, knowing furthermore at the departure time of the said sieur de Tonty, in addition to the men in his canoe, around 25 or 30 Frenchmen went up, some of whose names I have already discovered, which are those contained in the attached statement;[17] and having inquired today of sieur Dupré, a Montreal merchant and a very honest man who recently arrived in Quebec, if he had any knowledge of those who went up with sieur de Tonty And of the merchants who provided them with merchandise, he declared to me in good faith that he knew only the five merchants in sieur de Tonty's canoe and a man named Lorain aboard another canoe, and that it was true that he had provided the said sieur de Tonty with 3000#[18] of trade goods for the said trip, which he had by his order turned over to the said Lorain who was going up for him, but that that had not been until after having asked the pleasure of Monsieur de Callière who had told him that he could do it, which surprises me extremely, not appearing to me until now that my aforesaid sieur de Callière had facilitated any forbidden trade. The said sieur Dupré added that sieur de Coüagne a merchant in the aforesaid Montreal, had furnished the said sieur de Tonty with a much larger quantity of goods than he, And a man named Xaintonge,[19] who also recently came down from Montreal, told me that sieurs Pascaud and St. Germain[20] had likewise furnished merchandise and that six canoes had been loaded with it for the said sieur de Tonty. Thus there is no doubt whatever that all these goods are those that had been brought out of Montreal during the night, it being certain that the Indians never have them transported on draft animals, not having a good understanding of them[21] and always finding enough water in the river. Furthermore if that had been for them, the gates of Montreal would never have been opened for them during the night. Rather it must be said, speaking sincerely, that it is the execution of the plan that had been concocted during the summer during sieur de Tonty's two trips. It is good to note that sieur LeVerrier and his detachment had been ordered to leave only several days after the departure of all these Frenchmen, as it was pointed out previously in sieur de la Touche's letter.

Here then are the formal violations of the king's edict and declaration which set forth the abolition of congés and the prohibition for the French to go into the woods, on pain of the galleys. It is based on that [edict] that the intendant expects orders,[22] both in regard to the said sieur de Tonty and to the merchants embarked in his canoe without having had the Intendant['s] visa [or] Monsieur the governor's permit, and for having transported through the said sieur de Tonty a considerable quantity of trade goods; and in regard to all the other French who left furtively and without any permission or orders whatsoever, at least any known to the said Intendant.

decreed on the 25th of October 1697

Champigny

NOTES

1. Archives nationales de France, Archives des Colonies, series C11A, vol. 15: ff. 144r–46v.

2. Louis-Hector Callières was governor of Montreal from 1684 to 1698. Upon the death of Frontenac in 1698, he became governor-general of New France. After becoming governor-general, despite his role in the 1697 Tonty affair described in this manuscript, Callières strictly enforced the king's prohibition of the fur trade. *DCB* 2:112–17.

3. François Le Verrier de Rousson, the forty-one-year-old officer of the Troupes de la Marine in charge of the detachment sent to the Long Sault, was later criticized by Louis XIV for his "lack of zeal" in this assignment. *DCB*, 2:433.

4. In 1697 Charles-Gaspard Piot de Langloiserie was town major of Montreal, second in command after Governor Callières. *DCB*, 2:526–27.

5. The *long sault*, literally meaning "long rapids," is a reference to a place. The rapids are located about one day by canoe to the west of Montreal along the Ottawa River.

6. The Ottawa River was sometimes called *la grande Rivière*, the term used here, by the colonial French.

7. Alphonse de Tonty had been appointed Cadillac's successor as commandant of Michilimackinac, a post he held for one year.

8. Lachine was Montreal's port of embarkation for the upper country, located west of the Lachine Rapids. Freight for the west had to be carted about eight miles from Montreal to be loaded on the canoes at Lachine.

9. The *Chaudière* (boiling kettle), today called Chaudière Falls, is located in the Ottawa River at Ottawa, Ontario. The falls are about a day or so by canoe from the Long Sault.

10. An abatis, the English being taken from the French military term, is "a defensive obstacle formed by felled trees with sharpened branches facing the enemy." *Webster's Ninth New Collegiate Dictionary* (Springfield, Mass.: 1991), 44. The same Canadian regional term, *abatis*, refers to the land where a wooden abatis has been built, from which all the stumps have not been completely removed.

11. Jean Bochart de Champigny was intendant of New France from 1686 to 1702. His written endorsement (visa) was required by the king's edict on any trade license issued by the governor-general. An honest man, Champigny was persistently critical of Governor-General Frontenac. *DCB*, 2:71–80.

12. The original document consisted of several pages divided in half, with the report above on one side, and the following comments on the opposite side of the same page.

13. Louis Tantouin de La Touche was commissary of the Marine in Canada from 1690 to about 1700. He reported directly to Intendant Champigny and was scrupulously honest. *DCB*, 2:618–19.

14. This part of Champigny's letter is quoting directly from that which he received from La Touche. This section, thus, should be read as if La Touche is speaking.

15. The Canadian regionalism used here is *battures*, defined in *Le Nouveau Petit Robert* as "parts of the banks that the ebbing tide leaves exposed."

16. This ends the excerpt from la Touche's letter.

17. See document 41.

18. That is, 3000 livres of trade goods. It is not clear if the reference is to the value or weight of the cargo.

19. Possibly a misspelling of Saint-Ange. A merchant named Charly *dit* de Saint-Ange was listed in Tonty's canoe in the record of those accompanying Tonty on his illegal trip to Michilimackinac. For more on Charly, see document 41.

20. Antoine Pascaud was a prominent Montreal merchant. *DCB*, 2:508–9. A Ferdinand Saint-Germain was a soldier in LeVerrier's company who died in Montreal in 1702 at the age of nineteen. It is not likely that he, at the age of fourteen in 1697, was the "Sieur St. Germain" who furnished merchandise to Tonty. Jetté, *DG*, 1029.

21. not having a good understanding of them, *n'en ayant pas l'intelligence.*

22. That is, expects directions from France regarding how to deal with this situation and with the people involved in it.

Alphonse de Tonty's power of attorney to Pierre Lamoureux de St. Germain

1697, September 4, Montreal[1]

Before Anthoine Adhémar, royal notary of the island of Montreal residing in Ville Marie, undersigned, and the witnesses named below, there appeared in person sieur alphonse de Tonty, Esquire, Captain on the inactive list[2] in the Troupes de la Marine, living in the said town of ville marie, who has named and appointed as his special and general attorney pierre Lamoureux, sieur de St. Germain[3] to whom he is giving power and authority, in his name, to receive each and every one of the furs, beavers, and other things that will come down from the Ottawa countries belonging to him [Tonty], which beavers and furs the said attorney will deliver according to and in conformity with the orders that the said sieur de Tonty, the constituent, gives him by his missives, just as the said attorney will send such shipments of merchandise or other things that the constituent orders him to send, will purchase the said merchandise and sell the said beaver and furs as advantageously as possible; and generally the said attorney will carry out and manage all the other business that the said constituent could have in this country[4] and entirely in the same way that the constituent would do if he were personally present [. . .] the occasion were to require a more special order, even borrowing for the said constituent all and such amounts that the said attorney has in mind, to sign obligations or promissory notes for them and obligate the said constituent for the payment of the amounts that he borrows, with all his present and future possessions [as security] to the extent required by the occasion, promising etc., obligating etc. Drawn up and executed at the said ville marie in the office of the said notary in the year one thousand six hundred ninety-seven in the afternoon of the fourth day of September, in the presence of sieurs George Pruneau and Anthoine Galipau[5] residing at the said ville marie, undersigned with the said sieur de Tonty as constituent and the said notary in conformity with the ordinance.

Tonty

Pruneau paraph.

Galipeau paraph.

Adhémar paraph.

NOTES

1. Archives nationales du Québec à Montréal, Greffe d'Antoine Adhémar de Saint-Martin.
2. Captain on the inactive list, *Capitaine réformé*.
3. Pierre Lamoureux *dit* Saint-Germain was a Montreal merchant-entrepreneur who was born around 1644 and who died in 1709. Jetté, *DG*, 640.
4. That is, the lower colony as contrasted with the upper country.
5. Antoine Galipeau was a Montreal carpenter who died in 1722 at the age of seventy-six. Jetté, *DG*, 459.

Champigny to the Minister regarding Tonty's illegal trade to Michilimackinac

1697, October 27, Quebec[1]

Sieur [Alphonse] de Tonty, half-pay Captain, has been back from Missillimakinac for three days. He left from there before the arrival of the order that Monsieur de Frontenac sent there with sieur Boudor—about whom I informed you in the letter I had the honor to write you on the 14th of the present month—which makes me conclude in advance that he came down by another order sent beforehand. Whatever the case, he came with only the men who were necessary to man his canoe and he left there sieurs Vincennes, d'oleans, and de liette, junior officers,[2] a pair of soldiers from the garrisons, and the Frenchmen named in the list that I sent you, of whom the majority continue to have a rebellious spirit in requesting a postponement until next year,[3] declaring that it is because of the scarcity of Indians to help bring down their furs, and I have reason to believe that it is less that reason than finishing their trading, as I have had the honor of pointing out to you.

I have informed you, My Lord, that Monsieur de frontenac had Monsieur de Tonty paid 1,280# out of the King's funds for merchandise provided by him at Missilimakinac as presents to the Indians and I have sent you a report on it, marked "O." Since his return, he [Frontenac] again had him paid, on the same basis as the earlier one, some 1,080# according to another report, which is the second proof that he took merchandise against the King's express prohibitions. I have furthermore been assured by the Frenchmen who have just arrived from Missilimakinac that he had some 10 to 11,000# brought up, which have already produced two canoe loads of beaver that he had brought down behind our backs.

I found out from the same Frenchmen that sieurs Arnault, Boudor, Charly, Blondeau, and la Rose, merchants who left Montreal in his canoe under the pretext of taking him, sent, at the same time that they left, both by means of the Frenchmen who left without any permission and by Indians, to wit: Arnauld some 12,000# of merchandise which amounts to 4 Congés, that is to say 4 canoe loads; Boudor some 14,000#; Charly some 8 to 9,000#; Blondeau a considerable quantity that was never in fact found out, but which already produced some 8,000# of furs brought down secretly; La Rose some 5 to 6,000# with another Frenchman and thus with all the others who went up at the same time as sieur de Tonty, from whom I have been assured that he himself was taking out half the profits, that sieur d'argenteuil,[4] a lieutenant who was only to command and lead the Frenchmen who left Montreal around one month after sieur de Tonty to go only to pick up their furs in accordance with the permit which had been given to them, also secretly sent through a large amount of merchandise through some Frenchmen and Indians in several canoes, about which I have the details, besides what he had in his own which was seen on the way completely loaded with, among other things, a barrel of brandy as well as some Frenchmen whom he commanded. That is why you should not be astonished, My Lord, if after so many trade activities formally opposed to the King's orders and despite the threats of the galleys that they contain, there are so many Frenchmen who disobey the orders that were sent for them to come down.

You must not anticipate, My Lord, that we will be able to punish these Frenchmen by confiscating their things, because of the facility they have in entering the colony, either by various rivers, or through the woods at whatever location they want, from top to bottom, and the care and exactitude during the night, as in daytime, of sieur Quenet, controller of the farm[5] at Montreal, to whom I had secretly given the charge to be on the lookout with reliable people upon the arrival of the Frenchmen who have just come down, among whom there were some of those who went up without permission with sieur de Tonty last year, was of no use, [these men] having without difficulty taken steps not to let their furs be seen.

You must not believe either that when the Frenchmen who remained in the woods to finish their fur trading would come directly with their furs to Montreal as the ordinary place for their unloading it might be possible to arrest them without troops, because of their great numbers. Thus, My Lord, it is not within the power of an intendant who has little or no authority at all, to do it alone. However, if there is no punishment carried out against those who went up last year without permission, against those who only had permission to go get their furs and who smuggled a great amount of merchandise, against the rebels and against those who are disobeying the general order to come down this year only in order to complete their trading, they will violate with impunity all the King's orders and these disorders will continue and will increase to such a point that it will be impossible to remedy them.

I confess to you, My Lord, that I am profoundly mortified on seeing such disorders, very humbly begging you to remember what I have had the honor of writing you on this topic for several years, whose occurrence shows that, in order not to be confined by the King's orders which were so severely reiterated with regard to congés and fur trading in the woods, the Frenchmen who are disobeying and revolting only do it because they believe their acts will be tolerated as in the past with what was done in violating the same orders. As for me, if I had had sufficient authority, I can reply to you that the King would not have these just causes for dissatisfaction.

The beginning of the remedy for this evil and the surest, as I had the honor of informing you in my letter of the 14th of this month, and which I deem important to repeat, is absolutely to prevent all Frenchmen with no exception whatever, even le Sueur with his fifty men,[6] sieurs de la Forest and Tonty proprietors of fort St. Louis of the Illinois and their men,[7] from going up to the distant countries under any pretext whatever, except for only the missionaries, being Certain that they do not trade at all, and even to abandon fort frontenac,[8] where indubitably they will trade furs as they do at other places and principally when there will no longer be any advanced post but this one occupied by Frenchmen.

I had the honor of informing you in my letter of last July 12th about an ordinance that I had issued, inasmuch as it is under my authority, to require the French who were in the woods fur trading, to come back in conformity with the King's orders, but there was not one single man who was willing to, or who dared post it at Missilimakinac, where I had sent it. If I wanted to have those in such a case punished, It would be another painful matter for Monsieur de Frontenac, having told me himself that it [the ordinance] was not necessary. You see from that, My Lord, my willingness to carry it out and at the same time the impossibility of doing so. I am enclosing herewith a copy of this ordinance.

NOTES

1. Archives nationales de France, Archives des Colonies, series C11A, vol. 16: excerpts from ff. 131v–35v.

2. These junior officers included Second Ensign Jean-Baptiste Bissot de Vincennes, the French agent among the Miamis, whose eldest son, François-Marie, founded the post (now the city in Indiana) bearing the name Vincennes; and Pierre-Charles de Liette, Alphonse de Tonty's cousin, who was to spend decades living among the Illinois as an agent of New France. *DCB*, 2:68, 435–36.

3. That is, they want a postponement of the king's edict prohibiting trade at Michili-mackinac and to return to the colony.

4. D'Argenteuil is mentioned in a 1708 document as an officer with "much influence among them [the Indians], but [one who] has little management." *WHC*, 16:253.

5. Jean Quenet, born in 1647, was a carpenter, merchant-entrepreneur, and controller of the king's farm in Montreal. Jetté, *DG*, 953. "Farm" here refers to the farming (or collection) of taxes, under the authority of the intendant of New France.

6. Pierre Le Sueur, a successful trader, was appointed by Frontenac in 1693 to build a post at Chagouamigon (Ashland, Wisconsin). In 1697, despite Champigny's opposition, Le Sueur obtained permission to take 50 men into the Sioux country to establish mines and to trade in furs other than beaver. *DCB*, 2:427–28.

7. In 1690 François Dauphin de La Forest and Henri de Tonty, Alphonse de Tonty's older brother, both officers in the Troupes de la Marine and previously associates of the late René-Robert Cavelier de La Salle, were granted the latter's fur-trading concession in the Illinois country at Fort Saint-Louis. Due to a shortage of firewood, they moved the fort from Starved Rock to Pimitoui (now Peoria) in 1691. *DCB*, 2:633–36.

8. Now Kingston, Ont., at the source of the St. Lawrence River on the northeast shore of Lake Ontario.

Letter from the Minister to Callières

1698, May 21, Versailles[1]

Monsieur,

I[2] received the letter you wrote me on the 15th of this month and I reported what is in it to the King.

His Majesty was satisfied to see the detail you went into to report the things that occurred in your government last year. He hopes that you will take the greatest care and pay the closest attention of which you are capable to cooperate in the execution of his orders and his wishes although he has no reason to be satisfied with your conduct last year at the time that sieur Tonty was sent to Missilimakinac.

He was informed that instead of canoemen sieur de Tonty brought with him five of the principal merchants of Montreal; that the posts of that location were open for several nights in order to facilitate taking out the trade goods that these merchants sent into the woods; that under a general order that you gave sieur Le Verrier,[3] an officer of the troops that you put in charge of preventing the passage of people going to trade, to allow to pass all those who announced that they were with the aforesaid sieur de Tonty, a very large number of coureurs de bois went out and by that means they completely avoided carrying out His Majesty's ordinance which forbids congés and trading in the woods.

If you had knowledge of this disobedience of orders and if you had authorized it, His Majesty could not avoid giving you evidence of his indignation. He is more inclined to believe that you were taken by surprise, but as that is unworthy of an old and well-known officer, he hopes that you will take greater care in the future to have His Majesty's orders carried out, and being as you are at the head of the colony you will give such good ones in this regard that you will be able to answer for them to His Majesty.

I beg you to believe that, as for myself, I shall be very disposed to emphasize your good service when I have the opportunity to do so and when you do not create any obstacle in it, but I must warn you that nothing is so capable of making you lose the fruit of all the good service that you have given during your life as facilitating an abuse which His Majesty wants stopped at all costs.

I am etc.

NOTES

1. Archives nationales de France, Archives des Colonies, series B, vol. 20, renumbered ff. 100r–101r.

2. The minister of the Marine in this period, responsible for New France, was Louis Phélypeaux de Pontchartrain. He died in 1699, the year of this letter, and his son Jérôme Phélypeaux de Pontchartrain took over the position.

3. In 1697 Callières, as governor of Montreal, sent Lieutenant François Le Verrier de Rousson to the Long Sault west of Montreal on the Ottawa River in order to stop and examine all canoes. His son, Louis, served as commander of Fort St. Joseph in 1757–59, and possibly, briefly, as commandant of Michilimackinac in 1757. Lyle M. Stone, *Fort Michilimackinac, 1715–1781* (East Lansing: Publications of the Michigan State University Museum, 1974), 8.

Royal memoir to Callières and Champigny

1700, May 5, Versailles[1]

His Majesty has also granted to sieur de La Durantaye the appointment of Garde de la Marine which was given several years ago to his son, and they [Callières and Champigny] will find the order for it enclosed.

His Majesty was not willing to satisfy sieur de La Durantaye's expectations regarding the supplies he asserts he furnished to Missilimaquinac starting in the year 1683,[2] but he was willing to grant him a total of 1500 livres for all his claims in this matter, in return for which he no longer wants to hear anything about it. He has created this arrangement in the form of a gratuity[3] to reward him, although this is solely for the desired compensation, and that is what you must explain to him.

NOTES

1. Archives nationales de France, Archives des Colonies, series B, vol. 22, renumbered ff. 99r, 109r–109v.

2. See document 16 for La Durantaye's statement of his expenditures for 1683 and 1684.

3. The French term is *gratification*, which can be translated as gratuity, extra or supplementary pay, or bonus. Fort commanders in the upper country normally received a *gratification* for this duty because of their extra expenses. For a listing of such expenses and how they should be met, see the views of Chevalier de Raymond in Joseph L. Peyser, ed. and trans., *On the Eve of Conquest: The Chevalier De Raymond's Critique of New France in 1754* (East Lansing: Michigan State University Press, 1997), 80–82.

Minutes of the Enquiry of *Fezeret v. Boudor*

1700, May 27 and June 5, Montreal [1]

In the year 1700, on the twenty-seventh day of May, in the afternoon, before us Jacques Alexis de Fleury Deschambault, Esquire, king's councilor, judge in the royal court, court officer at the seat of the royal jurisdiction of the island of Montreal and other dependencies of the government of the said island, in the hearing room there appeared Marie Carlié, wife and agent of sieur Renne Fezeret who told us that in the legal proceeding sieur Fezeret, her husband, has pending at the Sovereign Council against sieur Jean Boudor, a merchant in this town, the said Fezeret obtained a decree at the said council, the twenty-sixth of April last, upon the petition that he had presented to the said council, by which, among other things, the said council allows the said Fezeret to present what appears reasonable to him before us, and to proceed to the enquiry and hearing the said witnesses, as she thus made clear to us by showing the said decree, and called for us to be agreeable to deliver to her our order to summon the witnesses whom she intends to have testify before us in fulfilment of the said decree, and to summon, at the same time, the said sieur Boudor to have the said witnesses appear and sworn in, signed,

Marie Carlié

Thereupon, we, the aforesaid judge and court officer, did record the appearance and above petition of the said Carlié in the said name, and have ordered that the witnesses that the said Fezeret wishes to be deposed in execution of the said decree of 26 April last, be summoned before us on the fifth of June next, in the morning, before us in the room where hearings are held, to testify truthfully in the enquiry which will be held by us. The said sieur Boudor is to be summoned, also, to that place, day, and hour, in order to have the said witnesses produced and sworn in. Done the day and year as noted above.

Deschambault

Marie Carlié

And the fifth of the month of June of the said year one thousand seven hundred, at ten o'clock in the morning before us, the aforesaid judge and court officer, in the room where we are holding the hearing.

There appeared the said Marie Carlié, wife and agent of sieur Renne Fezeret, who told us that, in accordance with our order of the twenty-seventh of May last, she did have summoned for this day, place and hour, in speaking to them personally in this town, Pierre Mauriceau and Dominique Estienne, voyageurs, to testify truthfully in the said enquiry and also had summoned for this day, place and hour, the said sieur Jean Boudor, at his home, by bailiff's writ of that day, which she showed us, against which writ sieur Boudor did not appear. She requested that we declare him to be in default, and in the interest of the latter [Boudor], given the presence of the said witnesses and given that ten o'clock had sounded, that we be agreeable to receiving their oath and proceeding to the said enquiry according to the said decree of the said day, the twenty-sixth April last, signed,

Marie Carlié

Thereupon we, the aforesaid, judge and court officer, have recorded the appearance and above petition of the said Carlié in the said name and the default against the said sieur Boudor who has not appeared nor any person duly summoned for him and because of this, given the presence of the said Pierre Mauriceau and Dominique Estienne, we ordered that he be considered present for us and we proceeded to the enquiry of the facts of the matter in accordance with the said decree of the said 26th April last, the oath previously taken by them in the customary manner.

In enforcing that order, we, the aforesaid judge and court officer, have, in the absence of the said sieur Boudor and by reason of the default declared by us against him, given and received the oath of Pierre Mauriceau, twenty-three years of age, or thereabouts, a voyageur, staying in this town with his mother on St.-Jean Baptiste street, and of Dominique Estienne, around twenty-six years old, a voyageur, at present staying at Longue Pointe on this island, and, after oaths taken by them separately to tell the truth, [we] have proceeded to their hearing, also separately, based upon the facts placed in our hands according to the said decree of the said day, twenty-sixth of April last, and have had their depositions written in copy books separate from our present proceedings. Done this day and year as above.

Deschambault

NOTE

1. Archives nationales du Québec à Montréal, Documents judiciaires de la juridiction royale de Montréal (1693–1760) [cote TL 4 S1]. This document was translated by José António Brandão with Joseph L. Peyser.

Fezeret v. Boudor: witnesses' testimony

1700, June 5, Montreal [1]

Enquiry conducted by us Jacques Alexis de Fleury Deschambault, Esquire, king's councilor, associate judge on the bench of the royal jurisdiction of the island of Montreal and other dependencies of the government of the said island, and commissioner by decree of our seigneurs of the Sovereign Council this past April 26, upon petition of René Fezeret against Jean Boudor, merchant in this town, in carrying out the said decree, we have proceeded in the inquiry as follows.

On the fifth day of June one thousand seven hundred at ten o'clock in the morning in the chamber where we hold hearings.

There appeared Pierre Mauriceau, twenty-three years old or thereabouts, a voyageur living in this town with his mother, who, after oath taken by him to say the truth & declaring that he is neither a relative, relative by marriage, servant, nor domestic of the parties, presented to us the summons given to him today to testify truthfully upon petition of the said Fezeret.

Testifies as to the facts that the said Fezeret handed us signed and initialed by us, numbered, which we had our clerk of the court read to him; that last year [1699] being at Michilimackinac in the service of the said Boudor he affirmed that the said Boudor and Fezeret always appeared to be good friends during all the time that he has known them living at Michilimackinac; that coming from Sault de Ste Marie and going to Michilimackinac he said he met Fezeret, his eldest son & several Indians in one single canoe en route to coming down here, and that it was at the island named Goose Island,[2] and that Fezeret senior asked him to please tell Guilhebaud his youngest son whom he had left at Michilimackinac, to send down no matter what the cost the thirteen packs of beaver that he had left for him in storage and that having arrived at Michilimackinac to carry out the said assignment he went to find the said Guilhebaud whom he met on the road with several other Frenchmen, and where Boudor arrived at the same time, in the presence of whom the witness told Guilhebaud what his father had instructed him to say to have him send down [to Montreal] no matter what the cost the thirteen packs of beaver that he had left him in storage, and that then Boudor said these words: by the way, your father had told me to tell you the same thing, to which Guilhebaud replied that he would do his best, and [the witness, Mauriceau] did not hear Fezeret speak about any furs other than the said thirteen packs, no more than Guilhebaud had in his sole possession; that after having stayed at Michilimackinac up to around the sixth or seventh of the month of August, Boudor is reported to have had him [Mauriceau] leave with orders to wait for him one league from there; that Boudor rejoined him only around the twelfth or thirteenth of August, which made him [Mauriceau] ask the man named Lagrave, a cano-eman in Boudor's canoe, the reason why he had delayed so long and made him wait six or seven days, to which Lagrave answered him: I will tell what it was but you must not say anything to anyone, after which, [Mauriceau] having promised to keep the secret, he [Lagrave] told him that the cause of their delay was the debauchery in which they had engaged, drinking brandy by the full bowl from which they were all drunk together, that during this debauchery Boudor had been gambling against Guilhebaud, from whom he [Boudor] had won the entire cost of the brandy to be paid for by ten packs of beaver, that afterwards approaching this town [Montreal], having encountered a band of Frenchmen and Indians who were going up with several ecclesiastics who gave them a keg of brandy, it was then that he, the deponent, said to Boudor that he [Boudor] was very pleased to have won so much, to which he answered nothing but what do you care, that it is also true that Lagrave told him that there had been a loss besides the above said ten packs of beaver, more than one hundred half-pints[3] of brandy, but that they had not been able to drink it all and that it was Guilhebaud who had lost everything, that Boudor did not forbid him to speak about it nor to give evidence, not even believing that Boudor was aware that the deponent knew about it, and that is still true that Boudor had said that he had had his beaver put in a hiding place, but that he [Mauriceau] had heard from Lagrave that that was not [so] but [it was] indeed the truth that Boudor had left it in the hands of [. . .] Cavelier at the rate of one crown[4] per pack for keeping it in the house where the deponent lives with Boudor[5] and in which the said Cavelier came to stay upon their departure, and to which Boudor had those aforesaid ten packs that he won from Guilhebaud sent, just as he likewise heard Lagrave say that it was he himself who had stacked them in the said house and that they were marked with Fezeret, the father's, mark; [the deponent] asserts that since then he heard the men named Domingue Estienne and Montour say that in another debauchery the said Cavelier had won from the said Guilhebaud a number of axes that [he] believes to be thirty-five axes and forty half-pints of brandy just as he had heard them say that at the time that Cavelier went to find Guilhebaud to be paid, Guilhebaud denied the loss of the said axes and [said] that he definitely did not remember having lost any but only several half-pints of brandy, and [the deponent said] that Fezeret, the father, then said that they should let him [Guilhebaud] sleep and that he was like a beast, and that it is true that it was through necessity that Fezeret, the father, left the thirteen packs of beaver in the hands of the said Guilhebaud his son in view of the fact that there was no opportunity to be able to send him down and the Indians would not go down saying the plague[6] was down here [in Montreal] and that Boudor was perfectly well aware of it since he was instructed to deliver the same aforesaid message that the deponent had, namely to tell Guilhebaud to send the said thirteen packs of beaver to him [Fezeret] no matter what the cost, which is all that he said he knew. Reading done for him [Mauriceau] of his deposition, [Mauriceau] said that it contains the truth, persisted in it, and declared that he does not know how to write or sign his name as required conforming to the ordinance, and after he requested remuneration[7] we awarded him twenty-two sols six deniers in money from France.

Deschambault

Adhémar paraph.

And whereas noon has arrived [we] have adjourned the said investigation until one o'clock this afternoon, done on the above day and year.

Deschambault

Adhémar paraph.

On the said fifth day of June one thousand seven hundred at one o'clock in the afternoon before us, the aforesaid judge and commissioner, in the room where we hold hearings, there appeared Dominique Estienne, voyageur, presently living at Longue Pointe on this island, around twenty-six years old, who after his oath to tell the truth and after telling us that he is not a relative, related by marriage, servant, nor domestic of the parties, presented to us the summons given to him to testify truthfully on this day upon the petition of the said Fezeret, testifies regarding the facts that the said Fezeret handed to us which we had our bailiff read to him item by item, that around the beginning of last August, not knowing positively the date that it might have been, the deponent [Estienne] being at that time at Michilimackinac, left his warehouse to go to the lakeshore which was nearby, [and] approaching the house into which a man named Duclos from Batiscan was going, he noticed inside Monsieur de Tonty[8] and most of all the voyageurs who were at that time at Michilimackinac, among whom he recognized perfectly well sieur Jean Boudor who was playing cards with Claude Fezeret dit Guilhebaud, not knowing right away what he found out shortly after he arrived, Boudor who told Guilhebaud as he believes, in his words, you owe for all the brandy that I had here, and afterwards [they] began to gamble for one pack of beaver in [each of] five games of Trump;[9] in next to no time at all the said Guilhebaud lost two games and wanted to continue to gamble; sieur Boudor told him to go get the two packs that he had lost before continuing, which Guilhebaud did and brought three that he threw into the room where they were gambling, saying there's another, [a] third one that I want to gamble in order to have the other two back, and [the deponent said] that if he had good reason to judge that Guilhebaud had drunk to excess, it would be because of the error that he noticed that [Guilhebaud] made in the way he played in this game, having lost with the Queen and the nine against the King and the ten all in trump, Guilhebaud having two tricks, sieur Boudor playing trump with his King, Guilhebaud letting go of his Queen and consequently losing the third trick which lost the game for him by his having failed to play the nine[10] which accompanied the Queen, and since the reason for this was so obvious the deponent was planning to go off and in leaving he heard Germain say quite loudly speaking about the said packs which were in the room, those are packs that do not belong to Guilhebaud but definitely belong to his father, which obliged the deponent to look at them and he recognized them as actually being marked with Fezeret his father's mark, that he believes to be from those [packs] that he saw going back from the edge of the water when the said Fezeret embarked to go down to this town [Montreal] to the man named La Chapelle's place with whom the said Guilhebaud had been living, and after the said game was over and lost by Guilhebaud purely through his own fault as stated above, the deponent [Estienne] left to go off to say his prayers. Upon leaving his prayers he passed by Makonchy's[11] hut where he encountered only Makonchy's wife and the man named Boisjoly his brother-in-law who asked him where he was going and the deponent replied that he was going to see those gentlemen gambling meaning sieurs Boudor and Guilhebaud, and then Boisjoly told him that it was useless seeing that they were no longer playing. Then the deponent asked him who had lost [and] the said Boisjoly told him that it was the said Guilhebaud who had lost nine packs of dry beaver against Monsieur Boudor and one against him by a ten-crown wager for each game in the same way he presumes as the first [game] that he witnessed, which did not prevent the deponent from going as far as the said location where they had played and there he saw the beaver in about the same number as that which Boisjoly had just stated, arranged in the said lodging against the partition,[12] that the next day he heard in the village that the said La Chapelle was going to write about it down here to tell about this thing and that if he had then been able, he would not have suffered the said beaver to be carried off by Guilhebaud in view of the fact that the said Fezeret the father had not entrusted it to Guilhebaud's safekeeping but rather to the woman,[13] that some time afterwards having embarked to come down here, he joined the said Boudor's fleet, Boudor having left before him, and caught up and slept together on Joachim's Island, where during the night, before falling asleep Boudor left his bed to come sit on the deponent's bed and then beseeched him to keep the secret down here and not to speak in any way whatever about the gambling he had done with Guilhebaud, [the deponent] declares that he does not positively know if it was Lagrave who was with Fezeret to go to La Chapelle's place to get the first three packs of beaver, but that there were certainly one or two people whose names he does not remember, that regarding the rest [of the beaver] neither does he know who went to get them in view of the fact that they were brought and lost while he was off saying his prayers, and that he does not know any number but the one that the said Boisjoly had told him, not having stopped to count them and that he has no other knowledge that they were not Guilhebaud's except from what was said by several people in the said house and from the said Fezeret the father's mark with which they were marked, which Boudor can well understand, without nevertheless having noticed at that time that he gave no proof [of origin] for them [the packs of beaver] and that the cards that they played with appeared newer rather than old, and that regarding the people present at the loss of the first three packs whom he still left there, going to pray as he said above, there were the said Germain; the above-mentioned Duclos; Boisjoly; sieur de Tonty;[14] and others whom he does not remember now, and whom he knew only down here; that the said Fezeret the father had asked the said sieur Boudor, encountered as he was coming back from Sault [Sainte-Marie] to Michilimackinac, to tell the said Guilhebaud to have the said beavers sent down for him in any manner whatever; that he still has perfect knowledge as if it were now and noting that Guilhebaud also allegedly gambled several days afterwards against Louis LeCavelier and lost forty-five axes and thirty and some odd half-pints of brandy and that it was only the noon hour when the deponent withdrew to his place, which Cavelier confirmed for him one or two hours later in Makouchy's house where the sieur de Tonty was then present, where he then said that he still had thirty half-pints to drink and that they invited them for as long as they lasted and that they were gambling a little liquor, that he truly heard Cavelier say that if Fezeret [the son] did not pay him he would take his fire tongs,[15] his anvil, and his hammers and would break his canoe in two, that then Monsieur de Tonty the elder told him that things were not done that way; declared furthermore that the Reverend Jesuit Fathers would not take out furs except for one of the Frenchmen who were up there, which is all that he said he knew. Reading was done of his deposition, [he] said that it was the truth and persisted in it and signed it with us and our clerk of the court and after he requested remuneration we awarded him the amount of thirty sols in money from France.

Dominique Estienne

Deschambault

Adhémar paraph.

NOTES

1. Archives nationales du Québec à Montréal, Documents judiciaires de la juridiction royale de Montréal (1693–1760) [cote TL 4 S1].
2. at the island named Goose Island, *lisle nommee des outardes.*
3. half-pints, *demi ars* (*demiards*).
4. A *petit écu* ("little crown"), sometimes known as an *écu blanc* ("white crown"), was a silver coin worth 3 livres, 6 sols. (A *gros écu* was worth 6 livres, 12 sols.)
5. This house was probably where they lived at Michilimackinac.
6. Indians died in large numbers from illnesses to which Europeans had built up immunities. Thus almost any outbreak of smallpox or illness producing high fever became like a plague to Natives.
7. As part of court costs to be paid by the party losing the case.

8. Alphonse de Tonty had been surreptitiously named commandant of Michilimackinac for 1697–1698 by Frontenac, despite the king's orders to withdraw the garrison and end the fur trade. In September 1697 Tonty went up to Michilimackinac with five Montreal traders, including Jean Boudor. They had been secretly preceded by a convoy of five or six canoes and twenty or thirty men. Pierre Lagrave, also mentioned in Mauriceau's (Morisseau's) deposition, was one of those who accompanied Tonty on this illegal trading voyage. See documents 41–43 for additional details on the illegal activities of these men and others, including the governor-general himself.

9. The word used here is *triomphe*, a card game of the period, translated as "trump" or "ruff." See "triomphe" in Cotgrave, *A Dictionarie of the French and English Tongues*. This game is similar to *la belote*, played in France today with 32 cards and two, three, or four players. See *Le Nouveau Petit Robert*, and *Grand Larousse en 5 volumes* (Paris: Larousse, 1987), 342.

10. Instead of playing the queen.

11. Possibly Jean Fafard *dit* Makoues, an interpreter at Michilimackinac. See Fr. Enjalran to.?, 7 mai 1684, AN, C11A, 6: f. 525r. His wife was Marguerite Couc, a métis woman and one of three sisters living at the post. Jetté, *DG*, 410.

12. A *cloison*, the term used here, is of lighter-weight construction than a wall and used as a room divider.

13. Up to this point, the testimony is that the furs were entrusted to Fezeret the son. No woman has been mentioned, and this point is not raised in the accounts that follow.

14. Both Alphonse de Tonty and his older brother, Henri, were at the Michilimackinac post in 1699, as evidenced by this manuscript. Alphonse appears to have been referred to on this page as "le sieur de Tonty," whereas his highly respected brother, Henri, was referred to later on this page as "monsieur de Tonty laisne [l'aîné]"— "monsieur" being a term of higher respect than "sieur," and "l'aîné" meaning "the elder." The previous witness, Mauriceau, appears, earlier in his deposition, to have referred to Alphonse also as "monsieur." The brothers were officers and of noble birth, and both could properly have been addressed as "monsieur." It is not always entirely clear which of the brothers is meant in the several references to one or the other in this document.

15. The word used here, *soufflet*, has a variety of meanings. It has been translated as "fire tongs" based upon the description and illustration of the *soufflet à bouche* in Nicole Gênet, Luce Vermette, and Louise Décarie-Audet, *Les objets familiers de nos ancêtres* (Montréal: Les Editions de l'Homme, 1974), 230. The photograph illustrating the *soufflet* shows a long metal tube (often an old gun barrel) mounted with two long, sharp prongs—potentially a wicked weapon. A Louis-Michel [Le] Cavelier, born in 1664 at Montreal, was the son of Robert Le Cavelier *dit* Deslauriers, an armorer. The tools mentioned by Louis Cavelier here suggest that he may have been in the same profession as Robert. See Jetté, *DG*, 211; *DCB*, 2:226.

Reversal by the Sovereign Council of the 1699 judgment in *Fezeret v. Boudor*

1701, October 3, Quebec[1]

[On October 3, 1701] the council considered a certain judgment rendered in the ordinary court of Montreal on December 19, 1699 between René Fezeret, a gunsmith, appealing this on the one hand, and Jean Boudor, the respondent, represented by Lepallieur[2] the bailiff on the other, from which and for the reasons contained therein the parties were sent back to formulate an appeal that they would think good, each party being assessed for its own [court] cost [. . .]. Having heard the king's attorney general together with Councilor de La Martinière's[3] report and everything considered, the Council annulled the said judgment, and, emending it, ordered and does order the said Boudor to return to the said Fezeret the said ten packs of beaver won by him gambling from the said Fezeret's son or pay him their just value if they are no longer in kind, [and the Council] also sentences Fezeret's son, who gambled the said beaver, to two months in jail for having gambled to this excess, and the said Boudor to pay the costs which will include the trips, stays, and return trips of the said Fezeret's wife[4] to be assessed by the said councilor-commissioner.

Bochart Champigny

NOTES

1. *Jugements et délibérations du Conseil souverain, 1663–1716*, CD-ROM, *Chronica 1* (Montréal: Archiv-Histo, 1999).

2. Michel Lepaillieur de Laferté.

3. Claude Bermen de La Martinière (1663–1719), a distinguished jurist, seigneur, and judge in New France, was a member of the Sovereign Council in Quebec from 1678 to 1719. In 1700 he was appointed keeper of the seal of the Sovereign Council, and in 1703, judge of the royal court of Quebec. *DCB*, 2:56–57.

4. Fezeret's wife, Marie Carlié, had to travel from Montreal to Quebec and back each time she was required to represent her husband at court. She actively participated in Fezeret's business and was often a litigant in the Montreal court and Sovereign Council, as in the above case where she successfully represented her husband in his appeal against Boudor. *DCB*, 2:221.

Minister to Callières regarding La Durantaye and La Dame de La Forest

1703, [May 30?][1]

Sieur de La Durantaye, a former captain, has proposed furnishing masts. His Majesty desires that they [Callières and Beauharnois][2] examine this closely. If they find that it is practicable, let them reduce it to the most advantageous terms possible for His Majesty and let him know their opinion.

La Dame Pachot[3] came to France to ask to be paid the sum of 1552 livres 10 sols that she claims sieur Pachot, her husband, loaned for the first Missilimaquina settlements claiming to be in the same situation as sieur de La Durantaye and the others whom His Majesty had reimbursed for the same expenditures. His Majesty's wish is that Messrs. de Callières and de Beauharnois have themselves apprised of what has happened in this matter and he wishes, should she prove that her debt is as legitimate as the debts of those who have received their reimbursement, that she be paid from the proceeds of the sale of the goods which are in the storehouse.[4]

This woman also claims that sieur de Champigny had a bark that she owned taken on his own authority for His Majesty's service and that the bark was lost during this service. She has received no damages for it and she is requesting them as something which she says is legitimately due to her. His Majesty also desires that they investigate with sieur Champigny what this affair is and that they do her the justice that they judge is due her.

NOTES

1. Archives nationales de France, Archives des Colonies, series B, vol. 23: renumbered ff. 69r–70v.

2. François de Beauharnois, intendant of New France from 1702 to 1705.

3. Charlotte-Françoise de Juchereau de Saint-Denis, known as the Countess of Saint Lawrence (*la comtesse de Saint-Laurent*), was perhaps the most colorful and contentious businesswoman in the history of New France. Born in 1660 in Quebec, she married in 1680 François Viennay-Pachot, a seigneur and businessman to whom she gave sixteen children. Pachot died in 1698, and in November of 1702 she married Captain Dauphin de La Forest, one of La Salle's officers and associates and future commander of Detroit. She was thus known first as "La Dame Pachot,"

then as "La Dame de La Forest" after her second marriage. In February 1702 she purchased the Ile d'Orléans, which permitted her to assume the title of countess. She could not, however, keep up the payments for the island (which was four miles downstream from Quebec) and finally lost it after nearly ten years of litigation. *DCB*, 2:305.

The appeal, mentioned in the above 1703 manuscript, by la Dame Pachot, or la Dame de La Forest, for payment of supplies provided at Michilimackinac in 1688 by her first husband, was to drag on until 1716, when the Council of the Marine in France denied her claim, finding that the evidence clearly showed that the debt had been paid in merchandise. AN Marine, B1, 9: 371. Her involvement in politics in New France was extensive and vitriolic. AN Col., C11A, 44: 356; Peyser, ed. and trans., *Letters from New France*, 113–14.

4. The enquiry was conducted, and the amount claimed was, in fact, 1552 livres. See AN C11A, 10: 239r.

Declaration by Marie Lesueur against Beaujeu accusing him of rape

1705, December 31, Montreal[1]

In the year one thousand seven hundred five on the thirty-first and last day of December in the afternoon before [us] Jacques Alexis de Fleury Deschambault, Esquire, king's councilor, judge in the royal court of Montreal island and other places under the governance of the said island, in our place.

There appeared Marie Lesueur daughter of the late Charles Lesueur and Marie Drouet presently married to Pierre Dagenest her third husband, around seventeen years of age accompanied by her mother the said Marie Drouet, which Marie Lesueur after swearing to tell us the truth said that since the day and holiday of last All Saints' Day [. . .] she had begun working at the home of Laurent Renaud for the amount of four livres per month, and left it the last day of November and also said that the said Renaud's wife had consented to her leaving her house, because she [Marie Lesueur] complained to her that sieur de Beaujeu,[2] a lieutenant in the Troupes de la Marine who was living in the home of the said Renaud, constantly asked her to go to bed with him, going to find her everywhere her housework took her, whether in the garret or the cellar or in the upstairs rooms and especially during the night when she was asleep because she slept in a single room where she did the cooking for the household. She declares that one night the said Beaujeu among other nights during the first two weeks or so of the said month of last November had come to find her as she was sleeping wanting to possess her carnally. She awakened and tried to prevent him from doing it by crying out, he threatened to put his sword through her body if she cried out which he did three separate times, and he had her carnally on three different nights, which obliged her to resolve to leave at the end of the said month as she did, after notifying the said Renaud's wife about this and the reason for it, which was caused by the said Beaujeu and his continually asking her to do wrong. She also declared that she believed she was pregnant from the above acts by the said sieur Beaujeu, of which she has called for a record [which was] granted to her to be used for legitimate purposes at the proper time and place and the said Marie Lesueur declared and the said Drouet her mother declares that they do not know how to write or sign, having been questioned as to this according to the ordinance, done on the above day and year.

Approved five words crossed out of no value.

Deschambault

Adhémar paraph.

NOTES

1. Archives nationales du Québec à Montréal, Documents judiciaires de la juridiction royale de Montréal (1693–1760) [cote TL 4 S1].

2. Louis Liénard de Beaujeu (1683–1750), a well-connected officer of noble lineage, commanded Michilimackinac from 1719 to 1722. *DCB*, 3:402–3.

Pontchartrain to Ramezay and Bégon regarding soldiers at Michilimackinac

1715, July 10, Marly[1]

Sieur de Louvigny wrote me that having spoken to you about the subsistence of the detachment of soldiers[2] heading for Michilimakinac you told him that you would have their pay given to them in card money[3] with which they could buy merchandise. Regarding that point, he has represented that considering the excessive price of the merchandise, these soldiers would not be able to live and would inevitably desert. He proposed having their pay given to them in goods from the storehouse on the basis of the goods on display, as stated in His Majesty's Regulation of 1696 and as carried out by Monsieur de Champigny. Since it is just to provide some relief to these soldiers and as the service to which they are destined is important, it is necessary for you to give them any consideration that you can.

NOTES

1. Archives nationales de France, Archives des Colonies, series B, vol. 37: ff. 176r–176v.

2. Louis de La Porte de Louvigny commanded Michilimackinac from 1690 to 1694, and from 1712 to 1720. These "soldiers" were largely unruly coureurs de bois and Indians, unsubsidized by the Crown, who were to take part in an expedition against the Foxes. The attack never materialized. *DCB*, 2:389.

3. See "monnaie de carte" in appendix 1.

Ramezay's orders regarding voyageur Verger dit Desjardins in prison for failing to go to war against the Fox Indians

1715, November 20, Montreal[1]

Claude de Ramesay, knight of the military order of St. Louis,[2] governor of the town of Montreal and its dependencies, king's commandant of all of New France

Sieur LaFerté,[3] jailer of this town's prisons, is ordered not to release the man named Desjardins who is in prison by our orders for having come down from the Ottawas in violation of the order that we had given him to come back only with an attestation from Monsieur de Lignery,[4] commandant of Michilimackinac, that he had served in the war against the Foxes, and since he did not carry it out, we order sieur LaFerté to hold him in prison until he is ordered to do otherwise, on pain of answering for it in his own and unofficial name.

Done at Montreal this 20th of November 1715.

NOTES

1. Archives nationales du Québec à Montréal, Documents judiciaires de la juridiction royale de Montréal (1693–1760) [cote TL 4 S1].

2. A much-coveted honor bestowed for distinguished military service.

3. Michel Lepallieur de Laferté.

4. Constant Le Marchand De Lignery commanded at Michilimackinac from 1712 to about 1718, and again from 1721 to 1728. The expedition that he failed to undertake, and for which Ramezay wants him jailed, fell apart due to poor planning (awaited supplies never arrived), and because the "army" of volunteers spent more time trading than preparing for war. *DCB*, 1:389–90. It should be remembered that until 1716, trading in the northern posts was banned, and these men at last had a legal excuse to be in the pays d'en haut. The temptation to trade was too much to resist.

Petition of Pierre Crevier dit Duvernay for Pay

*September 6 and October 19; January 30 and
February 20, 1717, Montreal, royal court*[1]

The associate judge of the royal court of Montreal Pierre Crevier Duvernay[2] humbly beseeches [the court], saying that last spring he hired himself out to sieur Pierre Trottier Desaunier[3] to go up to Detroit for a man named Philis on a contract drawn up before sieur Lepailleur, royal notary for the amount of four hundred livres during which voyage he carried out his duties in accordance with the said contract [and] went to war against the Foxes. Returning from the said war, he remained at Missilimakinac ill with an inflammation of the leg. He remained without provisions or the opportunity to come back to this town. Jacques Campau[4] who had orders from the said Philis, abandoned him at the said place so that he was at the point of remaining but for the generosity and helpfulness that sieur Laferté had toward him by putting him in one of his canoes and bringing him to this town where the said sieur Desonnier refuses to give him his pay, for which reason he is appealing to you.

Taking this into consideration, Monsieur, would you please permit the said supplicant to have the said sieur Desonnier summoned to be sentenced to pay him the amount of four hundred livres for his wages in accordance with his contract that he presented to you in order to obtain justice.

Pierre Crevier

*Permitted as requested. So ordered. Done at
Montreal this 19th day of October 1716.*

P. Raimbault[5]

In the year one thousand seven hundred sixteen on the twenty-first day of October upon the petition of sieur Pierre Crevier living in Ville Marie where he took up residence in the home of the widow Duvernay, his mother, situated on Rue St. François, I, the undersigned Royal Bailiff of the Montreal Jurisdiction, residing therein, officially conveyed to Pierre Trottier Desonnier, a merchant in the said location, by speaking to his spouse in his residence, the content of the petition for a ruling on the other page, in proper form and terms in order to come to a just conclusion, and I gave him a copy so that he would not be unaware of it. Furthermore and in accordance with the said ruling, by speaking to his spouse I gave sieur Desonniers the summons to appear next Friday at nine o'clock in the morning in the hearing chamber before the associate judge/clerk of the court on the bench of the said jurisdiction, in order to respond to the claims of the said petition and to see the latter prosecuted equitably, upon which I conclude with [a statement of] costs. I gave a copy on the day and year stated above.

J. Petit

Remuneration 17 sols in French coins or 3 livres in card money

September 6, 1716

Sir,

I am writing these lines to you to send my greetings and to inform you how I acted in regard to Duvernay whom you hired out to sieur Fillye. Having placed the Fox war goods[6] in my hands, I brought him to Michel Maquinac [Michilimackinac] in conformity to the king's orders in accordance with which he went on the Fox expedition with me. On returning from the war he told me that he did not want to go down [to Montreal] with the said Fily, saying that his time ended at the end of August. I brought him before Monsieur de Louvigny who ordered him to go down for the said Filye. Therefore Monsieur de Louvigny sentenced him to lose the month during which we had been at war. I wanted to hire him out to have him go down. Several persons offered me three hundred livres for going down. When he was informed he said that he could not go down because he was ill. I was therefore obliged to abandon him. A man named Boutillet and Robert Lafontaine would have given me three hundred livres if he had not said he was ill. Monsieur I did what I thought best having orders from Filis to hire him [and] not being able to have any furs taken down for us because it was too late in the season. I am with all my heart your most humble servant,
Jacques Campau

January 30, 1717

I certify that at Detroit Philis asked me in the presence of sieur Duvernay to hire Duvernay on behalf of the said Philis upon returning from the Fox campaign of the year one thousand seven hundred sixteen at such time as he arrived at Michilimackinac to go down to Montreal via the grande rivière [Ottawa River], but the said Duvernay, wanting to make problems for me during the above mentioned Fox war, said he was at the end of his obligation after four months. I brought him before Monsieur de Louvigny who ordered him to go down for Philis at such time as they arrived at the said Michilimackinac, which was agreed upon, and when we came back from the war I hired him out to Bourgis and La Fontaine in return for 300 livres in card money for going down, but Duvernay had such a pain in his leg that he could not even walk. That took on an appearance that led us to believe that it would not heal soon and consequently he was in no condition to serve them. After that I brought him again to Bouteiller who would have taken him but when he saw the leg he told me that that man could not work in the condition he was in as well as Bourgis and La Fontaine when I saw that he was too unwell I gave up on the trip down, and as a consequence sieur La Ferté, the son, asked me what I was going to do with Duvernay. I told him that I had abandoned him since he was in no condition to serve. He told me that he was going to take him since I could not make use of him and that he would pay him according to what he could do.

I can only praise him for having done everything that I wished. One can find nothing that needs to be redone. He was not able to come down as he was supposed to, but he absolutely was not able to do it.

I also certify that the said Philis, whom Duvernay had gone to see in person, received from Desrivières[7] thirty-five livres of dry beaver coming from Delorme[8] who had received the goods for his trip up, and along with the present declaration I am ready to provide testimony if need be when it is required.

Done at Montreal January 30, 1717.

In the year one thousand seven [hundred][9] seventeen on the twentieth day of February upon the petition of the widow Duvernay [whose late husband was] an entrepreneur of Ville Marie where she has taken up residence in his house located on rue St. François in whose name she is proceeding, I, Royal Bailiff of the royal jurisdiction of Montreal residing in Ville Marie on rue

St. Paul, undersigned, delivered a subpoena to sieur Pierre Trottier Dessonier, a merchant of this town, by speaking to [*blank space*] at his home, to come from there next Tuesday at nine o'clock in the morning at the hearing before the judge of the said royal jurisdiction in order to respond to the subpoena which was delivered to him by me upon the above mentioned petition on the date of the seventh of last [*blank space*] by me, the above bailiff, undersigned, upon which I conclude with the expenses.

J. Petit

NOTES

1. Archives nationales du Québec à Montréal, Documents judiciaires de la juridiction royale de Montréal (1693–1760) [cote TL 4 S1].

2. Pierre Crevier *dit* Duvernay was born in Montreal on June 8, 1699. He became an innkeeper and married Thérèse Chevalier in 1724. Jetté, *DG*, 293.

3. Pierre Trottier, sieur Desaulniers was a Montreal merchant-entrepreneur and seigneur of the Ile aux Hérons. Jetté, *DG*, 1092.

4. Jacques Campau (Campot, Campeau) (1677–1751) was a trader, merchant, and blacksmith who settled in Detroit with his family soon after its founding. *DCB*, 3:96; Jetté, *DG*, 195.

5. Pierre Raimbault was a cabinetmaker who went on to serve as a notary at Montreal from 1697 to 1727. He added titles and commissions, each of increasing importance in the legal system, almost until his death in 1740. *DCB*, 2:541–42.

6. Following Louvigny's successful attack against the Foxes in Wisconsin in 1716, and the peace treaty negotiated with them, many of Louvigny's men, including coureurs de bois, traded for furs with the Green Bay tribes. The expedition returned to Michilimackinac with a rich haul of these furs. Louvigny was subsequently heavily criticized for turning the expedition into a large-scale trading venture, but was nevertheless rewarded by the French court for forcing the Foxes to sue for peace. Edmunds and Peyser, *The Fox Wars: The Mesquakie Challenge to New France*, 84–86.

7. Possibly Julien Trottier *dit* Desrivières, a merchant, the brother of Pierre Trottier, sieur Desaulniers.

8. Pierre Delorme *dit* Sanscrainte, a soldier in the Merville company. Jetté, *DG*, 323. His nickname, "without fear," seems very apt for a soldier and suggests something of how he was viewed by others.

9. The omission of certain words suggests that this brief document, although signed, is a preliminary version of a subpoena drawn up by the bailiff.

King's attorney's complaint against various voyageurs for failing to go to war against the Fox Indians

1716, January 13, Montreal[1]

To the civil and criminal judge of the royal jurisdiction of Montreal the king's attorney at the said bench points out to you that for the infractions committed regarding the orders of the governor who ordered all the voyageurs who went up to the Ottawa country last summer to go to war against the Foxes under the command of Monsieur de Lignery, commandant of Michilimackinac, the men named Desjardins, LeBoeuf, Mongeault, Gautier[2] and several others who were at the said Michilimackinac allegedly removed themselves from the said sieur de Lignery's command and came down to this town with no orders for which reason the governor made the said Desjardins, LeBoeuf, Gauthier and Mongeault prisoners. As a result of these proceedings, Monsieur, may it please you to proceed to the said prisons with your clerk of the court in order to interrogate the said Desjardins, LeBoeuf, Mongeault and Gautier about the said violation and other cases the king's attorney shall wish to be heard, as well as the other violators who will be arrested for the said interrogations [to apply the law?] as is appropriate and do justice.

Le Paillieur paraph.

In view of the above brief we order that we proceed presently to the jail chamber to interrogate the prisoners named in the said brief.

Done at Montreal this 13th of January 1716.

NOTES

1. Archives nationales du Québec à Montréal, Documents judiciaires de la juridiction royale de Montréal (1693–1760) [cote TL 4 S1].
2. These men are identified here and in the following document.

Record of interrogations of LeBoeuf and other voyageurs charged with not fighting against the Fox Indians

1716, January 13, Montreal[1]

In the year one thousand sixteen on the thirteenth day of January at three o'clock in the afternoon, questioned about his name, age, occupation and residence, he said he was named Pierre LeBoeuf forty-two years old, a voyageur by occupation ordinarily living in this town. Questioned as to how long he has been back from the last voyage he made to Michilimackinac, he said that he has been back since the month of last August. Questioned as to how long ago he left this town to go up there and whether it was with permission, [he] said it was two years ago last spring and that it was without a congé. Questioned whether he had a congé to come down, he said no. Questioned if he went to the commandant to have permission [to take this trip], he said no.

P. Le boeuf

Questioned why he did not request a congé he said that having stayed at Michilimackinac for a month upon his return from fur trading, he used up the little that they had to wait for everyone to be assembled and having learned that the voyageurs from Detroit instead of going up to Michilimackinac to go to the rendezvous had left in a convoy with sieur Dubuisson[2] to go to Montreal and seeing from all appearances that there was nothing they could accomplish, he thought he did not do anything very wrong in leaving secretly, planning to go back up immediately if it had been necessary and indeed after having placed in a safe place the few belongings that he had, he left immediately to go to Michilimackinac where he would have arrived earlier than Monsieur Deschaillon[3] if he had not fallen ill on the way which obliged him to stay ashore until he was ready to complete this trip and go to war against the Foxes upon the first orders given to him never having planned to disobey them.

Reading done to the said LeBoeuf [. . .] etc.] and the said LeBoeuf was taken back to prison.

P. Lebeuf

P. Raimbault paraph.

Adhémar paraph.

Order[4] to the king's attorney and clerk for his summation, what he advises, and to report to us what is to be ordered that has been decided. Done on the above said day and year.

P. Raimbault paraph.

Adhémar paraph.

In the year one thousand seven hundred sixteen on the thirteenth day of January at ten o'clock in the morning upon the petition of the king's attorney and clerk, we Pierre Raimbault, king's councilor and his attorney at the bench of the royal jurisdiction of Montreal [and] clerk of the court performing the functions of assistant judge, having proceeded to the jail chamber of the royal prisons of this jurisdiction, had Jean Vergé dit Desjardins, a prisoner in this jail by order of the governor, who after his oath to tell the truth, was interrogated by us as follows.

Questioned as to his name, family name, age, occupation and residence, he said he was named Jean Vergé twenty-eight years of age, a voyageur by occupation ordinarily staying in this town.

Questioned as to the reason for which he was made a prisoner, he said that he was arrested because he had left Michilimackinac last summer before the convoy that came down from there.

Questioned as to why he left before the said convoy and whether he had the commandant's permission, he said that having gone up last spring with the governor's permission in order to carry orders with sieur Laurent Renaud and not being one of the coureurs de bois he did not believe he was absolutely obliged perhaps to remain at Michilimackinac to the detriment of his business, that seeing the lateness of the season, that the convoy that was to go up through Detroit was not arriving so that already it no longer appeared that the expedition against the Foxes could be undertaken, and that furthermore he had his canoe with part of his things at Nepissing[5] from where two Indians were to bring them down here with a French engagé of sieur Duval[6] but were not however to leave without his order or the sieur Duval's, and having heard that his engagé had left without his order with the said Indians he left Michilimackinac planning only to go after the said canoe to try to reach it and stop it not trusting the said engagé and Indians enough to take it and having also encountered a canoe that was going up to Michilimackinac carrying powder and those who were in it told him that as to having greasy beaver taken down from Michilimackinac they no longer doubted that the expedition was put off until the present year [1716] and with this in mind he continued on his way to try to catch up with his canoe fearing that it had been wrecked, [he said] that he could not catch up however with the said canoe which arrived seven or eight days before [at?] this island [of Montreal] and that indeed it is true that the convoy from Detroit having arrived too late at Michilimackinac made no expedition and the voyageurs came back from there some time after he did.

Questioned as to why he did not make known the reasons he had for taking the trip to Nepissing and for not asking permission for this from the Michilimackinac commandant, he said that fearing a refusal and having no other plan but the one that he told us about and that this trip was of the greatest consequence to him, he effectively did not speak to him about it, not believing furthermore that he was causing great harm since he still planned to go to war against the Foxes, or that he was a deserter, having always gone up to the upper country with permission to go to Detroit and that he is ready to go to war at his own expense with two men if necessary whenever it pleases the governor. Questioned as to how many men he had taken with him and how many he brought back. He said that he had taken four with him and that he brought back only one of them with another the previous year. Asked to tell us the names of the said engagés he said they are the men named Jean Catin,[7] Joseph of English nationality and the son of Seraphin Lauzon,[8] and the man named Monjeau also his engagé who was there from the previous year, that sieur Monjeau and Catin came down with him, the three others having remained up there. Reading of the present interrogation done for the said Vergé. He said and persisted that his answers were truthful and represented to us at the same time that he is suffering greatly from his detention having already contracted a sickness in prison for which reason he calls upon us to be willing to discharge and absolve him not believing that he is guilty and in the event there were some difficulty he offers to give whatever bail we please to guaranty his presence and his submission to going up there and to participating in the expeditions that will be made in the Fox war and he signed with us and our clerk of the court. Done on the above said day and year, and he was taken back to his prison. *Approved fifty words crossed out and null and void.*

Jean Vergé

P. Raimbault paraph.

Adhémar paraph.

To be sent to the king's attorney and clerk for summation and determination of what he will advise us and what has been decided to be ordered.

Done the above said day and year.

P. Raimbault paraph.

Adhémar paraph.

Clerk of the court

In the year one thousand seven hundred sixteen on the thirteenth day of January at two o'clock in the afternoon questioned as to his name, family name, age, occupation, and residence, he said he was named Jean Gautier, a habitant of Cap St. Michel living there, about forty years of age. Asked why he is in prison he said it is for having come down from Michilimackinac. Asked how long ago he had gone up there he said that he had gone up there last spring with a man named Landreville who had hired him to that end for the trip that he told him was to last only three months.

Questioned about whom he came down with and how long he remained at the said Michilimackinac, he said that he came down with the men named Quintal and LeBoeuf having remained up there one month. Asked by whose order and for whom he came down, he said it is his boss who sent him. Asked if he had leave from the Michilimackinac commandant, he said no only having obeyed his master being obligated by his contract to go where he wanted during the said trip.

Asked if he did not well know that it was not permitted of anyone whatever to leave the said place without leave, all those who came up to the said location having permission only on condition of being in the expedition that was to be made against the Foxes. He said that he did not hear any king's order on this topic made public up there, that he only heard several voyageurs say that they were going to war against the Foxes and that it was necessary to wait for everybody who was to come from several places to be assembled, and others who said in greater numbers that they were definitely not going to war, that nothing was ready having received no news from the commandants who were to be there.

Asked if it was not his canoe which was the first to leave without permission to come down here, he said yes.

Asked how much his wages were for his said voyage, he said that he had three hundred fifty livres in card money.

Asked if he already made several voyages to Michilimackinac, he said that it is the first voyage he had made in the upper country, never having gone on other voyages other than to go to war against the English.[9]

Asked if he left Michilimackinac long before the departure of the convoy of voyageurs who came down last autumn, he said that he knows nothing about it, that he remembers only that he arrived here during the harvest.

The reading was done for the said Gautier of the present interrogation; he said that his answers were truthful and persisted in this and declared that he did not know how to write or sign his name upon being questioned on this and the said Gautier was led back to his prison. Done on the above said day and year.

P. Raimbault paraph.

Adhémar paraph.

Clerk of the court

Order to the king's attorney and court employee for summing up and deciding on what he will advise and reporting to us what will be appropriate [for us] to order

In the year one thousand seven hundred sixteen
on the thirteenth day of January

Asked to give his name, surname, age, occupation, and residence, he said he was named Pierre Monjeau thirty years old a habitant of Cap de la Trinité ordinarily living there.

Asked how long it has been since he came down from Michilimackinac and how he had gone up there, he said that he had gone up there a year ago last spring, having been hired by Desjardins who had permission to go to Detroit and that he came back last summer with the said Desjardins.

Asked if he had permission to come down, he said no.

Asked why he came down without permission, he said that being hired and obligated by his contract to come down at the will of his master he obeyed him fearing that he would lose his wages which amounted to three hundred fifty livres in card money.

Asked if he did not know well that no one was permitted to come down last year before the Fox war expedition, he said no other than by hearsay not having heard the orders read and asked who were those who left Michilimackinac with him, he said that he left with the said Desjardins, a man named Catin and two Indians and, asked why he did not notify the Michilimackinac commandant about the said Desjardins's departure since he had heard it said that that was forbidden and that he could not have not known about it, instead of helping him and following him as he did, he said that being an engagé he did not believe he could do wrong in obeying his master and besides having no goods of his own to trade for his own profit and being paid by the said Desjardins only for going up and coming down he would have found himself in a state of dire necessity and obliged to hire himself out in order to live if it had been necessary for him to stay there any longer while his wife and children were down here at the mercy of God knows who and in utter destitution.

Asked by whose order he is in the said prisons, he said that it is by order of the governor who ordered him to proceed to prison which he immediately obeyed although his imprisonment is very unfortunate for him regarding his family which stays alive only through his work from day to day.

Reading of the present interrogation done to the said Monjeau, etc. [Monjeau] was sent back to his prison etc.

P. Raimbault paraph.

Adhémar paraph.

Clerk of the court

Order to the king's attorney and court employee etc.

In view of our request of yesterday and the assistant judge's ruling of the same day based on the interrogation undergone as a result of my petition before the assistant judge by the men named Jean Verger, Pierre LeBoeuf, Pierre Mongeault, and Jean Gautier dated this day, the order[10] also issued this day, I conclude that the said Mongeault and Gautier should be released from the prisons where they have been detained, with their being forbidden to commit further violations such as what they have done, also let the said Jean Verger and LeBoeuf be released from the said prisons by putting up good and sufficient bond for going up to Michilmackinac in the spring to follow the orders of Monsieur de Lignery commandant at the said place with their being prohibited from falling into similar disobedience on pain of punishment and the convicted to pay court costs. Montreal this 13th of January 1716.

Le Pallieur paraph.

NOTES

1. Archives nationales du Québec à Montréal, Documents judiciaires de la juridiction royale de Montréal (1693–1760) [cote TL 4 S1].

2. Jacques-Charles Renaud Dubuisson, active in the wars against the Fox Indians and commandant at Michilimackinac, 1729–30. *DCB*, 2:562–63.

3. Jean-Baptiste de Saint-Ours Deschaillons, officer in the Troupes de la Marine. He went to the pays d'en haut in 1717, and from 1721 to 1723 commanded the post at Kaministiquia (Thunder Bay, Ontario). He was very active in the fur trade with the merchant Jacques Le Ber. *DCB*, 3:578–79.

4. Order, *soit-communiqué*. See appendix 2.

5. Lake Nipissing, situated between Georgian Bay and the Ottawa River.

6. Possibly François Duval *dit* Duponthaut, a soldier in Louvigny's company. Jetté, *DG*, 399.

7. Jean was the son of Henri Catin, a butcher. Jean was about twenty-seven years old at this date. Jetté, *DG*, 208.

8. Seraphin Lauzon was a coppersmith. He had seventeen children through two marriages. His eldest son, Laurent, would have been about twenty-five years old at this time. Jetté, *DG*, 664.

9. The French and English had been vying for control of the Great Lakes interior since the early 1680s. Wars between France and England in Europe gave colonial authorities opportunities to try to extend their reach against their rivals in North America. The results were raids and counter-raids until the Treaty of Utrecht (1713) brought some thirty years of peace to the area. W. J. Eccles, *The Canadian Frontier, 1534–1760* (1969; Albuquerque: University of New Mexico Press, 1978), 119–42.

10. Order, *ordonnance de soit-communiqué*.

Sentence ordering four voyageurs to return to Michilimackinac to join in war against the Fox Indians

1716, January 14, Montreal[1]

In view of the brief of the king's attorney and clerk in this jurisdiction and our order being on the bottom of yesterday's [record of] interrogations undergone before us by the men named Jean Vergé dit Desjardins, Jean Gautier, Pierre Monjeau, and Pierre LeBoeuf, voyageurs and prisoners in the royal prisons of this jurisdiction, accused of having left Michilimackinac where they had gone for the Fox War and of having come down to this town with neither orders nor permission, containing their avowals, confessions, and denials of the same day, our order being at the bottom of the said interrogations stating that they would be conveyed to the king's attorney for the conclusions of the said king's attorney, all on yesterday, and all being considered we have ordered that the said Jean Verger and LeBoeuf be released from the said prisons provided that they go up next spring to the said Michilimackinac in order to place themselves under the orders of the commandant who will be in charge of the Fox war expedition and to bring with each of them two men, as a guarantee of which they will be required to post good and sufficient bail which will be received before us and submitted to the clerk of the court in accordance with the ordinance in the usual way just as the said Pierre Monjeaux and Jean Gautier will be released upon their sworn oath to present themselves again and join the expedition against the Foxes upon the first order given to them to do so, to which conditions they will submit in the office of the clerk of the court, setting forth their residence, furthermore forbidding them to repeat the offense on pain of punishment with the utmost rigor of the ordinances. We so order and done and given at Ville-Marie by us, above mentioned assistant judge and clerk the fourteenth of January one thousand seven hundred sixteen

P. Raimbault paraph.

Adhémar paraph.

In the year one thousand seven hundred sixteen on the fourteenth day of January at four o'clock in the afternoon we, the above assistant judge and clerk, having proceeded to the jail chamber of this jurisdiction's prisons, had the men named Jean Vergé, Pierre LeBoeuf, Pierre Monjaux and Jean Gautier, prisoners therein, brought before us, to whom we had our above sentence read, and at that very moment the said Vergé in order to comply with it said that he offers and presented as bond sieur François Poisset[2] a merchant in this town, and the said LeBoeuf, [presents as bond] Simon Réaume, personally, a merchant. We call for them to be received upon which was heard the king's attorney and clerk who said that he had nothing to say nor any objection which would prevent the proffered bond from being accepted. We received as bond guaranteeing the execution of our said sentence to wit the said sieur Poisset personally for the said Jean Vergé and sieur Réaume personally for the said LeBoeuf, these guarantors to formalize their offers with the clerk of the court in conformity with the ordinance, and [the following] have signed.

Le Pailleur paraph.

Pier Le Beuf

Jean Vergé

P Raimbault paraph.

Adhémar paraph.

clerk of the court

NOTES

1. Archives nationales du Québec à Montréal, Documents judiciaires de la juridiction royale de Montréal (1693–1760) [cote TL 4 S1].
2. Jacques-François Poisset, a recruiter in the fur trade. Jetté, *DG*, 932.

Appearance in the clerk of the court's office of François Poisset as bond for Jean Vergé, etc.

1716, January 14, Montreal[1]

Today in the clerk of the court's office in the royal jurisdiction of Montreal there appeared sieur François Poisset, a merchant in this town, who is coming forward as bond for Jean Vergé dit Desjardins to the king's attorney clerk of the said jurisdiction to carry out his sentence given in this court on this date and has submitted to it, designating as his residence the house in which he is living situated on Rue St. Paul. Done at the said office of the clerk of the court the fourteenth day of January one thousand seven hundred sixteen, and signed

F Poisset

Adhémar paraph.

clerk of the court

Today in the clerk of the court's office in the royal jurisdiction of Montreal there appeared Pierre Monjeau who in carrying out the sentence of the assistant judge on this day has submitted as promised and does promise to present himself again each and every time and declared that he does not know how to write or sign his name having been questioned on this. Done in the clerk of the court's office the fourteenth of January one thousand seven hundred sixteen.

Adhémar paraph.

Clerk of the court

[Following the above is an identical statement for Jean Gautier who also did not know how to write, signed by Adhémar.]

Today in the clerk of the court's office in the royal jurisdiction of Montreal there appeared Simon Réaume, a merchant-entrepreneur in this town, who said that he is coming forward as bond for Pierre LeBoeuf to carry out the sentence given in this court on this day and submitted to it, designating as his residence in this town the house in which he is living situated on Rue St. Paul. Done in the said clerk of the court's office the fourteenth day of January one thousand seven hundred sixteen, and signed

Simon Réaume

Adhémar paraph.

Clerk of the court

NOTE

1. Archives nationales du Québec à Montréal, Documents judiciaires de la juridiction royale de Montréal (1693–1760) [cote TL 4 S1].

Louvigny's statement regarding engagés's pay dispute over serving against the Foxes

1716, November 7, Quebec[1]

I attest that at Missilimakinac regarding some difficulties going on between the foremen[2] and their engagés, the latter claiming to be at the end of their obligation, including the time they went to war and by this means abandoning the goods of the foremen and canoe heads,[3] I gave orders to obviate these difficulties.

I ordered the engagés as the king's subjects to go on the expedition against the Foxes and that the time would neither be counted nor paid for, but upon their return their going down [to Montreal] would be paid for like their going up to Michilimackinac according to the agreements they had made or would make with the canoe heads in witness whereof I have signed the present certificate to be used at the proper time and place.

At Quebec November 7, 1716.

Louvigny

NOTES

1. Archives nationales du Québec à Montréal, Documents judiciaires de la juridiction royale de Montréal (1693–1760) [cote TL 4 S1].
2. Foremen, *bourgeois voyageurs*.
3. Canoe heads, *chefs de canots*.

Statement by François Daragon dit Lafrance on the topic of the soldier Lafranchise who was robbed and buried alive about 42 years ago

1734, March 27, Montreal[1]

March 27, 1734. Daragon, for Monsieur Blainville[2]

Before [the royal notary] etc., appeared françois Daragon called Lafrance, resident of St. Laurent, a former soldier in the company of Monsieur Dugué[3], who, upon the request [to the court] of the honorable Jean B. Céloron de Blainville, Knight of the military Order of St. Louis, captain of a company of the detachment of the marine, commanding the aforesaid troops in Montreal, and after taking oath at the hands of the aforesaid notary, with witnesses present, said, affirmed, and declared what he knew, that around forty to forty-two years ago a certain Lafranchise, a soldier in Duplessis's company,[4] was robbed of the sum of one hundred fifty livres in silver during the night by three men, soldiers of the Marquis de Crisafy's[5] company, among whom was Jean Sargnat Lafond,[6] who since set himself up as an innkeeper having married a daughter of henry Catin,[7] a butcher in this town. The aforesaid Sargnat and his accomplices after having taken away and stolen the aforesaid Lafranchise's money buried him alive and weighted down with brushwood outside the town, in order to hide their crime, which, having been uncovered at night by some passers-by who, drawn by the moaning of the aforesaid Lafranchise, found him under the dirt and the brushwood. Monsieur Duplessis, the aforesaid Lafranchise's Captain, brought charges against the aforesaid three accused men. And the three were sentenced and convicted by court martial, one to the galleys, the second to have his head broken, and the third, [to have] his life [spared].

The troops assembled in the customary manner made the aforesaid three men draw lots by means of three slips of paper; and it fell to the aforesaid Sargnat's lot that he would have his life spared; one of his accomplices had his head broken immediately; and [he] does not know at all what became of the one who was sentenced to the galleys, which is all that he said he knows and with the present statement has legally made his declaration to be used by my aforesaid Monsieur de Blainville as it pertains to him. Drawn up in

Montreal [in the] office of the aforesaid notary [in] the year one thousand seven hundred thirty-four [on the] twenty-seventh of March in the forenoon. The witnesses present Laurens artus Guignard, corporal[8] in Monsieur Dufigué's[9] company and Jean Baptiste Decoste who have signed, the aforesaid Daragon declared that he did not know how to sign when questioned about this after the reading done in accordance with the regulation.

Five words with no value Crossed out.

Guignard

Decoste

Raimbault

clerk of the court

NOTES

1. Archives nationales du Québec à Montréal, Greffe de Raimbault.

2. Jean-Baptiste Céloron de Blainville. He was a captain in the Troupes de la Marine and eventually made a Knight of the Order of Saint-Louis, despite an apparently ordinary military career. He died in 1735 at Montreal. *DCB*, 2:124–25.

3. Captain Michel-Sidrac Dugué de Boisbriand died in 1688; his son, Jacques Du Gué de Boisbriand, was an ensign in 1688 and was promoted to lieutenant in 1692. Céloron de Blainville held the rank of captain as early as 1691 and undoubtedly knew the officers mentioned in this sworn statement. In 1730, Du Gué senior's granddaughter married Céloron de Blainville's grandson. *Bulletin des Rescherches Historiques* (hereafter *BRH*) 24:172.

4. Captain François Lefebvre Duplessis commanded at Fort Chambly, near Montreal, until 1689.

5. As a captain, the Marquis Antoine de Crisafy commanded the troops at Sault-Saint-Louis, near Montreal, in 1692. He became governor of Trois-Rivières in 1703. *DCB*, 2:162–63.

6. In 1706 Jean Sargnat *dit* Lafond married Marie Catin, the older sister of Thérèse and Catherine Catin. These two sisters had won a judgment against Céloron de Blainville in the Superior Council of Quebec, the highest court in New France, on February 7, 1734. See Blainville's appeal, ANQ-M, Greffe Pierre Raimbault, 23 mars 1734.

7. Following his conviction and sentencing, Sargnat was stationed at Michilimackinac, marrying Marie Catin upon his return to Montreal from that garrison. See document 62.

8. Arthur-Laurent Guignard had served in the troops before becoming a Montreal court officer in 1734. He served as a bailiff from 1738 to 1744. *BRH* 23:359 and 32:89.

9. Possibly René-Louis Fournier Du Figuier, an ensign in 1694. *BRH* 26:333 and 34:60.

Statement by Widow Dailleboust De Musseaux on the topic of the soldier who was robbed and buried alive about 43 years ago

1734, March 29, Montreal[1]

Before [the royal notary] etc. appeared Madame Anne Le Picard, widow of the late Jean-Baptiste Dailleboust Demusseaux, Esquire,[2] who at the request of the honorable Jean Baptiste Céloron de Blainville, Knight of the military Order of St. Louis, captain in command of the troops of the marine detachment in Montreal, and after oath taken by her at the hands of the aforesaid notary with witnesses present, said and affirmed that forty to forty-three years ago or thereabouts she has complete knowledge that due to a robbery and brutal treatment of a soldier, three men were charged with and convicted of the deed and sentenced, one to have his head broken, one to serve as a slave in the galleys, and that the other would have his life spared, that she does not know the one who was robbed and beaten black and blue, that the aforesaid accused were convicted, at the head of the assembled troops behind the emplacement of délauriers[3] [. . .], today on the land closed in by the fortifications then serving as a commons, drew three lots, by means of three slips of paper. When the slips were opened, the man named Pelgry, one of the aforesaid accomplices [was] sentenced to the galleys; another whose name she does not remember had his head broken at the head of the troops; the man named Jean Sargnat called Lafond, a soldier in Monsieur De Crisafy's company, nicknamed the [. . .] by his comrades because he was indeed very free after having opened his slip, found out that his life was spared, that Sarnat whom she knew well has since married a daughter of henry Cattin who, when he was alive, was a butcher in this city, and that she withdrew after the verdict was given and they were breaking the head of the aforesaid soldier whose name she previously stated she does not remember, suffering and being upset upon seeing justice of this kind being done. Of which statement she has called for a notarized copy to be granted to her for the use of Monsieur de Blainville as he finds it appropriate.

Drawn up in Montreal in the house of the aforesaid woman who has appeared [before the notary] in the year one thousand seven hundred thirty-four on the twenty-ninth of March in the afternoon in the presence of Messrs. Joseph Phelippeax, Jean Baptiste Guillon, schoolmaster, who have signed, with the exception of the aforesaid widow Demusseaux who stated that she was not able to sign because of her poor eyesight when she was questioned on this, after the reading was done. *Seven crossed-out words are null and void.*

J. Phelippeaux, witness

Guillon

Raimbault

NOTES

1. Archives nationales du Québec à Montréal, Greffe de Pierre Raimbault.
2. Jean-Baptiste D'Ailleboust des Musseaux (des Muceaux and other variations) (1666–1730) served in the military until 1691 when, as a lieutenant, he left the service in order to go into business. He lived in Montreal and frequently took trips to the upper country. In 1689 he married Anne Le Picard, who died in 1736. They had sixteen children. *DCB*, 2:14.
3. Robert Le Cavelier *dit* Deslauriers was a Montreal armorer. *DCB*, 2:226.

Statement by Pierre Martin dit La Douceur on the topic of soldier Lafranchise who was robbed and buried alive around forty-three years ago

1734, March 30, Montreal[1]

Today Before the royal notary of the royal jurisdiction of Montreal residing there and undersigned, appeared Pierre Martin called La Douceur, a habitant of the Coste Notre Dame des Neiges[2] on this island of montreal, a former soldier of the late Monsieur Dumesnil's[3] company, who upon the request of the honorable Jean Baptiste Céloron de Blainville, Knight of the military Order of St. Louis, captain in command of the troupes de la marine detachment maintained for the king's service in Montreal, after oath taken at the hands of the aforesaid notary in the presence of the undersigned witnesses, said, declared and affirmed upon his soul and conscience that around forty-three years ago as far as he can remember the man named Lafranchise, a soldier in Monsieur Duplessis's company, was robbed in the town of montreal and after the authors of this deed had left him naked and taken away his money, and having beaten him so severely and believing him dead from the blows covered him with earth and brushwood, Monsieur Duplessis after a search identified the authors of this crime and lodged his complaint with Monsieur de Callière, the Governor of montreal.

The men named Pelgry and Jean Sargnat called Lafond, a soldier of Monsieur De Crisafy and one other whose name he does not remember, taken and declared guilty, were made prisoners in the prison of the aforesaid montreal, with irons on their legs. Their charge was investigated and judged by Court Martial. They were sentenced one to have his head broken, one to the galleys, and the other would have his life spared, after having drawn lots. He does not remember the name of the one whose head was broken, having been informed of it by his comrades who did not say his name.

Then, the troops having been assembled, the aforesaid three men drew lots and when their eyes were opened it turned out to be Peldry who was the man sentenced to the galleys; the soldier whose name he said he does not remember had his head broken; and the aforesaid Sargnat, with the lot he drew, had his life spared. Then the aforesaid Lafond Sargnat whom he knew very well, went into the garrison at Missilimakinac and upon his return married a daughter of Henry Cattin, a butcher in the city of montreal. Of which statement and solemn declaration he [Martin] has called for a notarized copy from the aforesaid notary, granted to him for the use of my aforesaid Monsieur de Blainville, which is legitimate.

Done and drawn up in the house of the aforesaid Martin La Douceur at the aforesaid Coste Notre Dame des Neiges, in the year one thousand seven hundred thirty-four on this March thirtieth in the forenoon in the presence of sieurs. Gabriel Paille, master carpenter, and françois de Lestre, habitants called as witnesses who have signed with us the aforesaid notary with the exception of the aforesaid martin who stated that he did not know how after being questioned on this after the reading done in accordance with the regulation. One word crossed out is null and void.

gabriel paillez

françois De Laistre

Raimbault

royal Notary

NOTES

1. Archives nationales du Québec à Montréal, Greffe de Pierre Raimbault.
2. This is the proper name of a place and literally translates as "the Parish of Our Lady of the Snow."
3. Possibly Captain Jacques Le Picard Du Mesnil de Norrey, who in 1691 commanded Fort Lachine, about eight miles from Montreal. He became garrison adjutant of the troops in Canada in 1706. *DCB*, 2:415–16.

Appendix 1.
Untranslated French Terms

bourgeois: a merchant-entrepreneur, often associated with the fur trade as an outfitter who provided goods to be taken to the *pays d'en haut* to trade for furs

card money: see *monnaie de carte*

commandant: commanding officer of any rank

congé: a license to trade for furs with Indians in the western part of the colony

coureur de bois: lit. "a runner of the woods," the term referred to men who traveled into the wilderness to trade with Indians (When the fur trade became better regulated and licenses [*congés*] were required, the term came to refer to an illegal fur trader.)

denier: a unit of French money (There were 12 deniers to a *sol*. The abbreviation, used in price lists, etc., was "d".)

dit: lit. "called," but also carries the sense of "better known as"

écu: a *petit écu* ("little crown"), sometimes known as an *écu blanc* ("white crown"), was a silver coin worth 3 *livres*, 6 *sols* (A *gros écu* was worth 6 *livres*, 12 *sols*.)

engagé: someone engaged to work for someone else (In the fur trade, it referred to a person hired to work for a *congé* holder. The latter did not usually travel to trade with Indians.)

habitant: lit. a resident, but it refers to someone below the rank of *seigneur* who held land in the colony

intendant: the second leading official in the colony (The intendant was subordinate to the governor of the colony and responsible for its civil administration.)

league: see *lieue*

lieue: a unit of French measure (A French post league was equal to 2.42 English miles; the common league was 2.76 miles; the marine league equaled 3.45 miles.)

livre: the basic unit of money in France and New France (It did not exist as a coin; rather it was an accounting term. The written abbreviation was similar to the "#" symbol. Up to 1717, the *livre* in New France was worth three quarters of that of France, which was known as the *livre tournois* or *argent de France*. After that date, the value was the same. The word *livre* is also the term for a unit of weight. The context of the word's use serves as a clue to which meaning is intended. At times, however, it is not possible to ascertain whether money or weight is being discussed.)

louis d'argent: a silver coin worth 3 *livres*

louis d'or: a gold piece worth 25 *livres*

madame: the common way to refer to a married woman, usually reserved for addressing women from the "better" families, but not necessarily those of noble birth (Married *habitant* women, "common folk," were usually addressed by their names only [e.g., Marie Carlié, rather than *Madame* Carlié].)

monnaie de carte: a card used as currency (Coins were not minted in New France, and paper currency was not used in this time period. Shortages of coins led to use of playing cards, assigned values of up to 100 *livres*, in the place of coins. To prevent fraud, only cards signed by the *intendant* could be accepted as currency or be redeemed for coins.)

monsieur: sometimes translated as Sir or Mr., the term is a more polite form of *sieur*, and usually reserved for addressing someone of noble birth

pays d'en haut: upper country (The term was used to refer to land to the far west and north of Montreal—generally, the area today known as the Upper Great Lakes region.)

pistole: an accounting term referring to 10 *livres*

seigneur: someone who received a land grant, either directly or indirectly from the king, and who was obliged to attract settlers to that land (The latter was known as a *seigneury*. The seigneur had to provide certain services to his *habitants* in return for small payments.)

sieur: a common form of address, equivalent to "monsieur" in today's French, or "Mr." in English

sol: a unit of French currency (There were 20 sols to a *livre*. The abbreviation for sol was "s".)

Troupes de la Marine: colonial regular troops, under authority of the minister of the Marine, the Crown official responsible for colonial matters

voyageur: a canoe man employed in the fur trade to travel to trade with Indians

Appendix 2.
Seventeenth- and Eighteenth-Century Legal Terms

à la charge de: chargeable to, the responsibility of; the obligation to; on condition that

à l'encontre de: against or in opposition to (applicable to countercharges)

à titre de: by way of, by right of, on grounds of, by reason of, by virtue of, on the basis of

accusé(e) (noun): defendant in a criminal case

acquêt (m): acquest; property acquired by a spouse other than by inheritance, forming part of the communal estate; in contrast with *propre* (q.v.) (see also *conquêt* (m))

acquis (m): knowledge acquired

acquitter: to pay, settle

acte (m): (notarial) deed or certificate, instrument (see *donner acte de*)

acte (m) *d'arrivée*: formal delivery

acte (m) *de départ* (m): beginning of a proceeding or action

adjonction (f): addition, annex, appendix

adjournement (m): a summons to appear in court (*ajournement* in modern French)

affrètement (m): chartering, hiring (noun)

ainsi qu'il ensuit: as follows

aliéner: cede, transmit, convey, give away, give up, alienate (a right or property)

allié(e): relative by marriage

appartenir: see *ce qu'il appartiendra*

appel (m): appeal

appointement (m. singular): settling of an affair

appointements (m. plural): salary (of an officer)

arrêt (m): decree, decision, judgment

arrêté (m; noun): decree, order

arrêté de compte: settlement of (closing out) an account, or statement of account (to date)

arrêté(e) (adjective): agreed, decided

arrêter: to settle, draw up a statement of (an account)

assignation (f) (*à comparaître*) (*en justice* [f]): summons, subpoena

assigner: to summon, subpoena

audience (f): hearing

au vrai: in actual fact

ayant cause (m): assign, assignee (noun) being a party to (e.g., legal heirs in a property dispute)

ayant charge (f) *de*: being responsible for

ayant droit (m): see *ayant cause*

bail (m) (plural, *baux*): lease; sometimes used for a service indenture (*bail de service*)

bailler: to give; to rent out

bailleur (*bailleresse*): person who rents out, lessor

bailli (*baillif, bailly*) (m): bailiff, magistrate in a seigneurial jurisdiction

bailliage (m): bailiwick, seigneurial court's jurisdiction

bien (m): possession, property

biens immeubles (m. plural): real estate or property, landed property

biens meubles (m. plural): personal (movable) possessions, including crops in the field

biens propres: possessions belonging to the individual spouse, not in the communal estate

billet (m) (*à ordre*): promissory note

bourgeois (m) *entrepreneur* (*marchand bourgeois*): merchant-entrepreneur, used for a reputable and propertied townsman (not a transient) of that place

cause (f): lawsuit, case

caution (f) (*judiciaire*): bail, bond

caution (f) *juratoire*: sworn oath

cautionnement (m): security (in a contract), surety

céder: give up, make over, transfer (property), dispose of

céder à bail: to lease

ce que de raison: what is just, equitable, legitimate

ce qu'il appartiendra: what will have been decided

charges (f): expenses, costs (see also *à la charge de*)

charges (f): responsibilities, financial obligations

commandement (m): summons to appear delivered by a court officer (*huisser* or *sergent*)

comme de raison (f): as one might expect

commis (m): court employee or officer or legal agent

commis greffier: assistant to the clerk of the court

commissaire (m): judge, arbitrator

commissaire-priseur (m): auctioneer, appraiser

communauté (f) *des biens*: communal estate (opposite of *biens propres*) of a wedded couple

comparant(e): one who appears (in a legal proceeding)

comparaître: to appear (in court)

comparution (f): appearance (in court)

complaignant(e): complainant (noun), plaintiff

conclure: decide, come to a conclusion

conclusions (f): summation (by court attorney); findings, conclusions (by judge); submissions (plaintiff) *condamné(e)*: sentenced; ordered (as a noun: sentenced person; convict)

confesser: to declare, avow

conquêt (m): immoveable asset received by a couple under a community of goods (see *acquêt*)

consanguin (adjective): see *frères*

constitution (f): action of legally establishing

contracter: to incur, contract (debts)

contrat (m): agreement, contract

contravention (f): infraction, violation

contumace (f): see *par contumace*

côte (f): rural community; strip settlement

cousin(e) germain(e): first cousin

cousin(e) issu(e) de germains: second cousin

Coutume (f) *de Paris*: Common Law of Paris, the body of civil and criminal law governing New France

curatelle (f): guardianship

damoiselle (f): mistress (title of address), damsel, maiden (archaic form of *demoiselle*)

défaut (m): failure to appear before a judge; default

défendeur (*défenderesse*): defendant

délaisser: give up possession of, quit, abandon; to leave (an estate), relinquish

demandeur (*demanderesse*): plaintiff, petitioner

dépens (m. plural) *compensés*: each party taxed or assessed for its own costs

déposant(e): deponent, one who gives evidence

déposer: to testify

de relevée: in the afternoon

désister: see *se désister de*

dessaisir: see *se dessaisir de*

détourner: divert, embezzle

dictum: judicial opinion on an item in a case other than the main question

dictum (m) *de sentence* (f): statement of the sentence or judgment; judicial opinion

divertir: to misappropriate, divert

d'office (f): automatically, as a matter of course

donataire (m, f; noun): donee, a recipient of a gift

donner acte de: to record, note, take note of, acknowledge formally

douer: to endow

droit (m): a right

échanges (m. plural): trade, trading, exchanges

effet (m) *de commerce* (m): bill of exchange

effet au porteur: bill payable to the bearer

effets (plural): things, clothes, belongings

élire domicile (m) *à*: to select a legal place of residence to which writs may be delivered, not necessarily the same as one's actual home

embauchage (m): hiring (noun)

encontre: see *à l'encontre de*

en face de l'église: with the ceremony, and according to the conventions, of the Church

en foi (f) *de quoi*: in witness whereof

enquête (f): inquiry, investigation involving testimony of witnesses

en temps et lieu (m): at the proper time and place; in due course

ensaisinement (m): delivery of, putting into possession

en justice: in court

en vertu (f) *de*: in accordance with

estimer: to appraise

eu égard à: see *pour ce qui est*

exécutoire (m): a registered writ of execution; it can be an official authorization to seize a party's goods awarded for court costs, or for the fees due to the court

exercice (m): accounting period

exploit (m): writ or summons to appear before a judge, usually to enforce payment

faire acte de: to act as (e.g., *faire acte de commerçant*)

faire droit à: to grant or accede to (a petition)

faire une demande en justice: to petition the court

faute (f): offense, misdeed, misdemeanor

fidejussion (f): guarantee or security by a third party for a debt

frères utérins: (half) brothers born of the same mother

frères germains: (half) brothers born of the same father

frères consanguins: brothers born of the same father and mother

germain (adjective): see *frères*

greffe (m): office of the clerk of the court (where the court records are kept); also used for a file of legal documents from one source, such as a notary

greffier (m): clerk of the court

greffier commis (m): assistant or deputy clerk of the court (see also *commis greffier*)

grosse (f): engrossment, a verbatim and lawful copy of a deed or judgment provided to the winning party in a court action

heure (f) *de relevée* (f): P.M.; in the afternoon

hoir (m): heir

huissier (m): bailiff, court usher

icelui, icelle (singular), *iceux, icelles* (plural): old forms of modern *celui-ci, celle-ci, ceux-ci, celles-ci*

indivis(e): undivided (see *par indivis*)

information (f) *judiciaire*: judicial inquiry or investigation to gather information and testimony about a crime before prosecution, unless the offender was caught while committing the crime

informer: to investigate

instance (f): legal proceeding

interrogation (f): interrogation, questioning

interrogatoire (m): interrogation; a record of questions to the accused and responses relating to a criminal matter

interpeller: to question (someone), to summon someone before a judge to answer a question about a specific detail, such as a witness's inconsistency

intimé(e): respondent, appellee, one to whom formal notice is given

jugement (m): judgment, sentence, decree, (final) decision, order

juridiction (f): jurisdiction; court of law

justice (f): see *en justice*

légataire (m) *universel*: sole legatee

legs (m): legacy, bequest

les lieux (m): the premises

lettre (f) *de change* (m): bill of exchange

libeller: to draw up (a signed and dated document)

licitation (f): auction of an undivided property

lieutenant (m): deputy judge

lieutenant particulier (m): deputy (assistant) judge in royal court

lieutenant-général (*civil et criminel*) (m): judge in royal court

loyal et marchand: of legal and marketable quality

loyalement: faithfully, honestly, rightfully, lawfully, legally

mandat (m) *de perquisition* (f): search warrant

mander: to transmit, convey the news of something to somebody; to order, command, say by letter

mainlevée (f): legal instrument putting an end to a seizure, etc., or waiving a legal impediment to ownership

moyennant: in return for, in consideration of (usually for a monetary payment)

nul (*nulle*): null and void, nullified

obligation (f): acknowledgment of debt

obliger: to bind, commit

octroyé(e): granted, accorded

office: see *d'office*

ordonnance (f): ruling, regulatory order

par contumace (f): in default; in his/her absence; in willful contempt of court

paraphe (f): paraph, flourish, initial, signature

parapher: to initial, to sign

partir (transitive): to share (out)

passer: to draw up, execute (a document)

perquisition (f): search (see *mandat*)

plainte (f): complaint

pour ce qui est eu égard à: concerning, as regards to, regarding, in view of

pour copie (*conforme*): certified accurate (copy)

pourvoi (m): appeal

[*pourvoir*] *se pourvoir*: to lodge an appeal

préciput (m): surviving spouse's right to take out, before dividing up the deceased spouse's possessions, an amount of money from certain assets of the bulk to be divided, presumed to be equal to that individual's personal effects

préjudice (m): harm, damage, prejudice

préjudicier: to prejudice, impair

preneur (m), *preneuse* (f): person who rents (from someone), tenant, lessee, buyer

priser: to determine the value of something, as in an estate inventory

procédure (f): proceedings

procès (m): (legal) proceedings; court action; trial

procès-verbal (m): official report, statement, minutes

procuration (f): power of attorney

procureur (m), *procuratrice* (f): holder of a power of attorney to act for another; attorney, agent; prosecutor

procureur du roy: king's attorney, prosecutor

propre (m): property acquired by inheritance, therefore not part of the communal estate; belonging to the individual

qui de droit: person having a right

quittance (f): receipt acknowledging payment in full

raison: see *comme de raison* and *ce que de raison*

recel (m): receiving or possession of stolen goods

receler: to receive or conceal stolen goods

récolement (m) (*des témoins*): recall or reexamination of witnesses to affirm their recorded testimony in the presence of the accused

relevée (f): see *heure de relevée*

reliquat (m): the balance of a debt or account

reliquataire (m, f): person who owes the amount remaining

remise (f): remission, forgiveness (of debt)

renoncer: to relinquish

requérir: to call for, demand, sum up, make closing speech *requête* (f): petition

réquisition (f): request, petition

réquisitoire (f): closing speech for the prosecution; instruction, brief (to the judge) calling for a specific sentence

sauf à: reserving the right to

saisi (*être saisi de*): to be legally provided with the goods of another, which are to be administered by the party receiving them

saisie (f): seizure

saisine (f): formal taking of possession by the lawful recipient

saisir: to seize; to bring before (the judiciary)

se désister de: to withdraw

se dessaisir de: to give up (something), part with; relinquish

sentence (f): verdict, sentence, decree, judgment, opinion delivered

siège (m): bench (in court)

signification (f): official notification

soit-communiqué (m): order at the conclusion of the proceedings for the summary to be submitted to the presiding judge

solidairement: jointly, jointly and severally

sommation (f): summons

substitut (m): substitute magistrate

suppliant(e): supplicant, suppliant, (humble) petitioner

taxer: to tax, assess, set a certain price on, reprehend; accuse someone of (*taxer quelqu'un de*)

tel qu'il se poursuit et se comporte: such as it is, in "as is" condition

témoignage (m): testimony

témoin (m): witness

teneur (f): content, terms, substance

tenir compte de (*quelque chose*): to take (something) into account

tenue (f): holding (of a hearing, etc.)

titre (m): see *à titre de*

traite (*de fourrures*) (f): fur trade

traité (m): compact, covenant, contract

transporter (*une somme*): transfer (a sum of money)

tuteur, tutrice: guardian

utérin (adjective): see *frères*

vertu (f): see *en vertu de*

vrai: see *au vrai*

Appendix 3.
Missionaries Assigned to Michilimackinac

1671–1673	Fr. Jacques Marquette
1672–1681	Fr. Henri Nouvel (both times as superior)
1688–1695	(Nouvel)
1674	Brother Gilles Mazier
1681–1683	(Mazier)
1681–1683	Brother Louis le Boesme [Boheme]
1673–1683	Fr. Philippe Pierson
1683	Fr. Nicolas [Jean] Potier
1681–1688	Fr. Jean Enjalran (as superior)
1701	(Enjalran)
1686–1705	Fr. Étienne de Carheil
1687–1689	Fr. Jacques Gravier
1696–1700	(Gravier as superior)
1688	Fr. Joseph-Jacques Marest
1700–1705	(Marest as superior)
1706–1721	(Marest as superior)
1701	Fr. Jean-Baptiste Chardon
1711	(Chardon)
1711	Brother Louis Haren

Appendix 4.
Commanders at Michilimackinac

1683–1690	Olivier Morel de La Durantaye
1690–1694	Louis de La Porte de Louvigny
1694–1697	Antoine Laumet *dit* Lamothe Cadillac
1697–1698	Alphonse de Tonty
1712–1720	Louis de La Porte de Louvigny (did not take command until 1716)
1712–1716	Constant Le Marchand de Lignery (interim commander)

Bibliography

Manuscript Sources

CANADA

Archives nationales du Québec à Montréal

Greffe de Claude Maugue

Greffe d'Antoine Adhémar de Saint-Martin

Greffe de Pierre Raimbault

Documents judiciaires de la juridiction seigneuriale de Montréal (1651–1695) [cote TL 2, feuilles détachées, 1681–1693]

Documents judiciaires de la juridiction royale de Montréal (1693–1760) [cote TL 4 S1]

Registres du bailliage (période seigneuriale) (1644–1693) [cote TL 2]

Registres des audiences (période royale) (1693–1760) [cote TL 2]

Archives nationales du Québec à Québec

Greffe de Genaple

National Archives of Canada

Manuscript groups 1, 5, and 18, transcripts of materials from the Archives nationales de France

FRANCE

Archives nationales de France (Colonial materials now in Aix-en-Provence)

Archives des Colonies, series C11A

Archives des Colonies, series B

Archives des Colonies, series C11E

Ministère des Affaires étrangères (Paris)

Mémoires et documents, Amérique

UNITED STATES OF AMERICA

Newberry Library (Chicago)

Ayer Manuscript Collection

Printed Sources

Allaire, Bernard. *Pelletries, manchons et chapeaux de castor: Les fourrures nord-américaines à Paris, 1500–1632.* Sillery/Paris: Septentrion/Presses de l'Université de Paris-Sorbonne, 1999.

Allaire, Gratien. "Officiers et marchands: Les sociétés de commerce des fourrures, 1715–1760." *Revue d'histoire de l'Amérique française* 40, no. 3 (1987): 409–28.

———. "Les engagements pour la traite des fourrures." *Revue d'histoire de l'Amérique française* 34, no. 1 (1980): 3–26.

Armour, David A. *Colonial Michilimackinac.* Mackinac Island: Mackinac State Historic Parks, 2000.

———. *The Merchants of Albany, New York: 1686–1760.* New York and London: Garland Publishing, 1986.

Axtell, James. *The Invasion Within: The Contest of Cultures in Colonial North America.* New York: Oxford University Press, 1985.

Bentley, Jerry H., and Herbert F. Ziegler. *Traditions and Encounters: A Global Perspective on the Past.* 2nd edition. Boston: McGraw Hill, 2003.

Brandão, José António, ed. and trans. (with K. Janet Ritch). *Nation Iroquoise: A Seventeenth-Century Ethnography of the Iroquois.* Lincoln: University of Nebraska Press, 2003.

———. *"Your fyre shall burn no more": Iroquois Policy towards New France and Its Native Allies to 1701.* Lincoln: University of Nebraska Press, 1997.

Broshar, Helen. "The First Push Westward of the Albany Traders." *Mississippi Valley Historical Review* 7, no. 3 (December 1920): 228–41.

Brown, George W., et al., eds. *The Dictionary of Canadian Biography* [DCB]. 14 vols. to date. Toronto: University of Toronto Press, 1966– .

Brun, Josette. "Les femmes d'affaires en Nouvelle-France au 18ᵉ siècle: Le cas de l'île Royale." *Acadiensis* 27, no. 1 (Autumn 1997): 44–66

Buffinton, A. H. "The Policy of Albany and English Westward Expansion." *Mississippi Valley Historical Review* 8, no. 4 (March 1922): 327–66.

Bulletin des Recherches Historiques. 70 vols. Lévis, Québec: A. Roy, 1895–1968.

Campeau, Lucien, S.J. *Catastrophe démographique sur les Grands Lacs.* Montreal: Éditions Bellarmin, 1983.

Charbonneau, Hubert, et al. "Le comportement démographique des voyageurs sous le régime français." *Histoire sociale/Social History* 11, no. 21 (mai/May 1978): 120–33.

Charlevoix, Pierre-François-Xavier. *History and General Description of New France.* 6 vols. [1744]. Translated by John Gilmary Shea. Chicago: Loyola University Press, 1870.

———. *Journal of a Voyage to North America.* 2 vols. London: R. and J. Dodsley, 1761.

Clark, John G. *La Rochelle and Atlantic Economy during the Eighteenth Century.* Baltimore and London: Johns Hopkins University Press, 1981.

Collections of the Wisconsin Historical Society. 20 vols. Madison: State Historical Society of Wisconsin, 1855–1911.

Colpitts, George. "'Animated Like Us by Commercial Interests': Commercial Ethnology and Fur Trade Descriptions in New France, 1660–1760." *Canadian Historical Review* 83, no. 3 (September 2002): 305–37.

Cotgrave, Randle. *A Dictionarie of the French and English Tongues.* London: Adam Islip, 1611; repr., Columbia: University of South Carolina Press, 1968.

Dechêne, Louise. *Habitants et marchands de Montréal au xviie siècle.* Montréal: Librairie Plon, 1974.

Delanglez, Jean, S.J. "Antoine Laumet, *alias* Cadillac, Commandant at Michilimackinac: 1694–1697." *Mid-America: An Historical Review* 27 (1945): 108–32, 188–216, 232–56.

Dépatie, Sylvie. "Commerce et crédit à l'île Jésus, 1734–75: Le rôle des marchands dans l'économie des campagnes montréalaises." *Canadian Historical Review* 84, no. 2 (June 2003): 147–76.

——, ed. *Vingt ans après "Habitants et Marchands."* Montréal and Kingston: McGill-Queens University Press, 1998.

Dickinson, John. *Law in New France.* Winnipeg: University of Manitoba Canadian Legal History Project, Working Paper Series, 1992.

——. *Justice et justiciables: La procédure civile à la prévôté de Québec, 1667–1759.* Québec: Les Presses de l'Université Laval, 1982.

Dubé, Jean-Claude. *Les intendants de la Nouvelle-France.* Montréal: Fides, 1984.

Dumont, Micheline. "Les femmes de la Nouvelle-France étaient-elles favorisées?" *Atlantis* 8, no. 1 (Fall/automne 1982): 118–24.

Eccles, W. J. "French Exploration in North America, 1700–1800." In *North American Exploration*, vol. 2, *A Continent Defined*, ed. John Logan Allen. Lincoln: University of Nebraska Press, 1997.

——. *Essays on New France.* Toronto: Oxford University Press, 1987.

——. *The Canadian Frontier, 1534–1760.* 1969; Albuquerque: University of New Mexico Press, 1978.

——. *Canada under Louis XIV, 1663–1701.* Toronto: McClelland and Stewart, 1964.

——. *Frontenac: The Courtier Governor.* 1959; Lincoln: University of Nebraska Press, 2003.

Edmunds, R. David, and Joseph L. Peyser. *The Fox Wars: The Mesquakie Challenge to New France.* Norman: University of Oklahoma Press, 1993.

Frêlon, Elise. *Les pouvoirs du Conseil Souverain de la Nouvelle-France dans l'édiction de la norme (1663–1760).* Paris: L'Harmattan, 2002.

Gênet, Nicole, Luce Vermette, and Louise Décarie-Audet. *Les objets familiers de nos ancêtres.* Montréal: Les Editions de l'Homme, 1974.

Grand Larousse en 5 volumes. Paris: Larousse, 1987.

Greer, Allan. *The People of New France.* Toronto: University of Toronto Press, 1997.

Harris, R. Cole, ed. *The Historical Atlas of Canada: From the Beginning to 1800.* Vol. 1. Toronto: University of Toronto Press, 1987.

Havard, Gilles. *Empire et métissages: Indiens et Français dans le Pays d'en Haut, 1660–1715.* Sillery/Paris: Septentrion/Presses de l'Université de Paris-Sorbonne, 2003.

——. "Postes français et villages indiens: Un aspect de l'organisation de l'espace colonial français dans le Pays d'en Haut (1600–1715)." *Recherches amérindiennes au Québec* 30, no. 2 (2000): 11–22.

Heidenreich, Conrad. "Early French Exploration in the North American Interior." In *North American Exploration*, vol. 2, *A Continent Defined*, ed. John Logan Allen. Lincoln: University of Nebraska Press, 1997.

Idle, Dunning. *The Post of the St. Joseph River during the French Régime, 1679–1761.* [1946] Niles: Support the Fort Inc., 2003.

Innis, Harold A. *The Fur Trade in Canada.* Revised edition. Toronto: University of Toronto Press, 1956.

Jetté, René. *Dictionnaire généalogique des familles du Québec des origines à 1730.* Montréal: Les Presses de l'Université de Montréal, 1983.

Jugements et délibérations du Conseil Souverain, 1663–1716. In *Chronica 1.* Montréal: Archiv-Histo, 1999. CD-ROM.

Kent, Timothy J. *Rendezvous at the Straits: Fur Trade and Military Activities at Fort de Buade and Fort Michilimackinac, 1669–1781.* 2 vols. Ossineke, Mich.: Silver Fox Enterprises, 2004.

Konrad, Victor. "An Iroquois Frontier: The North Shore of Lake Ontario during the Late Seventeenth Century." *Journal of Historical Geography* 7, no. 2 (April 1981): 129–44.

Lachance, André. *Crimes et criminels en Nouvelle-France.* Montreal: Boréal Express, 1984.

———. *La justice criminelle du roi au Canada au xviiie siècle.* Québec: Les Presses de L'Université Laval, 1978.

Lafitau, J. F. *Customs of the American Indians Compared with the Customs of Primitive Times.* [1727] 2 vols. Edited by W. N. Fenton; translated by E. L. Moore. Toronto: Champlain Society Publication 48–49, 1974 and 1977.

Lahontan, Louis-Armand, baron de. *New Voyages to North America.* [1703] 2 vols. Edited and translated by R. G. Thwaites. Chicago: A. C. McClurg, 1905.

Landry, Yves, ed. *Pour le Christ et le Roi: La vie au temps des premiers Montréalais.* Québec: Éditions Libre Expression, 1992.

Lavallée, Louis. "La vie et la pratique d'un notaire rural sous le régime français: Le cas de Guillaume Barette, notaire à La Prairie entre 1709–1744." *Revue d'histoire de l'Amérique française* 47, no. 4 (1994): 499–519.

Le Nouveau Petit Robert: Dictionnaire de la langue française. Paris: Dictionnaires le Robert, 1993.

Le Roy de La Potherie [dit, Bacqueville de la Potherie], Claude-Charles. *Histoire de l'Amérique septentrionale.* 4 vols. Paris, 1722.

[Lotbinière, Michel Chartier de]. *Fort Michilimackinac in 1749: Lotbinière's Plan and Map.* Vol. 2, leaflet 5 of *Mackinac History.* Edited and translated by Marie Gérin-Lajoie. Mackinac Island, Mich.: Mackinac Island State Park Commission, 1976.

Mancall, Peter C. *Deadly Medicine: Indians and Alcohol in Early America.* Ithaca, N.Y.: Cornell University Press, 1995.

Margry, Pierre, ed. *Découvertes et établissements des Français dans l'ouest et dans le sud de l'Amérique septentrionale, 1614–1754.* 6 vols. Paris: D. Jouaust, 1876–1886.

———, ed. *Relations et mémoires inédits pour servir à l'histoire de la France dans les pays d'outremer.* Paris: Challamel Aimé, 1867.

Mathieu, Jacques. *La Nouvelle-France: Les Français en Amérique du Nord, xvie–xiiie siècles.* Sainte-Foy: Les Presses de l'Université Laval, 2002.

McDermott, John Francis. *A Glossary of Mississippi Valley French, 1673–1850.* St. Louis: Washington University Studies, new series, 1941.

Michigan Pioneer and Historical Society Collections.

Moogk, Peter N. "The Liturgy of Humiliation, Pain, and Death: The Execution of Criminals in New France," *The Canadian Historical Review* 88, 1 (March 2007): 89–112.

——. *La Nouvelle-France: The Making of French Canada—A Cultural History.* E. Lansing: Michigan State University Press, 2000.

——. "Rank in New France: Reconstructing a Society from Notarial Records." *Histoire sociale/Social History* 8, no. 15 (mai/May 1975): 34–53.

Noel, Jan. "'Nagging Wife' Revisited: Women and the Fur Trade in New France." *French Colonial History* 7 (2006): 45–60.

——. "Caste and Clientage in an Eighteenth-Century Quebec Convent." *Canadian Historical Review* 82, no. 3 (September 2001): 465–90.

——. "New-France: Les femmes favorisées." In *Rethinking Canada: The Promise of Women's History*, ed. Veronica Strong-Boag and Anita Clair Fellman. Toronto: Copp Clark Pitman, 1986.

——. "Women in New France: Further Reflections." *Atlantis* 8, no. 1 (Fall/automne 1982): 125–30.

Norton, Thomas E. *The Fur Trade in Colonial New York, 1686–1776.* Madison: University of Wisconsin Press, 1974.

O'Callaghan, E. B., ed. *Documents Relative to the Colonial History of the State of New York.* 15 vols. Albany, N.Y.: Weed, Parsons and Co., 1856–1883.

Oxford Dictionary of English. 2nd edition. Oxford: Oxford University Press, 2003.

Pease, Theodore Calvin, and Raymond C. Werner, eds. and trans. *The French Foundations, 1680–1693.* In *Collections of the Illinois State Historical Library*, vol. 23. Springfield: Illinois State Historical Library, 1934.

Peyser, Joseph L., ed. and trans. *On the Eve of Conquest: The Chevalier De Raymond's Critique of New France in 1754.* East Lansing/Mackinac Island: Michigan State University Press/Mackinac State Historic Parks, 1997.

——., ed. and trans. *Jacques Legardeur de Saint-Pierre: Officer, Gentleman, Entrepreneur.* East Lansing/Mackinac Island: Michigan State University Press/Mackinac State Historic Parks, 1996.

——. "The Fall and Rise of Thérèse Catin: A Portrait from Indiana's French and Canadian History." *Indiana Magazine of History* 91, no. 4 (December 1995): 378–79.

——., ed. and trans. *Letters from New France: The Upper Country, 1686–1783.* Urbana and Chicago: University of Illinois Press, 1992.

Phillips, Paul Chrisler. *The Fur Trade.* 2 vols. Norman: University of Oklahoma Press, 1961.

Plamondon, Lilianne. "A Businesswoman in New France: Marie-anne Barbel, the Widow Fornel." In *Rethinking Canada: The Promise of Women's History*, ed. Veronica Strong-Boag and Anita Clair Fellman. Toronto: Copp Clark Pitman, 1986.

Pritchard, James. *In Search of Empire: The French in the Americas, 1670–1730.* Cambridge: Cambridge University Press, 2004.

Pritzker, Barry M. *A Native American Encyclopedia: History, Culture, and Peoples.* Oxford and New York: Oxford University Press, 2000.

Quaife, Milo Milton, ed. and trans. *The Western Country in the 17th Century: The Memoirs of Lamothe Cadillac and Pierre Liette.* Chicago: Lakeside Press, 1947.

Rapporte de l'Archiviste de la Province de Québec.

Robert, Paul. *Le Petit Robert: Dictionnaire alphabétique & analogique de la langue française.* Paris: Société du Nouveau Littré, 1978.

Stone, Lyle M. *Fort Michilimackinac, 1715–1781.* East Lansing: Publications of the Michigan State University Museum, 1974.

———. *Archaeological Investigation of the Marquette Mission Site, St. Ignace, Michigan, 1971: A Preliminary Report.* Mackinac Island, Mich.: Mackinac Island State Park Commission, Reports in Mackinac History and Archaeology, no. 1, 1972.

Thwaites, Reuben Gold, ed. *The Jesuit Relations and Allied Documents, 1610–1791.* 73 vols. Cleveland: Burrows Bros., 1896–1901.

Trigger, B. G., ed. *Handbook of North American Indians.* Vol. 15, *The Northeast.* Washington, D.C.: Smithsonian Institution, 1978.

Trigger, Bruce, et al., eds. *Le castor fait tout: Selected Papers of the Fifth North American Fur Trade Conference, 1985.* Lake St. Louis Historical Society, 1987.

Trudel, Marcel. *La Nouvelle-France par les textes: Les cadres de vie.* Montreal: Éditions Hurtibise, 2003.

———. *Initiation à la Nouvelle-France.* Montreal: Les Éditions HRW, 1971.

Vachon, André. "Colliers et ceintures de porcelaine dans la diplomatie indienne." *Les Cahiers des Dix* 36 (1971): 179–92.

———. "Colliers et ceintures de porcelaine chez les indiens de la Nouvelle-France." *Les Cahiers des Dix* 35 (1970): 251–78.

———. *The Administration of New France, 1627–1760.* Toronto: University of Toronto Press, 1970.

Vogel, Virgil J. *Indian Names in Michigan.* Ann Arbor: University of Michigan Press, 1986.

White, Richard. *The Middle Ground: Indians, Empires, and Republics in the Great Lakes Region, 1650–1850.* Cambridge: Cambridge University Press, 1991.

Zitomersky, Joseph. "The Form and Function of French-Native Settlement Relations in Eighteenth-Century Louisiana." In his *French Americans-Native Americans in Eighteenth-Century French Colonial Louisiana: The Population Geography of the Illinois Indians, 1670s–1760s* (Lund, Sweden: Lund University Press, 1994), 359–87.

Zoltvany, Yves F. *Philippe de Rigaud de Vaudreuil, Governor of New France, 1703–1725.* Toronto: McClelland and Steward, 1974.

Index

Note: Because of the variant spelling of many personal and place names, they are listed below as they first appear in a document. The lack of first names in many documents has made it difficult to identify/link-up individuals with similar/same last names. In such instances, rather than create potentially false identifications, multiple entries have been created. Where it has been possible to clearly identify a person, place, etc., the accepted modern spelling is used as written in the note identifying the person/place in the document (e.g., Antoine Laumet *dit* Lamothe Cadillac, not La Motte de Cadillac; Michilimackinac, not Missilimakina, etc.), and the variant spelling is added in parenthesis. Spelling of names in the index, and in the text (as much as is practical), follows the practice of the *Dictionary of Canadian Biography*.

Gaillard, Mathieu, 83, 84
Galipau, Anthoine, 120
Galop (Galoppe), *dit* Viger, Jacques, 85
Ganetchitiagon, 48, 54 (n. 8)
Gautier, Jean, xiv, 149, 153, 154, 156, 157, 158, 159
Gay, *dit* Cascaret, Jean, 47–48, 49–50, 51, 52, 54 (n.15), 55
Genaple, François, 57, 58 (n. 2), 59, 60, 91
Germain, 134, 135
Gervaise, Jehan, 48, 49, 50, 51, 53, 56
Godfrey de Lintot (Linctot), Michel, 63
Grandmaison. *See* Borry de Grandmaison, Laurent
Green Bay (Baye des Puans), 1, 2 (n. 6), 43, 45 (n. 11)
Greysolon Dulhut (Du Luth, Duluth), Daniel, 17 (n. 8), 23 (n. 2), 28, 30 (n. 19), 45 (n. 13), 55, 63, 64 (n. 3), 83, 84
Guichard, Claude, 57, 58
Guignard, Arthur-Laurent, 163 (n. 8)
Guillet, 43
Guillet, Mathurin, 101, 102
Guillon, Jean-Baptiste, 165
Guillory, François, 99, 100 (n. 4)
Guillory (Guilory), Simon, 22, 23 (n. 2), 25, 26, 27, 28, 31, 32, 97, 98 (n. 11)
Guitault (Guito), *dit* Jolicoeur, Jacques, 24, 25, 26, 27, 29 (n. 3), 32
Guyon, Marie-Thérèse, 105, 106, 108, 110, 111
Guyotte, Étienne, 78

Hazeur, François, 26, 30 (n. 11)
Hébert, *dit* Deslauriers, Ignace, 95, 96, 98 (nn. 8, 10)
Hébert, Léger, 96, 98 (n. 10)
The Heel (Le Talon), 9, 10 (n. 11), 14
Hertel de La Fresnière, Joseph-François, 27, 30 (n. 15)
Hoyo8la, 96
Hudson, Henry, xxiii, xxiv
Hudson Bay, xxiii, xxvii, 1
Hudson River, xxiv
Huron (Wyandot, Ouendat) Indians, xxviii, xxix, 7, 9, 10 (nn. 2, 13), 11 (n. 14), 12, 14

Illinois Indians, 2 (n. 7), 42, 63
Indians. *See names of individual nations*; Fur trade; Michilimackinac
Iroquois blanket/jacket, 8, 42
Iroquois Indians, xxiii, xxviii, xxx, xxxix (n. 28), 9, 14, 41, 43, 44 (n. 3), 45 (n. 9), 98 (n. 12)

Jamestown, Virginia, xxiv
Janot, *dit* Lachapelle (La Chapelle), Pierre, 67, 71, 75, 134, 135
Jesuits, xxviii, xxix, xxx, xxxi, xxxii, xxxix (n. 29), xli (n. 64), 1, 15, 17 (n. 9), 18, 26, 41, 45 (n. 10), 46 (n. 17), 49, 136
Jolicoeur. *See* Guitault (Guito), *dit* Jolicoeur, Jacques
Juchereau, 94
Juchereau de Saint-Denis, Charlotte-Françoise de (La Dame Pachot, La Dame de La Forest), 139–140 (n.11)

Kickapoo (Quicapous) Indians, 41, 42, 45 (n. 9)

La Barre. *See* Le Febvre de La Barre, Joseph-Antoine
Lachapelle. *See* Janot de La Barre, Joseph-Antoine
La Chenaye, 43
Lachine (la Chine), 28, 30 (n .21), 94, 114, 115, 116, 118 (n. 8), 167 (n. 3)
La Durantaye. *See* Morel de La Durantaye, Olivier
Lafontaine, 49, 50, 51
Lafontaine (La Fontaine), Robert, 146, 147
Lagrave, Pierre, 112, 113 (n. 12), 132, 135, 137 (n. 8)
Lahontan, Baron de, xxix, xxx
Lake Erie, 87
Lake Huron, xxvi, xxviii, 1, 48, 103
Lake Michigan, xxvi, 2 (nn. 6, 7), 29 (n. 4), 45 (n. 9)
Lake Nipissing (Nepissing), 151, 152, 156 (n. 5)
Lake Ontario, 44 (n. 3), 48, 54 (n. 8), 124 (n. 8)
Lake Superior, xxvi, 1, 46 (n. 17)
Lalonde, *dit* l'Espérance, Jean, 108